"BROTHER WOODROW"

"BROTHER WOODROW"

❧

A Memoir of Woodrow Wilson

❧

Stockton Axson

SUPPLEMENTARY VOLUME TO THE

PAPERS OF WOODROW WILSON

Edited by

Arthur S. Link

With the Assistance of

John E. Little,

L. Kathleen Amon, *and*

Nancy Plum

PRINCETON UNIVERSITY PRESS · PRINCETON, NEW JERSEY

Library of Congress Cataloging-in-Publication Data

Axson, Stockton, 1867–1935
"Brother Woodrow" : a memoir of
Woodrow Wilson / by Stockton Axson;
edited by Arthur S. Link, with the assistance of John E. Little,
L. Kathleen Amon, and Nancy Plum.

p.   cm. — (Supplementary volumes to The Papers of Woodrow Wilson)
Includes index.
ISBN 0-691-03255-6
1. Wilson, Woodrow, 1856–1924.   2. Presidents—United States—
Biography.   I. Link, Arthur Stanley.   II. Title.   III. Series.
E767.A95   1993
973.91′3′092—dc20   [B]   92-45168

This book has been composed in Adobe Utopia
Designed by Frank Mahood

Printed in the United States of America

3   5   7   9   10   8   6   4   2

Contents

❧

Illustrations

❧

(All photographs courtesy of Princeton University Library)

Editor's Introduction

❧

STOCKTON AXSON, born on June 6, 1867, in Rome, Georgia, was baptized Isaac Stockton Keith Axson II but always called himself just plain Stockton Axson. He was born into the Presbyterian ministerial aristocracy of South Carolina and Georgia. His grandfather, Isaac Stockton Keith Axson, held pastorates in South Carolina and at Midway Presbyterian Church in Liberty County, Georgia; was president of Presbyterian female colleges in Greensboro, Georgia, and Rome, Georgia; and was pastor of the large and wealthy Independent Presbyterian Church in Savannah, Georgia, from 1857 to 1891. Sometimes called "The Great Axson," he numbered among his close acquaintances most of the leading ministers of the Presbyterian Church in the United States, commonly called the southern Presbyterian Church.

Among the four children born to the Rev. Dr. Axson and his wife, Rebecca Longstreet Randolph Axson, was Stockton Axson's father, Samuel Edward, born at Waltourville in Liberty County on December 23, 1836. He married Margaret Jane ("Janie") Hoyt, herself the daughter of a Presbyterian minister, in 1858; served his first pastorate in South Carolina, was chaplain to a Georgia infantry regiment during the Civil War; only a few months after the end of that conflict, he took up the pastorate at the First Presbyterian Church of Rome, Georgia. Their first child was Ellen Louise Axson, born on May 15, 1860, about whom we will hear a great deal in this book because she was destined to marry Woodrow Wilson. Stockton was the second child. The third, Edward William Axson, was born on March 1, 1876. The fourth, Margaret Randolph ("Madge") Axson, was born on October 10, 1881. Margaret Jane Hoyt Axson developed childbirth fever after Madge's birth and died on November 4, 1881. Ellen Louise Axson, or "Ellie Lou," as she was called, now became the mother to her brothers and sister and, as it sadly turned out, nurse to her father.

Before 1881, Samuel Edward Axson had a successful ministry in Rome, in spite of recurrent attacks of depression, but his wife's death devastated him and sent him into a depression so deep that he resigned from his church and moved his family into the commodious manse occupied by his father in Savannah. Early in 1884, Samuel Edward Axson became violent and was committed to the Georgia State Mental Hospital at Milledgeville on January 13. He committed suicide on May 28, 1884.

Samuel Edward Axson's violent death traumatized his entire family, but particularly Stockton, then age sixteen and a student at Fort Mill College, a Presbyterian preparatory school for boys in York County, South Carolina. Although surrounded and supported by an extended family, he suffered throughout his life from feelings of inadequacy and pathological depression. He entered Davidson College in North Carolina in September 1884 but was constantly ill and withdrew from that college in June 1885, after what must have been an unsuccessful year. A few months later, he went to work for his uncle, Randolph Axson, cotton broker of Savannah. Stockton was subject to recurrent attacks of nervousness, claimed that the Savannah climate did not agree with him, and, in the summer of 1887, moved into the household of his aunt, Louisa Cunningham Hoyt Brown, and her husband, Warren A. Brown, a businessman of Gainesville, Georgia. Stockton enrolled as an "eclectic" student at the University of Georgia and managed to remain at that institution for two years in spite of various maladies.

Stockton Axson's life took a radical new turn in the autumn of 1889, when he went to live with his sister and brother-in-law, Woodrow Wilson, in order to become a student at Wesleyan University in Middletown, Connecticut, where Wilson was at this time a professor. Axson had fallen in love with English literature and hoped to have a career teaching that subject, and Wilson had urged him to come to Wesleyan to study under the eminent professor of English literature, Caleb Thomas Winchester. He was graduated with the A.B. degree from Wesleyan in June 1890. According to Woodrow Wilson, Winchester regarded him as one of the best students he ever had.

Axson went to The Johns Hopkins University for graduate work in September 1890 but was not happy there because of his professors' emphasis, in the Germanic tradition, upon philology and the technical aspects of literary study. Lacking any graduate degree, he worked briefly for Albert Shaw on *The Review of Reviews* in New York during the summer of 1891 and, in the following September, came back to Wesleyan for a further year of graduate work with Professor Winchester. He received the M.A. degree from Wesleyan in 1892, made an abortive start on a doctoral dissertation that summer, and secured a one-year appointment at the University of Vermont in September 1892. He was so successful there that he was given an additional year's appointment, as Wilson put it, by popular demand. In the summer of 1894 he secured employment as a lecturer in English literature for the American Society for the Extension of University Teaching, whose headquarters were in Philadelphia. When Adelphi Academy in Brooklyn was transformed into Adelphi College in 1896, Axson was appointed assistant professor of English literature, perhaps because the president of Adelphi was a close friend of Woodrow Wilson. That first year at Adelphi seems to have been a near disaster for Axson, who suffered what may have been the first of his serious attacks of depression and was under the care of physicians in New York. Recovery came at a time we do not know, and Axson, promoted to professor, remained at Adelphi until 1899, when he was appointed assistant professor of English literature at Princeton. He was extremely successful as an undergraduate teacher and was promoted to professor in May 1904, but he had had another bad attack of nervous prostration and was hospitalized in Philadelphia in April 1903. The year 1905 was a particularly bad one for him. He spent at least three months at the beginning of that year in a hospital for mental disease in Philadelphia run by the pioneer alienist and neurologist, Dr. Francis Xavier Dercum. Writing later, his sister Ellen said that Stockton was almost hopelessly ill for the entire year of 1905.

Life took a new turn for Axson in 1906 with the return of health and increasing popularity as a teacher at Princeton. Ellen Wilson wrote in 1907 that he was the idol of students, who voted him their favorite professor almost every year, and that he was adored by women, young and old. During Woodrow Wilson's time of troubles at Princeton, from 1906 to 1910, Axson was a strong Wilson partisan. In 1913 he accepted appointment as professor of English literature at the new Rice Institute (now the William Marsh Rice University) in Houston and remained there as a kind of lecturer in residence until his death in Houston on February 26, 1935.

Axson gained something like a nationwide fame as a lecturer on and interpreter of English literature. He never published a serious scholarly work, but he did publish a number of essays on English and American writers, English poets, art, etc., in a series known as *The Rice Institute Pamphlet* and elsewhere. He was awarded honorary degrees by the University of Pittsburgh in 1909 and Knox College in 1920. He was also secretary of the American National Red Cross, 1917–1919, and was in Paris with Wilson for a time during the Paris Peace Conference. He never married; indeed, what few romantic relationships he had seemed to precipitate extreme nervousness and depression. His published works show that he was a voracious reader in many fields; and he was something of a spellbinder as a lecturer. But to the end of his life, he was hypochondriacal and subject to recurring attacks of pathological depression. By the account of everyone who knew him, he was a kind and gentle person.

Stockton Axson met Woodrow Wilson in 1884 and knew him intimately until Wilson's death in 1924. Indeed, Axson knew Wilson longer than any other single person except his father and brother. Woodrow Wilson was always "Brother Woodrow" to Axson—a friend, companion, and mentor. Wilson fully reciprocated Axson's affection and was always fiercely protective of him; indeed, Axson was one of the few persons to whom Wilson would unburden his mind without any reservation.

At some time during 1919—it was probably in the summer of that year—Axson and Wilson's personal physician and naval aide, Admiral Cary Travers Grayson, agreed to write a joint memoir of Wilson, Axson to cover the period of Wilson's life to his presidency of the United States and Grayson to cover the period from 1913 onward. They drafted two tables of contents and one elaborate outline of the book and two introductions. (These and other documents referred to herein unless otherwise noted are in the Papers of Cary T. Grayson in the possession of Cary T. Grayson, Jr., and James Gordon Grayson.) On December 29, 1920, they signed a contract with Wilson's secretary, Joseph Patrick Tumulty. In it, Grayson and Tumulty agreed to retain Axson "to prepare, write and put in form ready for publication, the personal stories of our several relationships with Woodrow Wilson, drawn from data and information which we agree, severally, to furnish Stockton Axson for the above purpose." This contract also said that Axson, Grayson, and Tumulty would collaborate in writing a second book, a biography of Wilson covering his entire life. It was a strange agreement, because Tumulty had already written his own memoir of Wilson, which was then being serialized and would be published in 1921 as *Woodrow Wilson As I Know Him* (Garden City,

N. Y.: Doubleday, Page & Co., 1921); moreover, Tumulty never wrote a word in collaboration with Axson and Grayson. Perhaps the three men agreed to annul the contract soon after signing it.

Axson dictated his chapters of the projected memoir (except for the final one, which he seems to have written) between August 1919 and December 1921; he obviously intended to revise them once Grayson had written his part of the book. As it turned out, Grayson wrote only two chapters, an extended personal portrait of Wilson, and a number of expanded outlines for chapters.

A copy of an undated letter in the Grayson Papers from Grayson to Axson may provide the clue to the reason why the Axson-Grayson memoir was never completed. In this letter, Grayson says that he and Axson should not publish a book about Wilson while he is still alive without Mrs. Wilson's consent. It is possible that she vetoed the project or asked Grayson and Axson to defer publication of the projected book. However this may have been, Axson and Grayson never got around to putting the book into final form.

The text of the memoir that follows is substantially that of the chapters that Axson dictated and wrote between 1919 and 1921, the manuscript of which is in the Woodrow Wilson Collection in the Seeley G. Mudd Library, Princeton University. We have made a number of additions. Axson read the manuscripts of volumes 1, 2, 3, and 4 of Ray Stannard Baker's *Woodrow Wilson: Life and Letters*, 8 vols. (Garden City, N. Y.: Doubleday, Page & Co., 1927–1939) and wrote more than three hundred pages of handwritten notes and commentaries on them. In addition, Axson, in 1933–1934, wrote seven chapters of a biography of Wilson, which he condensed into three lectures that he gave at the Rice Institute in 1934 and published in *The Rice Institute Pamphlet* as "Woodrow Wilson as Man of Letters." The manuscript of the biography is in the Stockton Axson Papers in the Fondren Library of William Marsh Rice University. Finally, between 1925 and 1931, R. S. Baker interviewed Axson thirteen times. Baker's memoranda of these interviews are in his papers in the Library of Congress. In a few instances, we have silently incorporated very brief selections from the Axson commentaries and biography into the text of the memoir printed below. We have used other, longer portions with attribution. Material used from Baker's memoranda are incorporated in footnotes.

Because the text of the main body of this book was a first draft, we have tried to put ourselves in Axson's position if he were preparing the manuscript for publication. Hence we have silently corrected errors of fact, filled in blanks in the text, and standardized spelling, punctuation, and capitalization. Since Axson dictated most of this book, he was often repetitious. We have deleted repetitive text when it was possible to do so. We hope we have succeeded in putting in good and readable form the important corpus of Axson's impressions of Woodrow Wilson as recorded in various forms.

As readers will soon discover, this is a warm but not uncritical memoir of Wilson by an intimate friend of nearly forty years. As such, it is intended mainly for readers who want to know the human side of Wilson. With them in mind, we have tried to provide annotation that is appropriate without being unnecessarily detailed.

We are grateful to Kendrick A. Clements, John Milton Cooper, Jr., William H. Harbaugh, August Heckscher, Richard W. Leopold, Margaret D. Link, Charles E. Neu, Bert E. Park, M.D., and Betty Miller Unterberger for reading the manuscript of this book and making helpful suggestions.

Arthur S. Link

Princeton, New Jersey
August 8, 1992

"BROTHER WOODROW"

1. Stockton Axson, ca. 1920

Preface by Stockton Axson

❧

THIS IS not a biography but a series of impressions of Mr. Wilson, some descriptive, some anecdotal, some analytical. Taken together, they constitute an attempt to portray a complex man living in a complex world. The author was a brother of the first Mrs. Wilson. From June 1884, until the first inauguration, his association with Mr. Wilson was unusually intimate, and Mr. Wilson did him the honor to call him his friend. During the presidency, and after, this contact was necessarily less close, but he continued to see the president frequently until his death.

Mr. Wilson was a many-sided man engaged in a variety of activities. He was a student, a teacher, a college president, a governor of a state, a president of the United States, an arbiter of the destinies of the nations of the civilized world. One would call him an internationalist were it not that the term has been abused, made inconsistent with patriotism, synonymous with what used to be called nihilism. Mr. Wilson was a passionate American patriot, but he believed that the events which began to unfold in the summer of 1914 demanded that nations, without sacrificing their nationalism, should seek and find new modes of procedure in their relations with each other. He was an advocate of a plan of open justice and equality among nations in place of secretive and insincere diplomacies. He was a master of words and therefore disliked the usage of words in false and fancied meanings. It seemed to him that adhesion to a League of Nations signified no more loss of "sovereignty" than is implied in any treaty. As a student of political science, he had studied sovereignty since he was a young man, and it irritated him to hear the word bandied about insincerely for partisan purposes in the prolonged debate in the Senate on the ratification of the League of Nations. He was a student of the Constitution of the United States and held it folly to argue that, by becoming a signatory to the Covenant of the League of Nations, we should sacrifice our sovereign right to enter or stay out of an international broil, for he knew that the Constitution of the United States had not been changed, that nothing had diminished the authority of the article of the Constitution which declares that "Congress shall have power . . . to declare war," etc. He reverenced the Constitution of the United States and had no thought of setting up a "superstate." When he was a young professor in Princeton he read a paper, "Sovereignty," at a faculty club. The aged Dr. McCosh, president emeritus, was in attendance, and at the conclusion of the paper said, "Umph! I have always understood that sovereignty is derived from God." Professor Wilson smiled and said, "So did I, Dr. McCosh, but in this paper I was not going back that far." Before that and after, indeed throughout his life, he was a student of sovereignty, its origins, developments, privileges, and obligations. Government as a human phenomenon was his favorite topic. To him the most interesting subject in the world was mankind's predisposition for self-government, the opportunity for which he desired to extend to all nations.

Mr. Wilson was by lineage Scotch and Scotch Irish, and he ran true to form. With all his brilliancy, there was in him a kernel of tough common sense. He was an idealist with a strong realization of the practical. He read the signs of the times and the prognosis of the morrow. In forming his opinions and decisions, he reckoned with circumstances as they were and as they promised to be. He sought to do justice impersonally. He sought to set the house in order, not by theory, but by a clear recognition of existent facts. He knew that prior to the Great War, immense progress had been made in the settlement of international disputes by arbitration. He knew, for instance, that the United States had entered into treaty relations with every state of South America, and that scores of troublesome questions which formerly would have led to bloodshed had been settled peaceably. He was familiar with the history of the Hague Tribunal and his own country's part in the establishment of it. But he saw the helplessness of the Hague Tribunal in the face of the Great War. He saw treaties torn to pieces. It seemed clear to him from the beginning of the war that there must follow the war a stronger bond of nations, something less sporadic, less purely legal. Though a lawyer, he distrusted mere legalistic settlements of international disputes. Behind whatsoever court the League might set up, he saw the necessity of a human bond, wherein nations would be educated to understand the interdependence of their interests. He had doubtless meditated on the fact that the Supreme Court of the United States has no means of enforcing its decisions, that it has succeeded because of a prevailing sentiment in its favor, a national acceptance of it as a national institution. He knew human nature, and therefore he knew that no international court could obtain a similar allegiance until an international sentiment in its favor had been created.

One of the words most frequently on his lips was "counsel." He believed that if representatives of the nations could be drawn into common counsel in an association or league, the nations would be gradually educated into an understanding or sentiment which would guarantee acceptance of the decisions of a court of their own creation.

In short, he looked at all matters in their basic human qualities. Human wisdom and justice were cardinal traits of his mind and spirit.

In Paris during the peace conference, a prominent American was surprised to hear it said that Mr. Wilson thoroughly disliked the Germans. He could not understand how a man could dislike a nation and at the same time resist concerted efforts to crush her economically.

It was this balance in Mr. Wilson which led many to think of him as "a man of mystery." Mr. Wilson's strong sense of fact and knowledge of history taught him that a policy of vengeance was never a policy of sentiment. It breeds new wars or at least reprisals. He knew that the sentiment of most of the world was with France in the Great War, partly because of the insolent terms which Germany had put upon France after the Franco-Prussian War. Reared in the South, he knew that the pains and resentments of Reconstruction under a policy dictated by haters of the South had made more lasting trouble than the war itself. He himself had written *Division and Reunion,* and he knew whereof he spoke.

The dignity of Mr. Wilson, the calm control of political passions by his will and reason, no matter how much the volcano was bubbling within, a touch of reserve that was natural to him, though his affections were deep and strong—these things and kindred things made Mr. Wilson a less spectacular person than Colonel Roosevelt. Colonel Roosevelt was "Teddy" to everybody. Few called Mr. Wilson "Woodrow." None called him "Woody" except in loving jest. People thought of him as they addressed him—as "Mr. President" or Mr. Wilson.

By temperament Mr. Wilson was conservative, by conviction progressive. He loved old things, reverenced the elders in religion and politics, had an affection for old modes of life, old customs, old books, old manuscripts, old buildings. He was by inheritance a Britisher, and though he despised Anglomaniacs and all brands of hyphenism, he loved to travel and sojourn in the old country, especially in the lake country which borders England and Scotland. He loved walled gardens and stone hedges and the English "quartered" style. The only home he ever built for himself was in Princeton and was in that style of architecture. He loved the Scotch Presbyterian form of worship, which he kept as his own all his life, and he also loved the English cathedral as an architectural and national monument and as a symbol of loving, patient workmanship. He loved the close loyalties of the past, and often spoke in admiration of Sir Walter Scott's devotion to the things of his country's history. He loved old books and old styles of writing, the prose of Sir Thomas Browne, Milton, and Charles Lamb. He was sometimes accused of affectation in the writing of the middle period of his authorship because he imported occasional archaisms into his own writing. But it was genuine love for the old forms, not affectation.

With all this he was a political progressive. He was a democrat—a truer one never lived, and he knew the logic of the Magna Carta and the Bill of Rights and the American Revolution and the English Industrial Revolution and the long history of America's struggles in the nineteenth century against privilege working through legislative processes for the entrenchment of itself and the ousting of the plain people from economic advantage.

After nearly thirty years of study of governmental institutions, he emerged from the academic world into the world of practical politics. His adaptation of fundamental principles to the practical problems and situations of his time is unparalleled in the history of American politics. As an active politician there was nothing "bookish" about him. He met experienced politicians on their own ground and usually worsted those who opposed him. He knew their wiles and their limitations. He was an accurate judge of men's motives. Therefore, his almost uncanny ability to know beforehand what people would do—not only his own people, the people of America, but also the people of foreign lands. He who had never been in Germany judged the German mind and temper clearer than any other statesman of the Allies. Ludendorff has testified that President Wilson's

messages did more to break down the German morale than did all
the armed forces of the Allies. He sought to drive a wedge between
the German people and their leaders, and he succeeded, because he
knew human nature, knew how to appeal to people in the mass.

Though an intellectual aristocrat, he championed the cause of the
plain people, of labor, of the oppressed everywhere. He believed in
leadership, but he also believed in the capacity of the people to be
led without demagoguery. He believed in the people even when they
seemed to reject him, as in 1920. The day the election returns came
in he said, "I have lost none of my faith in the people." A 7,000,000
plurality staggered the faith of many in democracy, but Woodrow
Wilson's faith remained serene. The people could be temporarily
confused and inflamed, but back of sudden eruptions there was, he
believed, a steady judgment that would reassert itself.

He had an extraordinary mind, a lofty and somewhat reserved
spirit, but the outstanding fact about him was that he was a human
being. As a young man and a middle-aged man he was fond of quoting one of his favored authors—perhaps it was Augustine Birrell—to
the effect that "the only way to write was to write like a human
being."

He was a lover of letters, with the old humanistic love. He despised
pedantry. He lectured in the university on political theory, but he so
packed his lectures with human interest that the students crowded
the classroom to the doors. As governor of New Jersey, he presented
to the masses in language which the simplest could understand the
fundamental principles of self-government.

His messages as president of the United States were masterpieces
of exposition and interpretation. As the supreme leader of the councils in Europe, he reduced the complicated and technical reports of
his advisers to simplified human language which all the world could
follow.

To present the humanistic character of this man's mind and spirit
is the object of the present undertaking.

Woodrow Wilson and His Father

～

ONE DAY during the peace conference in Paris, when President Wilson was entertaining some American friends, one of whom had a son preparing for college, conversation turned to the education of boys, the types of teachers, the methods of teaching, and the varieties of colleges and courses from which boys may derive most benefit, and presently one of the company asked the president from what teacher he had received the best training; prompt was the answer: "My father![1] I got ten times more from my father than I got at college. He was a rare teacher." One who was closely associated with the president in Paris[2] remarked that the memory of his father seemed continually with the president in the perplexities and aspirations of his peace conference negotiations. "I believe," said this friend, "that every night when he lays his head on the pillow, his last thought is, 'I wonder if my father would have approved of what I did today and the way I did it.'"

When the English border city of Carlisle entertained President Wilson and extended to him the freedom of the city, less because he was president of the United States and a commanding figure in the world negotiations about to open in Paris than because his grandfather[3] had preached in Carlisle and his mother[4] was born there, Woodrow Wilson visited his grandfather's house, stood in reverent silence in the room in which his mother was born, and later from his pew made brief and delicate reference to her. Jessie Woodrow, who was born of Scotland's intellectual aristocracy, some of whose forebears had assisted in making Scottish history, especially in the kirk, sailed for America when she was a little girl, accompanying her parents to the then comparatively new country, was almost lost at sea when a great wave swept her from the deck, was saved by her own Scottish pluck, for she seized a rope that was trailing and was drawn aboard, landed in America, lived in Chillicothe, Ohio, grew up to be

2. Wilson's birthplace, Staunton, Virginia

a beautiful woman, married Joseph R. Wilson, a young Presbyterian minister, was a devoted wife and mother, carefully reared her two sons and two daughters,[5] all of whom except the youngest, Joseph, she saw happily married before her death, in 1888, in Clarksville, Tennessee, where her husband was engaged in his last professional task as lecturer in the theological seminary. Mrs. Wilson had the strength of character of the Woodrows, and their superior intellectuality, combined with grace and gentleness of manner which is clearly remembered even by those who when they were young knew her but slightly. She was a type of "pastor's wife" which the world cannot lose without impoverishment; bred in an older school, she probably knew little about modern church "organization" and "efficiency" and "church institutionalism," but she did know and practice the fine art of personal sympathy and understanding of the individual parishioners, supplementing church doctrines with quiet good deeds. From this strong and gentle mother Woodrow Wilson derived all that is best of mother love and mother training. Unobtrusive, delicate, all-involving was the influence of the mother on the son, scarcely so susceptible of analysis and assessment as the father's influence, the father who made systematic intellectual as well as moral education of the boy a definite business.

Dr. Joseph Ruggles Wilson was educated in the old school, wherein a prime object of education was to develop mind and character, to cultivate clear thinking, clear expression, and sound principles of living. Vocational education, in the modern sense, was unknown in Dr. Wilson's youth. If a young man was to be a minister of the gospel or a physician, he would, after his college course, study the technicalities of his "learned profession" in a theological or medical school; if he was to be a lawyer he might go to a law school or "read law" in the office of some luminary of the local bar. But the academic courses were practically the same in all the colleges of the country, whether Jefferson College at Allegheny, Pennsylvania, where Dr. Wilson studied, or Harvard or Yale or Princeton. Colleges were much alike in those days, all serving the same general purpose, namely, the training of the minds and characters of young men and the preparation of them for later study of one of the three learned professions.

Greek and Latin and mathematics formed the tripod on which sound education was supposed to rest, with some additional but secondary and rather incidental study of "natural philosophy," which generally meant whatever the professor in charge was best able to teach of elementary chemistry, or physics, or astronomy, or all three. As for English, that was not taught, for it was supposed, and it was a fairly sound supposition, that he who should learn Latin grammar thoroughly would need nothing more than it and his common sense to apply the principles of it to English speech, and that he who had learned to appreciate Homer and Aeschylus and Cicero would be able to appreciate, without further pedagogical guidance, Milton and Shakespeare and Burke. Sometimes rhetoric or "principles of criticism" might be studied, in Campbell or Lord Kames, but it really was not necessary if one knew his Quintillian. Joseph Wilson was sound in his classics and to his last days took pleasure in the old-fashioned manner of weaving Latin quotations into his conversation and especial delight in tracing an English word to its Latin or Greek root. But in his college days he also had a keen relish for the natural sciences, especially physics and chemistry.

When he went for his professional training to the Princeton Theological Seminary, the most distinguished figure in Princeton College, then the College of New Jersey, was Professor Joseph Henry, the eminent physicist, whose studies in electromagnetism had important bearings on the development of the electric telegraph; there is a Princeton tradition that the first message ever transmitted over a telegraph wire was sent from Professor Henry's house on the Princeton campus to the house of a colleague across the way. Fortunately for the young theological student, with the strong bent toward scientific study, Dr. Henry had not yet left Princeton to become the first secretary of the Smithsonian Institution in Washington, and Joseph Wilson not only attended Dr. Henry's lectures but formed a personal friendship with the older man and was admitted to the laboratory where he could watch, perhaps assist in humble ways, the important investigations which the great man was making. When Joseph Wilson was for a brief time a professional teacher in Hampden-Sydney College in Virginia, it was as a teacher of science, especially chemistry. There can be no question that he was a good teacher of chemistry, with his enthusiasm for the subject (to the end of his life his face would light up with interest when he talked of chemistry), with his extraordinary power of clear and forceful exposition, and with his strict and sometimes strenuous ideas of discipline. On at least one occasion, when he was dealing with a young man not only recalcitrant but aggressively impertinent, young Professor Wilson first knocked the student down and then taught him some chemistry.

Because in Augusta, Georgia, Columbia, South Carolina, and Wilmington, North Carolina, the southern cities in which Woodrow Wilson lived after he left Staunton, Virginia, his birthplace, there were no public schools in his day, he studied at private schools and under tutors, but with most stimulation from his father. The boy was not precocious, learned to read unusually late,[6] but long before he could read for himself he was being read to by his father and mother, and his father early taught him respect for literary style, stressed the idea that it was extremely important to have something to say, but also important to say it well, to select his words with care, rejecting

3. Joseph Ruggles Wilson, father of Woodrow Wilson, ca. 1860

4. Woodrow Wilson, ca. 1872

those which merely approximated his meaning and choosing those which would express his thought most accurately and most force-fully.

Certainly by no other teacher was he so systematically drilled in thought and expression, and it was in part as a result of this early training that Woodrow Wilson in his maturity placed much empha-sis on literary style; indeed, at one period of his authorship, when he was writing *George Washington* (1896), his critics accused him of being too attentive to style. As a university student at the Johns Hopkins, he used to complain that one of the lecturers under whom he sat most frequently "had a genius for selecting the weakest forms of expression."[7] Subsequently, each new book that he read, whether a solid work on history, jurisprudence, or economics, or a slight bit of fiction, had to pass muster as to its style. He would sometimes ask a younger acquaintance about the style of some book of which the young man was talking. The answer would frequently be a laughing retort: "Why, it has no style, I never thought of style in connection with the book." But Mr. Wilson always thought of style, at least in the earlier days of his faithful apprenticeship to the profession of letters. This was all due in part, of course, to inherent and developed tastes, but also in a considerable degree to the father who made it his business to cultivate the critical literary faculty in his boy. This chapter concerns the father's relationships to one of his children. Undoubtedly there was the same loving care for all the others, though none of the other children proved to have the inherent literary and scholastic tastes of the elder son.

To Dr. Wilson's systematic teaching of his son there was added the force of example. He himself wrote well, preached well, talked well, and daily read aloud in the presence of his son and the rest of his family a chapter from the Bible in the King James translation, than which, with all our modern methods, we have found no better means of developing youthful appreciation for noble language.

When Dr. Wilson was an old man he used frequently to say that one of the most gratifying things in his life was a letter from his boy who was then in Princeton College, which contained the sentence, "Father, I have made a discovery; I have found that I have a mind." Over the development of that mind Dr. Wilson watched with loving pride in the last ten years of his life when he was growing old and the son was growing distinguished as a marked man in the Princeton faculty and among young American authors. When Woodrow Wilson read to his father a portion of the manuscript of one of his earlier books—it may have been *Congressional Government* (1885)—the older man rose from his chair and kissed his son and with proud tears in his eyes congratulated him on the scholastic and literary excellence of the book, and then, quite unexpectedly, added: "I wish, my boy, you had been a preacher."

Because Dr. Wilson was himself humorous, sometimes sarcastic, sometimes frankly contemptuous of the "Praise-God barebones" pietistic type, people sometimes thought him lacking in what the

elect call "devoutness," but this little episode indicates that he held
to the old tradition of the Scotch Presbyterian Church that the lofti-
est mission on earth is the Christian ministry.

Each of Woodrow Wilson's succeeding books was read by the father with close attention and sometimes with a curt comment of criticism or commendation, as when referring to *The State* (1889) he
said, "Woodrow, couldn't you have put a little more juice into that
book?" Or, as when he said of *George Washington*, "I am glad you let
George Washington do his own dying."

No one personally acquainted with Dr. Joseph Wilson could be
mystified by the son's greatness, for Dr. Joseph Wilson was himself a
great man, although he did not achieve a great fame. He lived prior
to the day when every intellectual person, and frequently the un-
intellectual, feels under a compulsion to write a book. Dr. Wilson did
not write books. From southern pulpits he preached orthodox sermons, "sound" in theology, rich in Biblical lore, eloquent in phraseology, permeated and illuminated with flashes of insight into the
complexities of human nature; he was a learned professor of theology, at one time in Columbia, South Carolina, many years later at
Clarksville, Tennessee; he was stated clerk of the General Assembly
of the southern Presbyterian Church; but beyond an occasional article in one of the church papers, such as *The Southern Presbyterian*,
edited by his brother-in-law, Dr. James Woodrow,[8] he published
nothing, and the modern scholar who does not publish cannot have
an extensive fame. With all his pride in his son, he winced when he
came to be referred to as Woodrow Wilson's father. The son would
laugh and say, "It is your own fault, Father, for you would not publish." But he who came in personal contact with Dr. Wilson knew
that he was in the presence of a great personality.

He looked like a great man and he talked like a great man. He was
strikingly handsome and, because of his massive frame, gave the appearance of a larger man than he really was. Though only about five
feet, ten inches in height, his broad shoulders, deep chest, and leo-
nine head gave him a massive, dominating appearance. In his last
years his hair, which had not thinned, was a thick mane of the color
of Sea Island cotton, white with yellowish tinges in it. The eyebrows
were heavy, the eyes dark and penetrating, the nose straight, not so
long as his son's nose, but with the same sensitive flexible tip which
moved when he spoke with decision or emphasis. His mouth was
large and firm, at times fringed with a close-cropped mustache, at

other times close-shaven. He had enormous ears and feet, about both of which he frequently jested in his whimsical fashion.

Like the great old talkers of the leisurely eighteenth century, Dr. Wilson regarded conversation as one of the fine arts. He contended that if one would write well he must also talk well, that he could not be sloppy in conversation and classic in composition, that he who would protect himself from slovenly writing must take the pains to speak with care and precision. Withal there was no impression of pedantry in his conversation. His was racy talk in which the world of books, the world of men, and the world of everyday trivialities met together in agreeable fashion. He was bookish without being pedantic, and he could use a bit of current slang with a fine dignity of utterance. He was full of anecdote and as incorrigible a punster as Shakespeare himself. His puns were sometimes clever and quite as often very bad, and the bad ones were as funny as the clever ones. He would pun indiscriminately, with his intimates or with the stranger in the street, with the policeman on the corner, or the railway conductor on the train to whom he would hand his ticket with the remark that he would "like a little punch." His puns were spontaneous. Someone told him that the Delaware "peach belt" was moving southward annually: "Can't they buckle it?" he asked.

He doted on anecdotes about preachers. One concerned a Scottish divine who was giving the Lord much information in a very long prayer, but not long enough to contain all he wanted to tell, and so he concluded with "as thou knowest, O Lord, was published last month fully in the *Edinburgh Review*." He had infinite anecdotes about the General Assembly of the southern Presbyterian Church. One of these related to a Dr. McFarland,[9] who had an unusually long nose, and who on one occasion was in a minority of one on a question put by the presiding officer, the moderator of the assembly. After a roar of "ayes," the moderator called for the negative vote, and Dr. McFarland sprang to his feet and excitedly shouted "No! No!" several times, whereupon the moderator said, "The motion is carried, notwithstanding Dr. McFarland's nose."

The satiric quality of Dr. Wilson sometimes suggested Dean Swift, but there was a closer parallel to Dr. Samuel Johnson. There was in Dr. Wilson's ordinary conversation the same deliberateness, the same careful attention to language, without the impression of self-consciousness or display of erudition, because, like Dr. Johnson, Dr. Wilson was thoroughly human and humanly interested in everything that he saw or came in contact with. Like Dr. Johnson, he in his latter years loved "to fold his legs and have his talk out," and sometimes would be a little impatient in a good-natured way with his purposeful son saying, "Woodrow is always in a hurry," the same complaint Dr. Johnson made of John Wesley, whom Dr. Johnson loved but with whom he could never "have his talk out," because Wesley must be up and away to meet his next engagement. Woodrow Wilson, engrossed in college duties, in study and writing, in family and community responsibilities, had not the leisure for long hours of drifting conversation, no matter how stimulating, in front of the open fireplace in winter, on the porch in mild weather. After lunch he would pause for twenty or thirty minutes of conversation and then be off to his desk, or classroom, or committee meeting.

Dr. Wilson, widowed, retired from active professional pursuits (his son always said that the father made a mistake in retiring while his mind maintained all its vigor and extraordinary activity), social by inclination, but not one to go out in search of companionship (he once said that all his life he had suffered agonies from shyness, though the casual observer would not have guessed it in the big forceful man), a confirmed lover of that genial assistant to leisurely talk, tobacco, which the son never used, welcomed the companionship of a much younger man, a frequent member of the Wilson household,[10] who, like the doctor, was an habitual smoker, who had, or made, leisure for long talking, and who, also like the doctor, was fond of speculative conversation, not so much caring to what conclusion or terminus the conversation led, as that it was a pleasant road to jaunt along.

Purely speculative conversation, like the habit of musing, is the pastime of youth and age. Middle life is occupied with things practical, with getting results. Woodrow Wilson himself, as a young man, had enjoyed rambling speculative conversation, but as he grew older, as his ambitions and plans of authorship became more clearly defined, he had less interest in abstract theories and talk about theories. He was ready to discuss a principle, but it must be apparent that the principle was leading to something either in action or constructive thinking. There was work to be done in the world, and his share of it was becoming clearer to his vision.

Dr. Wilson, whose systematic work was ended, loved to discuss abstract, even abstruse problems. Though a clergyman and an orthodox theologian, he was delightfully unprofessional in his talk. His religion was something to live by and die by, but he was too broad-minded to suppose that "our little systems," which "have their day and cease to be," can explain all things in the universe, not even the system of the logical Calvin in which he had been bred.[11] "There are more things in heaven and earth than are dreamt of in your philosophy." His mind was liberal, free to range far in inquiry; in conversation he was the least contentious of people, loved to assume a proposition and follow it to its conclusions. He belonged to that older generation which treasured "table talk," and it is a pity that his youthful companion took no written notes on those wise, humorous, pithy, sometimes profound, sometimes searching, always human conversations. There has been only one Boswell, but even an ordinary reporter could out of such notes have made an illuminating chapter on this great personality and great talker.

Articulation was one of his hobbies. He had always stressed its value, and as semideafness overtook him he naturally valued it the more. He would sometimes say: "People shout at me, which is quite unnecessary, for I can understand every word that Woodrow says, and he never raises his voice in addressing me. He articulates." And that was quite true. If other members of the family circle would begin to speak hurriedly in his presence he would look at the speaker, with a slow turn of the head, keen look from his dark eyes, and quiet smile, and pronounce slowly the word, divided by deliberate pauses into its constituent syllables, "ar-tic-u-la-tion!"

Doubtless, this high valuation of spoken discourse was due, in part, to his training and profession as a public speaker. His was the tradition of the old Presbyterianism, whose ministers were supposed to be ripe scholars and trained, and if possible, eloquent preachers. Oratory was to Dr. Wilson one very important form of literature. In the older South to which he belonged, there was not an essential difference between the habits of mind of great preachers and great statesmen. In the South Carolina of Dr. Wilson's early days, one of the names most frequently associated with the name of John C. Calhoun was that of the distinguished theologian, James H. Thornwell,[12] with whom, by the way, Dr. Wilson had had a close friendship and for whom he retained to the end of his life an unqualified reverence, for though like his son he was critically minded, not given over to sudden enthusiasms, more likely to extend friendship than unrestricted admiration to an acquaintance, he nevertheless retained to his dying day an admiration amounting to hero worship for a few orators, including some preachers. Speaking of Dr. Benjamin Palmer,[13] one of the most eloquent of southern Presbyterian divines, formerly of South Carolina, latterly of New Orleans, whose facial features were not comely, Dr. Wilson said, "When he begins to speak you think he looks like a gorilla, but when he ends you think he looks like a god."

In Dr. Wilson's youth, a great statesman and a great divine, at least in the South, were cut on much the same pattern. Both were philosophers: the statesman with fundamental views on the relationship of government to individuals and the scope and meaning of the Constitution of the United States; the preacher with fundamental theological concepts and far-reaching theories about church government. Both the statesmen and the preachers tended to trace their dogmas back to first principles, to metaphysics. The South produced little antebellum literature in the sense of belles-lettres, but oratory was itself often literature. A sermon or a speech in Congress by an eminent man was an event which people anticipated beforehand and remembered and talked of afterwards. Passages of eloquence from sermons and political orations were discussed in the home and in the places of business and were sometimes memorized and recited. Even as late as the time in which Woodrow Wilson was getting his early formulative mental impressions, the son of a prominent Presbyterian preacher, conspicuous not only in his pastorate but in the stirring debates of the Presbyterian General Assembly, would unconsciously absorb from his father's account of the last meeting of the General Assembly a number of things destined to have a bearing on a later political career.

It was from his father that Woodrow Wilson derived his taste for Burke and Webster. In Paris, President Wilson was one day telling some friends how his father in his young days had taken to pieces the speeches of Webster, carefully analyzing their formations and their sentence structures and trying to substitute other and better words in place of some of Webster's words, but always finding that he could not improve the Webster diction, that Webster himself had found the strong word and put it in the strong place.

Once Dr. Wilson had heard the great Webster speak, nor had he forgotten the thrill of it half a century later when he described the blazing summer heat, the stand erected in front of the Capitol at Washington, the majesty of the Olympian Webster when he stepped to the front of the platform, slowly extended his hand toward the sun, and in sonorous tones uttered a salutation, and the opening sentence of his address, "Hail, thou sun of liberty." "And," said Dr. Wilson, "do you know, I thought the sun winked back at him," meaning that the sun recognized a peer in Webster.

It was in the old school of forensics that Dr. Wilson had trained himself, both in composition and delivery. The movement of his sentences was stately, and, though he liked the "strong Saxon word," he was too good a classicist to forgo the advantageous occasional use of Latin derivatives, with their dignity and rhythm. His style was neither floral nor familiar, but classic, with power held in reserve. He studied delivery as carefully as he studied composition, for in his day it was no more assumed that "anybody could make a speech" than that anybody could make a watch. Writing and speaking were arts to be studied and practiced as one would study and practice music or painting. His favorite place of rehearsal was an old barn, and one day, in a reminiscent mood, he described in detail the scene of his labors, the barn, the hayloft, the corncrib, and the old red cow that lay in one corner chewing the cud and mildly turning her head to look over her shoulder at the young orator when his delivery became frenetic. The old gentleman recited the incident and painted the picture as one who muses aloud, reconstructing the scene in his mind's eye, and then, gradually coming back to the present, he turned to his companion with a characteristic slow movement of the head and remarked, in his deliberate way, "And she was about as intelligent as my later audiences."

His flashes of sarcastic humor were droll rather than cruel, resultants of his clear recognition of the stupidities, absurdities, and vainglories of the human race. These were the moments when he reminded one of Dean Swift. Like Swift, he had no personal vanities, "was," as Swift said of himself, "too proud to be vain." Like Swift, he spoke plainly and to the point, was sometimes curt, sometimes sardonic, but he was not intentionally cruel, and he was not embittered. Mankind's pettiness, malice, and foolishness, which enraged Swift, amused Dr. Wilson. He had a *bubbling* humor, which Swift had not; in good temper and with those he liked, it bubbled genially, like a pleasant spring, in repartee and kindly teasing. If Dr. Wilson teased you, it was a sure sign that he liked you. If he was displeased by a person, his humor bubbled *hot*, in scalding sarcasms.

His repartee was quick and ready. One of the many stories which Woodrow Wilson has frequently related of his father was of a ready reply which Dr. Wilson made to a parishioner in Augusta, Georgia, who rashly undertook to "have a little fun with the dominie": Dr. Wilson drove a good horse in those days and on one occasion, while he was watering the animal at a town trough, the parishioner, in passing, noted that Dr. Wilson's coat was not in its pristine youth or as carefully brushed as usual; whereupon he said, "Why, doctor, your horse is better cared for than yourself." "Good reason," said the doctor, "I take care of my horse, and my congregation takes care of me."

He was ready to acknowledge defeat when he was worsted in a verbal encounter. One day, when Woodrow Wilson was living at Bryn Mawr, his first teaching post, in the newly founded college for women, he and his father and mother had been spending a naive afternoon in visiting the historic sights of Philadelphia. Dr. Wilson, whose animal spirits were sometimes lively, was in a mood for wild fun; all afternoon he showered miscellaneous Philadelphians with puns and repartee, like an exploding skyrocket. A fresh whim seized him when he reached Broad Street Station, and, in going down the platform to the local train, he walked in an elaborately bowlegged fashion, his enormous feet spread wide, at right angles to the plane of his legs. If his more sedate son disapproved this hilarious behavior he made no sign; his filial respect would not have permitted him to remonstrate with his parent. Now, it so happened that an enormous Negro man who had been cleaning car windows with a long-handled swab was standing with his mop over one shoulder, his pail in the other hand, looking vacantly up at the beams of the train shed, with the vacuous expression of the primitive Negro type, a ludicrous figure, and a challenge to Dr. Wilson in his mood for horse play. As soon as the doctor saw the man, he straightened his own figure, walked up to him, put his arms akimbo, raised his eyes to the dark face that towered above him, cocked his head on one side, and said, "Well, what are you going to do about it?" The gigantic Negro slowly bent his eyes down on the doctor, his immobile face betraying no surprise and his mouth no flicker of a smile. "I'se gwine do what's right about it," he answered. Dr. Wilson turned away, grunted softly, and said, "I rather think he had the best of that."

A little silent comedy was played periodically in the Wilson home in Princeton on occasional visits from a relative of Mrs. Woodrow Wilson's,[14] of whom both she and her husband were very fond, but whom Dr. Wilson did not cordially like, and who, in turn, was not enamored of the doctor. This relative was also a distinguished Presbyterian clergyman, of approximately Dr. Wilson's age. They both belonged to the more conservative school of Presbyterianism, both had been ardent sympathizers of the South in the war, both were strong personalities, given to clear thinking and straightforward speaking. It is said that opposites attract; perhaps these two strong men were too much alike for mutual attraction. They genuinely respected each other and frankly did not like each other. Each knew that in the other he had a foeman worthy of his steel, and each hesitated to deliver the first blow in a verbal combat. Each was a ready, easy talker with other people, but as soon as they began to talk to each other they became restrained and elaborately polite, exchanging guarded courtesies, like two big dogs, each determined to behave until the other "starts something," and then let bystanders beware!

Dr. Wilson was an incorrigible humorist of the sort that finds delight in repeating the same jest or pun or bit of teasing with infinite reiteration. When he once "got a joke on you" he never "let up"; he followed one of his loving and admiring victims[15] for a dozen years with the same joke, which referred to an anecdotal incident related by the youngster in an unlucky moment, the truth of which Dr. Wilson took leave to doubt. It was a story about a mule;[16] for a decade and more when the younger man would begin to tell a story, the doctor would gravely ask to be assured beforehand whether it had anything to do with that mule.

His "ruling passion was strong in death," for he jested on what was practically his deathbed. One day the little Wilson girls ran into the apartments of a relative in Princeton with the message that "Mother wants you to come at once; we fear Grandfather is dying." He had been ill for several years with arteriosclerosis, but on this particular afternoon the crisis seemed to have arrived. Woodrow Wilson, then president of the university, was out of town on business, but when the relative arrived in the bedchamber he found assembled Mrs. Wilson, Mrs. Annie Howe, Dr. Wilson's daughter, and his younger son, Mr. Joseph Wilson, who had arrived from his home in Nashville several days before. The immediate crisis had passed, but the doctor was only semiconscious. The relative stood at the foot of the bed and was aware that the sick man was scrutinizing him, as one peers through a mist, trying to identify him. "Who is that?" the doctor presently asked in hoarse, weak tones. "It is I, doctor." "Who is I?" The visitor gave his name. "Why, what are you doing here?" the old man asked. "Oh, I just dropped in," said the other. "Umph," grunted the doctor, "I am a little dropsical myself."

As a matter of fact, he did not die that afternoon, though he had journeyed to the threshold of the terrible gate. When his death came several weeks later, his son Woodrow was with him, and the old man's last intelligible words were, "My dear, dear son!"

The love between these two was lifelong, tender, deep, and understanding. His father has always been Woodrow Wilson's true hero, for, added to filial affection and the respect which he maintained to the end of his father's life in all its original simple quality of deference, there was profound admiration for the character and the mind of his father.

Mr. Tumulty[17] has several times related this incident: one afternoon as the cabinet was assembling, there arrived at the White House offices an old man, who said that he had known Dr. Joseph Wilson and would like to see his son, the president. Visitors may not usually be permitted to interrupt or delay a cabinet session, but Mr. Tumulty felt that this was an exception. He went into the cabinet room, whispered a few words to the president, who immediately came out and shook hands with the old gentleman, who, in turn, told the president the circumstances under which he had known his father, and, laying his hand on the president's shoulder, gently turned his face to the light, saying, "I want to look at you." As the visitor talked, the president was seen to bow his head and press both hands over his eyes. After a brief conversation the old visitor gently patted the president on the arm and said, "I have just one thing to say to you: take good care of yourself," and the two parted company. At the door of the cabinet room, the president was seen to pause an instant and brush his hand rapidly across his eyes. Then he threw back his shoulders, lifted his head, and stepped firmly and briskly into the cabinet chamber, to take up the nation's business for the day.

Dr. Wilson lived to hear his son mentioned for the presidency of the United States.[18] Sitting in his dressing gown in an easy chair, in a pleasant upper room in Prospect, the official residence of the president of the university, the French windows open on a mild autumn afternoon, with a long stretch of New Jersey landscape undulating to the far horizon, he talked with a visitor of various things, and presently, with an abrupt change of conversation, said, "They are talking about Woodrow for president—of the United States," and then,

5. Joseph Ruggles Wilson, ca. 1890

after a moment's pause, "but the politicians will never let him be president."

During his last dozen or fifteen years he was, either intermittently, or regularly, a member of his son's household. When he first retired from his professorship in the Southwestern Theological Seminary at Clarksville, Tennessee, he divided his time between New York[19] and Princeton. He loved New York, its libraries, a few valued friends there, and the crowded life of the city's streets. But as he began to grow feeble, his stays in New York were shortened, those in Princeton lengthened, then even the brief visits to New York became infrequent, and at last he settled quietly down in his son's house, clearly recognizing the fact that the end was slowly drawing on. He saw the family move from a rented house in Library Place to the home which they built on an adjoining lot, a house in which he always found his room ready for him on arrival, and when Woodrow Wilson was made president of the university, in 1902, Dr. Wilson, of course, moved with the family to Prospect, where he lived, now a confirmed invalid, until his death, in January 1903, at the age of eighty-one.

In those later Princeton years he read omnivorously but unsystematically. He had the taste of his generation for Walter Scott's novels, which he had read entire several times during his vigor, and he again reread them all a year or two before his death. He was a more rapid reader than his son, and his tastes were more miscellaneous, ranging from theology, philosophy, and history to novels of slightest merit. It became an advertised fact that President Wilson frequently rested his mind with detective stories. These were also a taste and habit with Dr. Wilson, and increasingly so as he grew older. But in the days of his vigor, when he also was "resting his mind," he added to his reading that type of adventure fiction known as "dime novels." Usually the literary style of these books is poor, but occasionally one is well written. Dr. Wilson was accustomed to buy them in bulk, saying, "It is like buying cheap razors; if you buy enough you are likely to find one good one."

He read much history in his latter years, occasionally a book of science, seldom a work of theology, which had been his life's specialty. Occasionally, he would read a book of devotion, but grunted contemptuously over those that were morbidly introspective or gloomy in tone. Even Thomas à Kempis did not appeal to him. In one of his less reverent moods he said that "if Thomas à Kempis had taken a blue mass pill,[20] he would not have written that book." His religion was healthy, robust. On the table in his bedroom his Bible, with a flexible cover, always rested, and its worn back and crumpled pages gave the evidence of its constant use.

His feet were firmly planted on the ground, and he never had much sympathy for the transcendentalists. Though he loved Carlyle's *French Revolution*, it is doubtful if he cared much for Carlyle's mystical writings. He certainly was not fond of Emerson. He saw the

sage of Concord once, and his sole reminiscence was rather shock-
ing to the ardent admirer of Emerson to whom Dr. Wilson related the
manner of this encounter. It was on a railway train, in a day coach.
Emerson, doubtless on a journey to deliver one of his immortal lectures, was asleep, his head thrown back, his mouth open, snoring. "It
was the biggest mouth I ever looked into," said Dr. Wilson. Certainly
not a luminous recollection of Emerson.

To Dr. Wilson, the writings of Emerson seemed tenuous, nebu-
lous. Between the transcendentalists, with their blithe indifference
to logic, and the stern dogmas and strict logic of Calvin, there is a
fixed gulf, and Dr. Wilson was on the side of the Calvinists, if not
in the terrors of their teachings, at least in their respect for close
reasoning.

Woodrow Wilson, who necessarily derived prejudices as well as
admirations from his father, may have received in his father's house
his lifelong lukewarmness toward Emerson, an indifference which
some admirers of both Emerson and Woodrow Wilson have regret-
ted. There is similarity in the serene idealism of the two men, and in
the clear confident prose of Emerson one sometimes hears a voice
which reminds him of the tones of Woodrow Wilson, when he is expressing the vision and the aspirations of a new age in the world's
international relations.

A student of American history and of Woodrow Wilson's career
once asked a man who had known Mr. Wilson in his young days,
"Was Woodrow Wilson in his youth taught to dislike Thomas Jefferson?" There was in President Wilson a disposition to distrust some of
the Jeffersonian doctrines as too theoretical, some of the generaliza-
tions as too loose. Whether or not Woodrow Wilson had derived
from his father a particular distrust of Jefferson's political philosophy, he had certainly learned from his father to keep in close touch
with actualities, to plant the base of his ladder in the firm ground, no
matter how high into the heavens its upper rungs may reach. Political theory never interested Woodrow Wilson, though political principles, deduced from racial and national experience, since his college
days at Princeton, engaged much of his thinking.

Dr. Wilson's own most vivid political experience had been in connection with the events and interpretations which led to the War between the States. For him, as for most southern men, there was a
definite Constitution of the United States to be reckoned with and a
consequent tendency to reject that invisible "higher law" than the

Constitution of which some Unionists had talked prior to the conflict. Not that Woodrow Wilson himself, in his maturity, was a "strict constructionist," quite the contrary, for he became the most important advocate of the "biological," "developmental" view of the Constitution. But in earlier days, Dr. Wilson, true to his environment, had been a strict constructionist.

Though northern-born and married to a wife of Scottish ancestry, also reared in the North, Dr. Wilson, like so many northern men who lived in the South, became thoroughly convinced of the right of the southern states to secede, and Lee and Jackson were as much his heroes as if he had been born in Virginia instead of being only for a few years a resident there. One associates him more with Georgia and South Carolina than with Virginia. He was loyal to South Carolina and respected South Carolina's traditions. He was completely reconstructed after the war, and, in all likelihood, held his son's view that the success of secession would, in the light of events, have been a catastrophe. But this did not destroy his historical loyalty to South Carolina's cause in the days of question, hesitation, and decision, before "hindsight" had made clear what was then concealed from "foresight."

He had the South Carolinian's pride in South Carolina, and sometimes in Princeton he crossed swords with men of his own generation, whose triumphant Unionism had made them bigoted. One of these[21] had the poor taste to tell Dr. Wilson, "I am happy to say that I was never in the state of South Carolina." Prompt was the retort, dignified but stinging, "I have no doubt, Sir, that the state of South Carolina reciprocates."

Like Dr. Samuel Johnson, once more to draw the parallel, Dr. Wilson was "a good hater." He possessed some old antagonisms which he kept like jewels in a casket, something precious, not to be lost, occasionally to be set forth for the joy of contemplation. In anticipation of his death he was giving his son some directions about his funeral, to which he added, "And don't let So-and-So come to it," So-and-So being an eminent divine for whom Dr. Wilson cherished those "imperfect sympathies" of which Charles Lamb wrote.

One day in his own prolonged illness, President Wilson remarked to a person who had known his father, "With all my devotion to my father, I cannot find that I have inherited any of his traits." The visitor was compelled to assume an abnormally grave look to keep from smiling. Woodrow Wilson, now one of the elders himself, his age accentuated by illness, is very much like his father: like him in little things, such as the love of anecdote and the habit of punning and the taste for detective stories, like him in moments of blunt speech and uncompromising disinclination to mollify or conciliate those with whom he differs fundamentally in views and convictions, like him in the stern consistency with which he holds to a faith or a prejudice. As a young man, exceptionally gentle, tender, courteous in his human and social contacts, one did not immediately recognize the resemblance between son and father, not until he had come to know the father well and discerned depths of tenderness in the older man beneath a gruff exterior. But as Woodrow Wilson himself under the weight of years and cares stiffened in fiber, the resemblance became obvious to one who had known both, and in each there was a greatness which underlay all qualities, acquisitions, and attainments, an essential greatness, marked in the son who achieved a world fame, marked in the father who was but little known outside his own communities and the circles of southern Presbyterianism, a greatness of personality.

Health and Recreations

❧

ORGANIZED play was unknown to southern boys of Woodrow Wilson's generation. They had no gymnastic teachers or "coaches," and community play was as unanticipated as the radio. They learned swimming, boat riding, shooting, and fishing as the boys in Squeer's School[1] learned window washing—by doing it. Boxing with gloves was a favorite sport, but there were no professional teachers of defense and attack. They formed themselves into baseball clubs, which usually bore fantastic names, and whose pitchers were innocent of the science of the curved ball. A sort of modified "association football" was played in scattered localities. In their backyards, they swung trapeze from tree limbs and erected horizontal bars, which they called "acting poles," and on which they taught themselves to hang by their legs, "do the giant swing," etc. It was the period of the vagrant tightrope walker, who would give his exhibition in the main street of the town or village and depend for revenue on volunteer offerings. After every such visit there was an eruption of tightrope walking among the boys of the town. Usually the "rope" was the backyard fence, and the local apothecaries did a thriving business in arnica.[2] The greatest annual event was the visit of the circus. The average boy was busy before the performance carrying pails of water for the animals, and after the showmen had folded their tents and ridden away, the boys engaged in various stunts in open lots.

Boys invented their own amusements, simple and primitive. It is astonishing how much pleasure they could get by laying two pins crosswise on a railway track for the locomotive or streetcar to press into scissors. Or they would go down to the cotton warehouse and play hide and seek among the cotton bales. Boys who read books of adventure taught their companions to play Indians and Indian fighters and highwaymen. The elders frowned on the popular dime novel literature of the day, but most boys read them nevertheless and found in their pages many hints for applied amusements. Bows and arrows as well as kites were skillfully fashioned, but they were home-made and not "store bought." Marbles were played and tops spun in regular season.

Life was simple, and amusements were inexpensive and spontane-ous. The discipline of organized sport was entirely lacking in a way that was unfortunate. Southern boys of those bygone days were fiercely individualistic. They fought at the drop of the hat and never learned the give and take of modern team play. On the other hand, it is possible that the modern boy is being too much standardized, sets too much store by good "form," relies too little on his own spontane-ous invention or idea. The marked individualism of the southern man of a generation ago may be due in part to this lack of standard-ized training in the days of his youth. He was by no means always superior to his more stereotyped brethren, but he was picturesquely different.

Woodrow Wilson was both different and superior. During his ac-tive political career, slightly younger men of different training than his complained that he did not do business like other people. It is at least a plausible theory that some of his marked individuality may have been due to the fact that as a child he was never pressed into a mold. As a clergyman's son, he was taught the sanctity of the moral law, and in his father's household he heard from earliest childhood high talk on serious matters. And yet, as has been remarked in this book and elsewhere, nobody forced him to learn his alphabet until he was nine years old. From early age he learned to think his own thoughts and practice his own devices.

There is more about play than about books in the record of Mr. Wilson's childhood. Mr. William Bayard Hale, who wrote a delightful brief biography of Mr. Wilson in 1912,[3] and who accumulated from original sources much pertinent matter concerning Mr. Wilson's childhood, says: "He was a real boy while he was a boy." He then proceeds to show that the child, "Tom" Wilson, found his amuse-ments in many of the typical forms which we have catalogued above. He had his baseball club, known as the "Lightfoot." He rode horse-back. He made friends with the drivers of the streetcars and felt the thrill of being allowed to work the brakes. He played Indian fre-quently with his tomboy cousin, Jessie Bones.[4] They would stain their skins with pokeberry juice, arm themselves with bows and arrows, and act out the *Leather Stocking Tales* to the terrorization of the pickaninnies whom they met on the roadway. "Tom" seems to have been a good bowman. On one occasion his aim was almost fatally accurate. His cousin Jessie was playing squirrel in a tree top, and Tom's arrow brought her tumbling to the ground unconscious. He took her to the house in his arms, exclaiming: "I am a murderer; it wasn't an accident; I killed her." But happily, his apprehensions were exaggerated, for in a few minutes she was conscious and herself again.

Mr. Hale relates a story known to all of Mr. Wilson's friends and connected with his boyish ambition to become an officer in the United States Navy. It is a rather unusual story because of the many months which the lad spent in one systematic game. Conceiving of himself as admiral of a United States war fleet under orders from the Navy Department to find and destroy the nest whence pirates sailed on marauding expeditions against American commerce, the boy wrote daily reports to the department in language so literal and de- tailed that it reminded Mr. Hale of DeFoe's realistic narratives. In those days, young Wilson had never visited a sea port, but he knew of types of sailing vessels and could tell the name and use of every spar and rope. That ambition to enter the country's naval service is testi- fied to in books still existent in the Wilson library—old books which bear the inscription in round, bold, clear boyish handwriting, "Thomas W. Wilson, Admiral," to which is appended as a concession to his younger brother, "Joseph R. Wilson, Jr., Commodore."

In the young admiral's idea of destroying the piratical fleet at its source, the old style biographer would have found a prophecy and a portent, for in August 1917, President Woodrow Wilson, commander in chief of America's navy, as well as her other armed forces, deliv- ered an address to the officers of the Atlantic Fleet, in which he as- serted that it was hopeless to try to destroy Germany's submarine power by sinking a vessel here and there, that the only way to end the menace was to find the harborage or "nest," for he used the same word he had used in his boyish report. "We are hunting hornets all over the farm and letting the nest alone," he said.[5] It was the civilian who had once played at being a naval officer who conceived and in- sisted upon the plan pronounced impossible by seamen of both the United States and Great Britain by which the German submarines menace was finally ended.[6] At Davidson College, which young Wil- son entered in 1873, he continued his general elective plan of both study and sport. He played on the college [freshman] baseball team, but the captain[7] told him that he "would make a dandy player if he were not so damn lazy." He walked a great deal in the country, and he seems to have read more in the books that he liked than in those prescribed by the college curriculum. It was at Davidson that we hear of his first serious illness, sufficiently serious to compel him to go to his father's home in Wilmington, North Carolina, before the end of the college year. An attack of measles went hard with him and left aftereffects from which he did not recover in many years.[8] He spent the next year in his father's home recuperating, reading and tutoring in Greek and other studies in order that he might enter Princeton College, then the College of New Jersey, in 1875. At Princeton he became immediately a leader in one of the most remarkable classes that has ever graduated from that institution, the famous class of 1879—not only an intellectual leader as we shall hear in other chapters, but a leader in sports. Because of his previous illness he was not sufficiently strong to play on either the football or baseball team—this to his great sorrow. But he was made president of the baseball association and in his senior year president of the athletic committee.

From Princeton he went to the University of Virginia to study law under the distinguished John B. Minor and had a brilliant career with which, however, we are not concerned in this chapter. The outstanding facts in the story of his recreations and health are that, though he played baseball a little, he sought his chief exercise in taking long walks, sometimes with companions, sometimes alone. But that exercise did not preserve him from an illness which forced him to leave the university without taking his degree in law.[9] Undoubtedly he worked harder at the University of Virginia than he had ever worked before, and it is quite possible that it was here that he acquired the indigestion with which he was troubled for many years.

In 1882–1883, he was a young lawyer in Atlanta, and there appears no record of the condition of his health during that period.

This brings us down to 1884 when I, the brother of the first Mrs. Wilson, became personally acquainted with Mr. Wilson. His and Ellen Axson's engagement was of a year's standing, and Mr. Wilson, who had abandoned the practice of law for graduate studies at Johns Hopkins University, was visiting Miss Axson in Rome, Georgia. I, a schoolboy, was at home for the summer vacation. Mr. Wilson was in his twenty-eighth year, five feet, eleven inches tall, of medium build,

6. Ellen Louise Axson, ca. 1883

with a remarkably long jaw but a counteracting smile which saved his face from severity. You would have had to travel a long day's journey to meet a man with more winning manners, more friendly courtesy. He was kind to me for his sweetheart's sake doubtless, but whatever the incentive, he was so very cordial that I lost my heart to him at once.

Probably in my callow youth I was less impressed by his large, luminous eyes—the eyes of genius—than by his long, flowing mustache. Such a copious and fluent mustache would have won the admiration of any boy in the early 1880s. And yet with all my enthusiasm for Mr. Wilson's mustache there was a mental reservation, a vague instinct, that an orator should be clean-shaven, though I have no idea why I then supposed he was an orator. In addition to the mustache, he wore short, close-clipped side whiskers, known in the vernacular as "paddies," and there protruded above the unusually low collar, which he affected, long unclipped hairs. His was the combination of refined features and much hair. In fact, his beard was so heavy that he had to shave twice in the day if he was attending a social function in the evening. When a professor at Bryn Mawr College he sacrificed his mustache, so he said, to enable the young ladies in his classes to know from the expression of his mouth when he was joking and when he was serious.

On a picnic in that summer of 1884, his cousin Jessie, who had married Mr. Brower,[10] challenged the men and boys of the party to a contest, the object of which was to throw a stone over the top of a tall pine tree which grew on a high ledge above the roadway—no small feat. Mrs. Brower, who could throw more like a man than most men, won, with Mr. Wilson a close second, as I remember.

After this visit I did not see him again until he came to Savannah to be married in June 1885. In the next summer I had my first prolonged visit with him in Gainesville, Georgia, where Mrs. Wilson, in anticipation of the birth of her first child,[11] had gone to be with her aunt, Mrs. Warren Brown, and here I learned of Mr. Wilson's indigestion, which was a remorseless enemy for many years. He exclaimed one day after a trying experience: "I suppose I have the worst stomach in the world." He was also subject to severe headaches, but he pluckily kept on his feet in spite of indispositions. I remember Mr. Wilson in much ill health, but I remember him seldom confined to his bed.[12]

In Gainesville our only exercise was walking, usually along the railway track to Holland Springs, then a crude but picturesque summer resort, now a great cotton manufacturing plant. It was on those walks that I got my first lessons in Burke and Bagehot—the young professor's favorite authors—and heard politics discussed on a high plane, more about principles than personalities, and learned that the young professor would dearly love a seat in the United States Senate but believed that his academic profession had permanently side-

7. Independent Presbyterian Church, Savannah, Georgia,
with the manse, where Woodrow Wilson and Ellen Axson were married
in 1885, in the foreground

tracked him from active politics. We walked leisurely, at a gait that permitted conversation. Mr. Wilson enjoyed exercising his mind more than exercising his body.

The increase of adult physical exercise since Mr. Wilson was a young man gives the generation succeeding his a better chance of longevity and health. Boys have always invented physical sports, but for men of Mr. Wilson's vintage, at least in the South, there was little planned systematic exercise. Men rode horseback in the country but not very much in the towns. Some men went on hunting and fishing expeditions but took little or no exercise between their trips. The southern climate did not encourage long cross-country "hikes." Golf was unheard of, and lawn tennis was just beginning to be played by youngsters. Grownup men with serious business thought it beneath their dignity. Mr. Wilson was never a hunter or a fisherman, and though he rode horseback well, he could seldom afford the luxury.

In Gainesville in 1886, and also in the following summer, for we all met again in 1887 in the little Georgia hill town, I saw him in his typical pursuits of those days, walking, conversing with friends, reading and writing books and articles, for a portion of each day was set apart for work. Mr. Wilson was amused to find that he had acquired a reputation for erudition in Gainesville, not by his published writings, for not many of the citizens of Gainesville bothered with those things, but because the postmaster noised it abroad that this young man who had married Warren Brown's niece received by post books from Europe published in foreign tongues.

I visited the Wilsons at their home in Bryn Mawr in the summer of 1888, and in the northern climate our walks were more frequent, more rapid and longer—sometimes ten miles—the distance from Bryn Mawr to Philadelphia, and this was still his one mode of exercise. If he played lawn tennis at all at Bryn Mawr, it was infrequently. His brother Joseph, familiarly known as "Josie," who also spent that summer in Bryn Mawr, rode with enthusiasm the old-style high bicycle, dressed in a natty suit of blue, with the letters, L.A.W. (League of American Wheelmen), woven on his blouse. But again it was a case of boys doing what men disdained. Among the numerous high wheels ridden by young men one occasionally glimpsed an odd-looking low bicycle which was called a "safety" bicycle. But it was regarded as an eccentricity favored by only a few timid people. Better not ride at all than ride a safety! In a few years this innovation displaced the old standard high wheel, and there came the bicycle craze of the early and middle 1890s. Mr. Wilson was not the sort of person to be infected by a craze, but he found the bicycle a convenient means of getting about, both in this country and in England.

On the whole his health at Bryn Mawr was better than it had been. There were still headaches and "nervous dyspepsia," but the attacks were less frequent and apparently less severe. Spending the summers with the Wilsons was a fixed habit with me, and so I was with them in Middletown, Connecticut, in the summer of 1889—indeed had helped them to move in the previous summer from Bryn Mawr.

By 1889, Mr. Wilson had become a tennis addict, playing nearly every afternoon during the summer, sometimes with one of his colleagues of the faculty, preferably his friend, Professor Winchester,[13] and sometimes with me. I was nearly always beaten, for he had a sure eye, a steady hand, and good coordination.

In 1889–1890 I was an undergraduate at Wesleyan University, a member of the Wilson household, and a student in some of Mr. Wilson's classes. Of his qualities as a teacher I shall speak elsewhere—the clarity of his exposition, the ease with which he made difficult things seem simple, the magical touch which humanized history and political economy.

But here I wish to speak of the effect of his teaching on himself, for that is part of the health story. My first distinct impression of his constitutional strength belongs to that college year—1889–1890—my first clear understanding that he was not a robust man. Throughout the year, he was not confined to his bed except for a few days during the period of what was then called "Russian Influenza," which first visited America in that year and prostrated nearly everybody. But he tired easily, so easily that after lecturing to a class of forty lads it was necessary for him to rest on a couch for half an hour—this not occasionally but frequently, I should say habitually. By a remarkable physical development, he was able to do at fifty-four things that would have exhausted him at thirty-four. To one who had known him in the intervening years it seemed almost impossible that the frail man of 1890 should have become the robust political campaigner of 1910, traveling up and down the state of New Jersey, speaking every day several times, and usually also in the evenings, returning to his home in Princeton for a short night's rest to renew the strenuous program the following day.

In 1890 he went to Princeton as professor. Here he took more exercise than he had taken since his boyhood. He played tennis frequently, rode his bicycle both for utility and exercise, played billiards occasionally, and took up golf, though it was not until he came to Washington under Dr. Grayson's care that he was persuaded to play golf regularly as a health measure. Some time during the 1890s he took up the Swoboda exercise.[14] Probably Mr. Wilson never played any game with as much distinction as he played billiards, his fine coordination already referred to doubtless making him proficient.

I remember first discovering his interest in billiards in the summer of 1886, when he and Mrs. Wilson, the baby, and I were traveling from Gainesville to Rome. We stopped over in Atlanta between trains at the old Kimball House, and Mr. Wilson led me to the billiard room, where we watched the players for some time. He with critical interest pointed out their errors to me, who at that time had never played the game. While on this subject, I might remark that he did the same thing when he and I were in England together in 1899. Several times he suggested that we watch the players in the inn billiards rooms, and I remember distinctly his disgust on one occasion with the clumsiness of the men who were playing the game.

At the Nassau Club in Princeton he played the game fairly frequently until he became president of the university, when he said that it was useless to go to the club for recreation because everybody there wanted to talk business with him. He had a contempt for pool, which he regarded as too easy, but he played billiards sufficiently well to engage the attention and respect of the best players in the club, such as Mr. Osborn,[15] the old treasurer of Princeton, and that engaging village character of those days, "Pete" van Doren,[16] an 1879 Princeton graduate whom Mr. Wilson seldom encountered except over the billiard table. Van Doren was acknowledged the most expert player in Princeton. Some said he played billiards too well to be a good lawyer, and on a night memorable in the club annals Mr. Van Doren defeated a well-known professional player who had come down from New York to give an exhibition. That Mr. Wilson played the game well enough to interest this man is sufficient tribute to his skill. In the long run Van Doren was of course the winner, but not infrequently Mr. Wilson could edge a game away from him.

It was in the college year, 1895–1896, that Mr. Wilson had his first "breakdown." I was living in Philadelphia at that time, paying occasional visits to Princeton, and I remember the anxiety of both my sister and Dr. Wilson. I particularly remember Dr. Wilson remarking that he was very much worried by a twitching of Woodrow's eye[17] that occurred frequently and sometimes continued. Dr. Wilson was an extraordinarily plain-spoken man, and I remember how I was shocked one day when he suddenly said in his blunt way: "I am afraid Woodrow is going to die."

There seemed nothing to warrant so serious an apprehension, but there is no doubt that he was suffering from stomach trouble and nervous debility, and at intervals his vitality ran so low that he had to take to his bed. The most serious symptom was a severe neuritis which at times rendered his right hand useless.[18] With customary determination, he set about learning to write with his left hand, and after a week's time noted with satisfaction that his left-hand signa-

ture was indistinguishable from his old right-hand signature. Since
he was a young man he had used shorthand and the typewriter, ac-
quirements which did him yeoman service in his illness. He put himself under the treatment of Dr. Delafield,[19] a well-known stomach
specialist in New York. Mr. Wilson would go periodically to the me-
tropolis to visit the doctor, staying at the old Everett Hotel in Union
Square. One day, following Dr. Delafield's directions, he attempted
to wash out his own stomach, but after he had filled it with water the
siphon refused to work. Whereupon he hastened to Dr. Delafield's
office only to be informed by the nurse in charge of the doctor's appointments that it was five minutes past one and the doctor's office
hours were over. Mr. Wilson was in no mood to stand on formalities,
and, having ascertained that the doctor was still in the building, he
insisted on seeing him and opened the conversation with the characteristic remark: "I will have to hold you up, doctor, I am water-
logged."

For the doctor, Mr. Wilson had the highest respect as physician
and man, but he laughingly complained that a sense of humor had
been left out of Dr. Delafield. He has frequently related with zest how
the doctor approached him on the occasion of his first treatment
with a long rubber tube in his hand saying: "You will find this extremely disagreeable but not intolerable." "His words and manner,"
said Mr. Wilson, "reminded one of an old Puritan parson about to
pronounce a benediction." During the entire period of treatment, it
was Mr. Wilson's whim to try to make Dr. Delafield laugh. It seems to
have been Mr. Wilson's luck to encounter people whose sense of
humor ran low or who were not appreciative of his particular brand
of humor. We heard a moment ago how some of the Bryn Mawr girls
could not see his jokes. When he was a lecturer at Johns Hopkins
University, there was one graduate student in the class who was so
phenomenally solemn that Mr. Wilson deliberately set himself to
extract a laugh from that particular man. One day at luncheon he
said jubilantly to some other members of the class with whom he
was talking: "I succeeded in my object today. Did you see him
laugh?" "Yes," was the comment of one of his companions, "it was
like the breaking up of a hard winter." Years afterward he spoke of
the same experience with the great artist, Mr. John S. Sargent, who
painted his portrait in the White House, asserting that no public
business gave him more trouble than the attempt to make Mr.
Sargent laugh. Of course, Mr. Sargent and his friends may say that it

was Mr. Wilson's particular type of humor to which Mr. Sargent was impervious. Be that as it may, in youth and in old age, in sickness and in health, Mr. Wilson dearly loved to make those laugh who seemed disinclined to laugh.

It was the breakdown of 1895–1896 which led Mr. Wilson to make his first journey abroad alone, for he was a poor college professor with three little children, whose mother could not leave them at home, while he in turn could not afford the expense of taking five people abroad. Mrs. Wilson had long urged this foreign journey and was delighted when he finally was persuaded by the physicians that it was necessary for the restoration of his health. So he took his bicycle, engaged passage on one of the smaller of the old Anchor Line boats sailing for Glasgow, a primitive little boat[20] which burned oil lamps and upon which passenger rates were low. Subsequently he made other journeys on larger and better equipped Anchor Line boats. It being his habit to do the same thing repeatedly rather than seek new experiences might account for his continued preference for the line by which he had made his first voyage between the two continents; also, it may be that he liked the Anchor Line boats because they were slow and he dearly loved prolonged sea voyages. But he himself stated his preference on the ground that he met with better conversation from the Americans of modest means but well-furnished minds who used to patronize those ships. It was the line by which college professors and preachers made the foreign tour, and no doubt Mr. Wilson's mind met and merged with theirs more readily than with the bankers and steel magnates who patronize the gilt-edge lines.

On this first journey he bicycled through portions of Scotland and England and was much in the company of an American lady and gentleman, Judge and Mrs. Charles A. Woods, of South Carolina, in whose conversation he delighted and whose familiarity with the literary and historical places and monuments of England stimulated him. When the wheel had become a full circuit and he was president of the United States, the Department of Justice sent over to him a list of eminent lawyers, one of whom was to be selected as United States circuit judge for the fourth circuit, and Judge Wood's name was on the list. The president smiled and said: "This is the time the bicycle wins." And he appointed his old traveling companion to the office.

The foreign journey as a health measure was entirely successful. In one of his letters to his wife, he said that he had not felt an ache or a pain since he reached England. As I know from the fact that I was his companion on a subsequent bicycle tour through Great Britain, he wrote Mrs. Wilson daily and at length, intimating to me that his letters were a journal of his travels and experiences. They will make good reading if they are still existent and should ever be published.

That first summer in England cured him, and he returned to Princeton more vigorous and more aggressive than I had ever seen him; likewise, a better American, which is no infrequent occurrence with the American who makes his first visit abroad. Sometimes we have to go away from home to find out how dear home is. Previous to this journey, Mr. Wilson had a tendency to idealize England.

We may pause a moment to consider what that meant. It was not Anglomania of the shallow, flashy sort. He was too genuine to admire in pose. Moreover, he was keenly aware, even as a young man, of the complacency of Englishmen—what Lowell calls "a certain condescension in foreigners." Mr. Wilson used to quote with relish W. S. Gilbert's satirical lines about the Englishman, who, in spite of all temptations to belong to other nations, remained an Englishman. Was this idealization then due to his pro-southernism—that tendency of most southerners of his generation to glorify England— one of the bequests of the War between the States? Woodrow Wilson was southern-born, southern-reared, in part southern-educated. His father, though born in Ohio, adopted the southern cause in toto. Woodrow Wilson has always loved the South, and yet apparently not as a partisan. As a Princeton student he does not seem to have been recognized as a southerner of any intense sectional feeling. From the time he began to reflect, he apparently came to the conclusion, which he subsequently so often expressed in his lectures, that as lawyers the southerners were constitutionally right, but that as statesmen they were wrong. In short, he seems early to have conceived of Abraham Lincoln's conception of the sanctity of the Union.

We probably must look deeper than pro-southernism for his idealization of Great Britain. Something there may have been in it of the literary mind's predilection for an old and settled civilization, for the England that Walter Scott loved so dearly—Mr. Wilson has often been heard to comment with appreciation of Scott's loyalty to the ancient British civilization. But, above all, there was probably a political cause for this idealization of England. In his first writings, he made it frankly known that he believed that the English cabinet form

of government was more democratic because more directly responsible to the people than the congressional form of government by
committees. His reading of Burke and of Bagehot and his long study
of the constitutional and parliamentary history of England had given
him a high respect for the statesmanship of England. Whatever the
truth of the analysis, the fact is that, when Woodrow Wilson in the
summer of 1896 faced the actualities of England, he found out what
a thoroughgoing American he really was.

Mr. Wilson also became more energetic after his trip to England,
more purposeful, with less time to sit down for prolonged talks in the
old, easy, gossiping way. He was just as companionable as ever, but
he was like a man who had things to attend to and could not spend
the hours in rambling talk which I had so much enjoyed. And I am
very much inclined to think that this change came after this illness
and after this restoration and after this visit to England.[21] This new
purposefulness, this less time for prolonged and rambling talk, I am
very much inclined to think dates from the autumn of 1896 after the
poor health of the preceding year, after the restoration of the summer. He was very busy with his literary work. He had his time well
systematized. He had his college lectures all in the first two days of
the week, and, except when he was out of town delivering public lectures or speeches, he was systematically busy writing his books.

Mr. Wilson's physical troubles were not over. It was about 1898
that his stomach difficulties again made him a patient of a New York
specialist—this time Dr. Van Valzah[22]—an obedient patient, as he always was. Mrs. Wilson would sometimes argue that a certain single
dish could not possibly hurt him, whereupon Mr. Wilson would
draw from his pocketbook Dr. Van Valzah's dietary and if the dish
was not specifically mentioned would say: "No, I am not permitted
to eat that." He remained under Dr. Van Valzah's occasional treatment for at least two years and his strength increased. There was no
longer the exhaustion after lectures, and there was much more activity outside of Princeton in the way of lectures and addresses. The
process of growing stronger was a progressive one. He still complained occasionally of headaches, and he and the family suffered
annually from grippy colds—concerning which there is another
small anecdote about another of Mr. Wilson's physicians. This was
old Dr. Wikoff,[23] of Princeton, a general practitioner of the old
school, in whom Mrs. Wilson had confidence because of his long ex-

perience in treating sick people. Dr. Wikoff's pessimistic attitude toward diseases in general and grippe in particular caused Mr. Wilson much merriment. After the family had been prostrated for several successive years by late winter colds, Mr. Wilson accompanied Dr. Wikoff to the front door one morning and said: "Doctor, is there any reason to suppose that this grippe epidemic will ever cease?" And Dr. Wikoff responded in his queer, abrupt way: "I see none, Sir; good morning, Sir."

In the winter or spring of 1905 Mr. Wilson, then President Wilson of Princeton University, suffered an illness which necessitated an operation by Dr. [Andrew James] McCosh at the Presbyterian Hospital in New York for hernia and hemorrhoids, followed by phlebitis in the left leg. It was in 1906 that his worst breakdown up to date occurred, which was regarded as extremely serious.[24] One morning he waked up not feeling in the least ill but casually passed his hands over his eyes and suddenly discovered that he was unable to see out of one of the eyes. Medical examination discovered the fact that a blood vessel had ruptured in the eye. He went under the treatment of Dr. Alfred Stengel and Dr. George Edmund de Schweinitz of Philadelphia. The physicians were serious about the case and told Mrs. Wilson very plainly how critically they regarded the situation. Mr. Wilson as usual remained quite calm. It might be said that when he was told that he was dangerously ill, he turned on his side and went to sleep. Mrs. Wilson could not take the case so philosophically, and on one occasion asked Mr. Hibben,[25] then the most intimate friend of the family, to go down to Philadelphia and interview the physicians. Upon his return, I met Mr. Hibben at the station and asked him to tell me what they had said. He told me, and it was all rather alarming. I begged him not to make a full report to my sister, for, in my judgment, she was already sufficiently on the rack and could do nothing more than she was doing to protect and nurse her beloved husband. But probably because he was unable to avoid cross-questioning (Mrs. Wilson was a sharp cross-examiner), Mr. Hibben finally divulged to her all the information he had received, which was not good for her.

At this time Mr. Wilson was held in the highest esteem by the members of the board of trustees and no one of them was more concerned than Mr. Moses Taylor Pyne,[26] at that time one of Mr. Wilson's closest personal friends on the board of trustees and one of his most ardent supporters, though afterwards he became the leader of the antagonists against Mr. Wilson in the struggles over the quadrangle and graduate school plans. On one of his visits to Prospect, Mr. Pyne summoned me and we walked back and forth between the front door and the gate for the better part of an hour while Mr. Pyne disclosed his solicitude and anxiety, saying that the death or disablement of Mr. Wilson would be an extreme catastrophe for the university. He seemed to think that Mr. Wilson's immediate family were not fully aware of the seriousness of the malady. I combated that idea, telling him, as I told Mr. Hibben, that Mrs. Wilson was herself bearing up by sheer force of will, and that I hoped no one would add unnecessarily to her present alarms. Mr. Pyne stressed the fact that Mr. Wilson did not take sufficient physical exercise, to which I agreed in general but added that daily walks had been his habit previous to the breakdown, to which Mr. Pyne responded with some excitement: "Walks! He doesn't walk, he only saunters." And he added that he hoped after the illness Mr. Wilson would be compelled by somebody to take daily, systematic, and vigorous exercise.

It should be mentioned here that after Mr. Wilson became president of the university the increase of responsibility upon him and the necessity of being away from Princeton a great deal on college business did lead him to slacken in physical exercise. He abandoned the bicycle, played golf seldom, and billiards practically not at all.

In the summer of 1906, he and his entire family went to Great Britain, where he consulted a physician at Edinburgh. An incident on the eve of his voyage has to do with his relationship with the board of trustees then and thereafter. Several friends, including my younger sister[27] and myself, accompanied the family to New York. One of the friends told me with delight that the trustees had voted a sum of money to Mr. Wilson to defray his expenses abroad during the summer, and, I think, added that the check was to be handed him on the ship. But before the vessel left the dock, my sister told me that the check had been declined with thanks. He appreciated the good will of the trustees, all of whom were then his friends, but both his pride and his foresight prevented acceptance. He said to Mrs. Wilson: "I cannot afford to let the trustees do this. The relationship between them and myself is now delightful, but none of us can foresee the future. A time may come when I shall have to oppose them on some point of college policy, and I must therefore keep myself a free man.

My obligations are to the best interests of the college as I see them, and it would be a mistake to permit any personal favors to stand between me and the discharge of those duties."

That is a good example of Mr. Wilson's character, foresight, and philosophy of leadership. He did not then contemplate any rift between himself and the board of trustees, but in the presidency of the university, as in the governorship of New Jersey and in the presidency of the United States, he held that only what he called "a free man" could be a fearless leader. With regard to politics, he said some time before holding electoral office: "What this country needs is a new set of men in office, but the trouble is that the present office-holders are all tied up with promises. I do not mean that they have been bought with money, but I do mean that the conditions of their nominations and elections have put them in a position where they must pay off favors."

Many years later he was commenting on the generous offer of the Princeton board of trustees, but added: "My refusal to accept their bounty was one of my wisest acts."

Mr. Wilson returned from England in the autumn apparently quite restored to health, and I have nothing to add to this informal narrative except one minor point which is interesting because of a sequence and a coincidence. I myself had had more than one breakdown in which Dr. Francis X. Dercum, the eminent Philadelphia neurologist, had been my physician. Dr. Dercum had become acquainted with the Wilson family, and Mrs. Wilson had consulted him about an aggravating neuritis from which her husband suffered sporadically. Dr. Dercum talked to her of baking, etc., but said that the real cure would be a hot, dry climate, which of course was not procurable in New Jersey. Though Dr. Dercum did not know Mr. Wilson intimately, he had become fascinated by him as a public figure; and one day, when the doctor and I chanced to be lunching together, he expressed his enthusiasm for the ideas newly broached that Mr. Wilson should be nominated for the presidency of the United States, adding that he had no doubt that he could be elected. I demurred on the score of his health and asked the doctor if he thought that a man of Mr. Wilson's constitution could carry the load. Dr. de Schweinitz and Dr. Dercum were close friends, and Dr. Dercum was therefore familiar with the history of the ruptured blood vessel in the eye, but he did not seem to think that this or any other of Mr. Wilson's illnesses would make the presidency perilous to his life. It was this same Dr. Dercum whom Admiral Grayson called in as consultant when the great break came in 1919. It is mere truism to say that no better man could have been drawn into the case. He was preeminent as a neurologist, and his kindness, generosity, and self-sacrificing service were as notable as his scientific skill. He told me that when he got the first intimation from Admiral Grayson that he might be needed at the White House, he packed up and made ready to stay indefinitely in Washington, as he put it, "to camp out so long as my services were needed." His interest in Mr. Wilson never ceased. After the president's term of office had expired, Dr. Dercum held himself ready at any time to confer with Admiral Grayson.

Woodrow Wilson's Educational Career

❧

OF THE PRESIDENT'S preparatory schooling I know practically nothing, except that he attended certain private schools, and I think had at one time or another private tutors. But, as is now generally known, his real teacher was his father. Dr. Wilson had become pastor of the Presbyterian Church at Wilmington, North Carolina, when his son was ready to enter college. It was perfectly natural that the lad should be sent to Davidson College at Davidson, North Carolina, a few miles from Charlotte. This was an old Presbyterian institution, in which there was a very small faculty, but in which the teaching, as I can personally testify from my own experience ten years later, was very sound indeed. In fact, I can remember in my own days at Davidson this extraordinary circumstance, that the boys were so grounded in Greek and Latin that it was not uncommon to hear Latin phrases on the baseball field, of course, jocosely uttered, but it simply meant that, like English boys, they were saturated in the classics. Mr. Wilson spent only his freshman year in this college. While there he was active in athletics and played center field in baseball.

It was in the autumn of 1875 that he went to Princeton, then officially known as the College of New Jersey. Princeton before the Civil War had been almost as much of a southern as northern college, a great many of the students coming from the southern states. By 1875 southerners had begun to drift back to it in considerable numbers.

Mr. Wilson was not an especially hard student, but, like a great many young men of fine qualities, he found his own way in the college library and began to read in history and political philosophy, with a special interest in English parliamentary history and English political authors—above all Edmund Burke. If it is possible to say that Mr. Wilson has ever had an intellectual master among authors, we have to say it was Edmund Burke. Certainly, Burke has influenced his thinking and his style of writing more than any other writer. Next to Burke was Walter Bagehot, whom Woodrow Wilson was destined practically to introduce to the American public in his own writings. It might be interesting to mention here that considerably later he formed a very strong attachment for the writings of a much less conspicuous English figure, namely, Augustine Birrell, who was a young author and advocate in England when Mr. Wilson was himself practically just beginning his own career. Subsequently, Augustine Birrell became a member of the British cabinet.

Woodrow Wilson joined the Whig Society at Princeton, to which most southern boys gravitated, rather than to the rival society, Clio. He became a leader in the debates and the parliamentary affairs of old Whig. In his senior year he was one of the editors, I think the editor in chief, of the *Nassau Literary Magazine*.[1] He was a leader in college life, but I never gathered from my own literary associations and the old members of the faculty who had been teachers in Wilson's undergraduate days that he had made an especially strong impression on his teachers in his classroom. And none of the faculty seems to have made an especially strong impression on him, with the exception, of course, of Dr. McCosh, the great old Scotch president.[2] Even this impression on Mr. Wilson was rather the impression of a personality than of a teacher, for the simple reason that Dr. McCosh was a metaphysician, and I should say that perhaps the most interesting thing about Mr. Wilson's mental constitution is that, while he is profoundly philosophical, he is absolutely *non*-metaphysical and has not had much interest in metaphysics.

He graduated from Princeton with his class in 1879, but without taking signal honors,[3] though undoubtedly the most respected member of the Whig Society, where he had given the best evidence of his mental powers. All this I think simply means that Mr. Wilson developed slowly but very surely. As he often tells his friends, he was nine years old before he began to read. But certainly one of the most remarkable things about him is the steadiness of his development. At sixty-odd years of age he is growing as ordinary people are supposed to grow only in their twenties. His development has never ceased.

I do not know when it was that Mr. Wilson decided that he was going to be a lawyer, but by the time he had graduated from Princeton this was his fixed determination, and he went for the study of law to the University of Virginia, where he came under the influence of perhaps the only teacher except his father who made a profound and lasting impression upon him, namely, the great old law professor, John B. Minor. At the University of Virginia he probably studied harder than he ever studied before, because he was studying the thing that he was most interested in, namely, law. Here again he was active in one of the literary societies—the Jefferson Literary Society— and, incidentally, he was a member of the University of Virginia Glee Club and sang in the choir. He won the debater's medal, the chief distinction of this sort at the University of Virginia.[4]

After two years at the University of Virginia he went to Atlanta, Georgia, to begin the practice of law. Here he entered a partnership with Edward I. Renick. But he was destined to find that law as it was practiced in those days in Georgia had no real satisfaction for one of his quality of mind, for law had become simply a matter of business. And this young legal philosopher was more interested in what lies behind law—the mind of the people, the history and the philosophy of law.

I have heard him so often say that when he would talk to fellow lawyers in Atlanta about the side of law which most interested him, they would look at him with uncomprehending eyes. To them it was sufficient that a thing was on the statute books. To Wilson it was a matter of supreme interest as to how such a thing got on the statute books, what process of social and political development had led to the making of laws.

It was while he was a young lawyer in Atlanta that he was called on to testify before a commission appointed by Congress to inquire into the tariff question.[5] By some curious political accident, a member of this commission was a certain Judge Underwood,[6] of my own town of Rome, Georgia. Judge Underwood was then a member of Congress and a typical expansive pompous old type of southern congressman, rather absurd even in his own town. I have so often heard Mr. Wilson say that while he was testifying before this committee, he made objection to the tariff that was put on English books brought into America and instanced as an example the amount of tariff that had to be paid in order to import a book by Huxley or Spencer, then in the height of their scientific and literary fame. And old Judge Underwood, blowing himself up like a porpoise, said: "But Mr. Wilson, do you mean to say you want *in-fie-del* books to come in free of charge?" Mr. Wilson replied that he did.

It was during this interval of his practice of law in Atlanta that he became engaged to Ellen Axson, whom he had known when they were both children by reason of the fact that the Axsons and the Bones family were great friends. He was visiting his cousins in Rome when he and Miss Axson met after a long interval.

My father, Edward Axson, received a visit from young Woodrow Wilson, then a briefless attorney-at-law in Atlanta.[7] Mr. Axson thought the visit was intended for him, and was gratified by this attention from the son of his old friend, Dr. Joseph R. Wilson. Mr. Axson and Dr. Joseph Wilson were not intimate friends; in age Dr. Wilson was midway between the ages of Mr. Edward Axson of Rome, Georgia, and his father, Dr. I.S.K. Axson, of Savannah. But Presbyterianism was a bond between Georgians in far-gone days, and Dr. Joseph Wilson was a power in the southern Presbyterian Church. Mr. Edward Axson had known Dr. Wilson as a younger man knows an older, had possibly, I do not know for a certainty, been a guest in Dr. Wilson's Augusta, Georgia, home. Certain it is that Mrs. Edward Axson had taken the baby Ellen for a visit to Dr. Wilson's sister, Mrs. James Bones, then living in Augusta. It was a family tradition that little "Tommy" Wilson had asked for and received the privilege of holding in his lap the tiny Ellen, some four years his junior. Certain it is that there were ties direct and indirect between the Wilsons and the Axsons. So Mr. Edward Axson of Rome was pleased that the young lawyer should call upon him, entered innocently upon family talk and a grave conversation about midweek prayer meetings, was visibly surprised when young Mr. Wilson asked if he might see Miss Axson, promptly summoned his daughter without thought of ulterior motive, for Mr. Axson was no matchmaker, had probably dreamily assumed that his daughter would always be the chatelaine of his own home, her mother having died. However, Mr. Axson saw enough of young Mr. Wilson to inspire a letter to me, then a schoolboy in South Carolina.

The letter was for my admonition, though my father did not say so. Though Mr. Axson was a preacher, he did not preach much to me, trusted to his own example and occasional use of a stout leather strap to keep me in the narrow path. The letter, a long one for my father to write, was almost exclusively about this admirable young man who was visiting his relatives in Rome, and contained a sentence which I have not forgotten, however far short I have fallen of its intent: "I could wish myself no better fortune than a son like that," Mr. Axson not guessing that after his own too early death this young Wilson would be a son-in-law.

Jessie Bones Brower made the match if it was not made by "a higher power than we can contradict." Mr. and Mrs. James Bones and their children had moved to Rome, and Jessie when absurdly young had married Mr. Brower, a banker. A year or so ago, Helen Bones, the youngest of the family, born after the removal to Rome, by the way, told me that it was obvious to everyone that young Wilson was being smitten by Ellen Axson, and that Jessie Brower kept busy arranging occasions for the two to meet—picnics, straw rides, boating parties, and all the simple diversions of those simple days.

After Mr. Wilson had returned to Atlanta, the high-spirited Jessie called at the Axson home, and as she was leaving produced a photograph of her cousin Woodrow and presented it to Ellen. Ellen exclaimed: "Why, Jessie, I can't take that!" "Very well, let it rot in the strawberry patch," said Jessie, tossing it among the berries and striding away. Ellen retrieved it, and it was among her treasured possessions until her death.

Except for the large, luminous oval blue-gray eyes, I don't think anybody could have called him handsome in those days—of course I am not accountable for what Ellen Axson thought. Mrs. Edith Reid of Baltimore,[8] who came to know him a little later, reproduces a conversation with him: "'Tell me something of Ellen Axson,' I asked. 'Why, you know, of course,' he said, 'that she is the most beautiful woman in the world?' 'That we will take as matter of course,'" answered Mrs. Reid. There was rather more basis for that than for a corresponding opinion which she may have had of him. When he was old and broken and tottering toward death he called his daughter Margaret, and, not seeming to realize that Margaret was a grown woman when her mother died, asked with emphasis: "Margaret, *do* you remember your mother?" "Why, of course, Father dear," said Margaret, and he responded: "Wasn't she the most radiant person you ever saw?"

Mrs. Reid writes that the Johns Hopkins student once lamented "the cut of my face; it's too bad," and, then with a woman's perception, she writes thus:

"It was a remarkable face, I thought, strong and heavily marked, naively young but full of power. It must have been drawn, one might

think, for the caricature of a Scotch Covenanter and then transformed by an idealistic inner light that obliterated everything that
might have been ugly."

It was many years after this, toward the close of his term as president of Princeton, that a man with intuitions (men have them sometimes) said: "The Lord set out to make Woodrow ugly, but he turned
round and made himself handsome." When Wilson was president of
the United States he was a sight to please the eye when he stood up
to address the Congress in joint session. He was clean-shaven and
perfectly tailored, thanks to the oversight of his valet, Major Brooks,[9]
utter gentleman though colored, "dapper," said a lady of fashion beside whom I chanced to be seated at a dinner table.

But the chief usher at the White House, Hoover ("Ike") who died a
few months ago, hit it off better, I thought, when he said after one of
the congressional addresses: "And wasn't he handsome while he was
speaking!"

Apparently, the president never realized the change in his appearance that had come with the years, which may have been a reason
for his supreme preference among the limericks he quoted of that
one which has been reprinted *ad nauseam*, "For beauty I am not a
star" and so forth. By the way, there appears a current notion that
Mr. Wilson composed many original limericks. He composed very
few, but remembered those that were recited to him. That particular
one about "beauty" and "star" was recited by a guest at the wedding
of his niece in Princeton, the purveyor not foreseeing the world-
flung fame the homely little rhyme was to attain.[10]

The interrupted theme has been the personal attractiveness of
Mr. Wilson as he grew older. The shaving and the tailoring were only
adjuncts. There was something more germane, an indwelling spirit,
lofty living in things of the mind. So long ago I heard a woman say of
another: "If one would be as beautiful as she one must be as good as
she." The pure thoughtful spirit in Mr. Wilson, expanding with the
years, ennobled and illuminated the strong mobile countenance. So
many Washington sojourners who are newspaper headliners are
drearily commonplace when you see them and hear them. President
Wilson "looked the part." One knew he was in the presence of a great
man as soon as he heard him utter one sentence. He dwelt in mountain tops and dewey airs baptized him. There used to be a saying in
Washington that some grow, others swell. Mr. Wilson grew.

Johns Hopkins University had been founded in Baltimore a few

8. Daniel Coit Gilman, first president of The Johns Hopkins University,
ca. 1876

years before under the presidency of Dr. Gilman,[11] and, incidentally, very strongly under the influence of the German idea of university teaching. It was unquestionably Johns Hopkins which gave to our American education for some twenty years the strong German influence which it had until there came a natural revolt against the German method.

In Paris, during the peace conference, President Wilson said to me, with more bitterness than was customary with him in those days of counsel and conference: "Because I stand for a plain principle of justice, the men with whom I am dealing and with whom I am in closest daily contact sometimes charge me with being 'pro-German,' whereas I am the only one of the whole group who had always all my life long been consistently opposed to Germany and all that Germany represents. I have never been in Germany, and I never went to Germany because I have always disliked German people. I have despised their educational ideas and have distrusted their writers on political science."

On another occasion, in conversation with a group of men, among whom if I am not mistaken were Ambassador Davis and Ambassador Wallace,[12] I heard President Wilson say that Professor Georg Jellinek[13] was the only sound German expositor of political science. Mr. Wilson said that Jellinek once wrote of a certain political idea that it "rationalizes and *therefore* falsifies." Mr. Wilson's comment was that Jellinek was the only one of the Germans who could see that a systematic rationalization of politics is of necessity a falsification. And this leads me to add that ever since I have known Mr. Wilson I have been impressed by the fact that one of the many reasons why he so much admires Edmund Burke is that Burke was always suspicious of political *theory*. I heard Mr. Wilson say that the trouble with the French revolutionists was that they set up elaborate theories of government, and that sound government is not conducted according to ingenious theories but is a development which keeps in close touch with the facts.

However, there can be no question that The Johns Hopkins University was one of the most important influences in American educational life in that it gave to educational ideas a greater seriousness than they had ever had in America before. It was undoubtedly Johns Hopkins University that put postgraduate education and special training for teachers on a higher level than had ever been known in America up to this time. It was Johns Hopkins University, it may be said, which made the teaching profession a definite and distinct profession in America. Previous to that there had been too much of the idea in America that teaching was the thing adopted by men whose ill health prevented them from doing anything more robust, and professorships were largely filled by preachers whose throats had failed. There were a great many fine young men in America who began to realize that Johns Hopkins University was offering them just the thing they wanted to satisfy their own natural ambitions, and to this university already were flocking men who were destined to be a very strong influence on American public life. I cannot at the moment enumerate them, though it would make rather a long catalogue. Eminently among them is Albert Shaw, who became subsequently the editor of the *Review of Reviews*. He has been a conspicuous figure in American intellectual life.

The young Atlanta lawyer, Wilson, dissatisfied with law as he had practiced it in Atlanta, began to realize that his real career should be that of teacher and writer, expounder of law in its deeper meanings and deeper relationships, rather than simply a pleader in the lower courts. And so to Baltimore he went and became a student in The Johns Hopkins University. Here, again, as at Davidson, I followed in Mr. Wilson's wake many years later, and I think I can testify that this is true about Johns Hopkins University—that it was a great educational institution in which the majority of the teachers were not in and of themselves especially great personalities. There were exceptions, particularly in the field of natural science, such as Rowland[14] in physics and Martin[15] in biology; but in the departments with which Mr. Wilson and I became familiar, the chief teachers were fine scholars without being especially impressive men personally.

Mr. Wilson's chief teachers were Herbert Baxter Adams[16] in history and Richard T. Ely[17] in economics. For Ely he had no admiration whatsoever, and for Herbert Adams only a limited admiration. But the point of it all is that these were modern men with modern methods of study and were able to guide Mr. Wilson and assist him in finding out things for himself.

It was at Johns Hopkins University that he wrote his first book— that notable volume—*Congressional Government*. In this book he made an analysis of the difference between the theory and the practice of government under the American Constitution, and he made that strong plea for responsible government, which has been one of his most insistent ideas throughout his whole career, and of which he has been the most notable example in his own career as president of the United States. In *Congressional Government*, he very frankly criticized the irresponsible American method as compared with the British cabinet, which is directly responsible to the British people. This book was written not as a university task but because Mr. Wilson had something he very much wanted to say. Subsequently, the book was accepted as his thesis for his degree of Doctor of Philosophy, which degree he did not immediately take. He was in a great

9. Herbert Baxter Adams, Wilson's chief mentor at
The Johns Hopkins University, ca. 1885

hurry to be married; in fact, he wanted to marry even a year earlier than he actually did marry. And he left Johns Hopkins University without his degree to become a member of the little faculty of the brand new college for women at Bryn Mawr, a college founded on the model of Johns Hopkins University itself. The president of this college was an amiable old Quaker gentleman, named Dr. Rhoads,[18] but the real power from the start was Miss Thomas,[19] who was at this time officially the dean of the college, but became very shortly the president of the college. Mr. Wilson was professor of history and economics.[20] He made an arrangement by which he was permitted to lecture at Johns Hopkins University once a week and traveled back and forth between Bryn Mawr and Baltimore. It was Miss Thomas who insisted on his taking his doctor's degree from Johns Hopkins. And so, even after he had become a professor, he stood the form of examinations, presented *Congressional Government* as his thesis in 1886, and received the Ph.D. degree—a thing to which he himself was personally indifferent. Mr. Wilson used to say that the young women students at Bryn Mawr were docile rather than actively interested; too ready to take as final gospel whatever "the professor" chose to say; too little inclined to challenge him in the manner of young men students of the same age. And it is questionable if Mr. Wilson ever really found his teaching duties at Bryn Mawr thoroughly interesting. But he was busy studying and writing, and, of course, he was absolutely faithful to his classroom duties.

He was married in the June preceding the beginning of his professorship at Bryn Mawr, which began in September 1885. It was characteristic of the young couple after one year of boarding life at Bryn Mawr, and when they had taken a little home of their own, that they should have brought into their household two members of Mrs. Wilson's family: Miss Mary Hoyt,[21] a first cousin of Mrs. Wilson, and a young women of eager, intellectual ambitions, who was enabled by this kindness to become a student at Bryn Mawr; and little Edward Axson,[22] Mrs. Wilson's younger brother, who had been living with an uncle in Georgia since the death of his father and mother, and who now became a member of the Wilson family, and more like Mrs. Wilson's son than brother. He was about thirteen years younger than she. Young Edward remained a member of the family until he himself had grown up and graduated from college and was married and started on his own professional career, which was cut short by a tragic accident in which he and his young wife and his young baby were all drowned together, these deaths giving Mrs. Wilson perhaps the greatest shock of her whole life.

Margaret Wilson was born in April 1886, and now the little family, consisting of Mr. and Mrs. Wilson, the baby, Mary Hoyt, and Edward Axson lived in the Baptist parsonage, just back of the college, on Gulph Road in Bryn Mawr, the pastor of the Baptist church for some reason not needing the manse for his own dwelling.

It was in this cottage that I visited them in the summer of 1888, the third and last year of their residence at Bryn Mawr. Dr. Wilson and young Joseph, precisely my own age, were also visitors at the house during the earlier part of the summer. I was with them while they were packing up their household effects preparatory to moving to Middletown, Connecticut, where Mr. Wilson was to become professor in the autumn. Mr. Wilson and I personally packed up all the household affairs, boxing furniture, books, bedding, etc., with our own hands.

It was in the closing days of this residence at Bryn Mawr that a rather curious adventure befell us. Told in detail and chronologically, it was something like this. One pleasant summer's night, Dr. Wilson, his son, Mr. Woodrow Wilson, and I were out on the little front porch watching a partial eclipse of the moon, when suddenly a setter dog, which Mr. Wilson had been keeping over the summer for one of his colleagues who had gone away on his vacation, began barking madly and ran into a wood against which the Baptist parsonage was built—rather an extensive bit of forest. That was the beginning of a good deal of agitation on the part of this dog, and it presently became evident that night after night some prowler was infesting these woods. Back of the manse there was the house of the janitor of the church, and he and family reported a stranger who was doing very curious things night after night.

One night I was awakened by a sound without my window, and I saw the outside blind opened and just got a glimpse of a pair of eyes looking in. I got Mr. Wilson and Joe, both of whom had pistols. I had none, but went before them with the candle, and we searched the house from upper story to basement but found nothing. Several nights we three men stayed on a little back porch for several hours, hid behind a huge water cask which stood on the porch, and waited for this prowler. One night we thought we heard him, and Mr. Wilson fired and then was terribly anxious lest he might by chance have hit somebody. One afternoon, after Dr. Wilson and Joe had returned south, Mr. Wilson and I went out for a walk in the same forest which I have spoken of, with this beautiful Irish setter dog as our companion. Suddenly the dog left us, running and barking excitedly, and we called and chased him but were unable to catch up with him. Presently we heard a howl of anguish from the dog, went in the direction, but were unable to find him. By a circuit we returned to the house when little Edward Axson met us with his eyes very large, his face very grave, and said that Dash had come back cut all to pieces. We went to the cellar where little Edward had taken the dog and found it lying there, literally ripped from his throat to his tail, as if he had sprung at the man, who had met him with a sharp knife laying his belly open. We got a veterinary surgeon and nursed the dog for all the remaining days that we were in Bryn Mawr, and curiously enough the dog recovered. There were many curious things that happened, but we never saw our man. The time came for moving to Middletown, Connecticut, and I went on with the family to help them get established in their new home before returning to my own college, the University of Georgia. It was in a New York paper that we read several days after we had been in Middletown that a maniac had been captured in these woods at Bryn Mawr, one who had escaped from a neighboring insane asylum, and this, of course, explained all our adventures.

Mr. Wilson was professor in Wesleyan University for two years—from 1888 to 1890—when he joined the faculty of his own college of Princeton. It was in the autumn of 1889 that I became a member of the family, because Mr. Wilson himself had urged that if I intended to be a teacher of English I ought to come to Wesleyan and study with the man who, he believed, was the best teacher of English in America, Professor C. T. Winchester. And I may remark here that to this day President Wilson still contends that Professor Winchester is the greatest of all teachers of English. So I went there for my senior year, and from there I graduated in 1890. Though naturally in the circumstances the bulk of my work was with Mr. Winchester, I had the good sense to elect two of my courses with Mr. Wilson, the general course in economics and the course in American history. And so I had the privilege for one year of being a member of his classes.

Though Mr. Wilson had been now five years a professor, three at Bryn Mawr and two at Wesleyan, he still had not had an opportunity to teach the things for which he really most cared, namely, political institutions. He never considered himself either a historian or a political economist. I remember how he once said, laughingly, at Wesleyan that he would like to say something original about political economy if only something original would occur to him to say. We used as a textbook the classic of those days—General Francis Walker's general book on economics[23]—a fascinating volume it was too—and Mr. Wilson's commentaries were always deeply and humanly interesting.

Of course he had the great art of quizzing students, of drawing them out by degrees, and of leading them to show what it was they did not understand in the text. He would clarify their own rudimen-

10. Caleb Thomas Winchester, professor of English literature and
Wilson's closest friend at Wesleyan University, ca. 1888

tary notions. He would constantly illuminate an economic theory
with a pat, concrete illustration. But as I look back now, I realize that
he was right in his own judgment when he said that he was not con-
tributing any original ideas to the science of political economy. He
was a wonderful commentator on the things in the book. The classes
at Wesleyan were small, and Mr. Wilson lectured formally comparatively little, though he did preface his course in political economy
with an historical sketch of the history of political economy. He

began this with about six lectures, but they grew from year to year until they constituted a course by themselves—a course in the history of political economy. And I can testify from personal experience that by 1889 this had developed into a fascinating narrative.

It was in the course in American history, however, that he gave us more of himself. Even though he did not at that time consider himself a professional historian, he naturally felt very much at home in expounding for us boys the true political significance of the great epochs of American history, such as the Revolution, the Jacksonian period, the Civil War, and the Reconstruction period. In 1889, in New England, there were still some fairly stiff ideas about the South and the so-called "War of the Rebellion." And Mr. Wilson's dealing with the whole thing with these northern students was very wonderful, because he was so frank and at the same time so reasonable that these young Yankees found themselves getting a new revelation without quite knowing just how they were getting it. They began to see for the first time that the "rebels" really had a case and were not just simply the wanton rascals which they had been led to suppose by what they had heard at home and in the New England schools. I remember how Mr. Wilson on one occasion expounded that view of his, that in the matter of secession the South was absolutely right from the point of view of a lawyer, though quite wrong from the point of view of a statesman.

We crude and callowed college boys—whether northern-born like the great majority or southern-born like myself—began to understand something we never understood before, namely, that the American Constitution is not merely a document written down on paper but is a living and organic thing, which, like all living organisms, grows and adapts itself to the circumstances of its environment. And the point Mr. Wilson was making with us in his illuminating talk was that the southern statesmen had taken a strict-construction view, which regarded the Constitution merely as a legal document which was to be interpreted strictly according to its phraseology, just as a lawyer would interpret any other document, but that meanwhile the nation had been growing, expanding, changing, and the Constitution had been taking on new and larger meanings than the meanings that appear merely on the surface. The northern boys began to see that the southern statesmen were absolutely honest in their contention that the Constitution gave them the right to secede, and the very few southern boys, including myself, began to see that the northern statesmen had a larger vision of a greater United States than had been perceived when the colonies formed themselves into a Union.

I have stated all this very badly, but perhaps I have given some hint of how Mr. Wilson used to open up great vistas for us and put a new life into old things. I remember one day leaving the classroom, when one of my northern companions said: "What would he have done himself if he had been old enough to fight when the war broke out?" "Why," I said, "I suppose he would have fought." "On which side?" asked my companion. "Why," I said, "on the southern side." "Well, then don't you see," said my companion, "he would according to his own judgment have committed a wrong act of statesmanship." I said, "Yes, I suppose he would, but he certainly would have been human enough to go the way of his father and his friends." And then I told the boy what he had not known—that strictly speaking Mr. Wilson was not of southern stock. His mother was a Scotch lady; his father was born and reared and educated in Ohio; they had moved south, and, like practically all people who moved south, they had become entirely southern in their sympathies. Though I did not understand it then, I see now what my friend and I were getting at—the essential tragedy of the whole Civil War situation—that whichever way you chose, you had to choose something which was essentially tragic in itself. That was the situation which was laid upon the southern people.

The students had what they thought was one good joke on Mr. Wilson at Wesleyan. We students were all required to attend chapel morning exercises, and I can recall some desperate races that I had to get there before the bell stopped ringing; it rang for five minutes, and I had arisen from bed after it had begun ringing and had been in my seat in chapel, moderately clothed, when the last stroke sounded. The *College Annual* published a record of the faculty in attending morning exercises. Some ingenious rascal had kept this record religiously day by day, marking all the faculty absent or present, according as they appeared or did not appear. It was the custom for the morning exercises to be conducted in rotation by different members of the faculty. And when the record of faculty attendance was published at the end of the year, the lowest attendance was that of Mr. Woodrow Wilson, who had appeared in chapel exactly the number of times it was his duty to read the morning service. What the boys did not know was that this young professor had three babies and a

wife, who had been cruelly burned several months before by the up-
setting of some grease in the kitchen,[24] and that he himself had had
to be nurse to wife and babies, as well as many other things, while
conducting his college duties, and his nights were often very broken
nights, indeed.

To this day Mr. Wilson still tells some stories of the Wesleyan experience. Two of his favorites are not very creditable to the intelligence
or manners of Wesleyan students. One is of a student who met him
at a reception one night and told him that his roommate was so delighted with Mr. Wilson's lectures and was so especially pleased with
the agricultural references, because his roommate was himself a
farmer's son. He had come back with delight from a recent lecture to
tell his chum that Mr. Wilson had said that something had occurred
in the *heyday* of a man's power!

Another is this: it was the custom for a class to wait for the appearance of the professor for five minutes after the classroom bells had
sounded. If he did not appear in five minutes, the class had a right to
adjourn, and whenever it did so it always cheered lustily. Mr. Wilson
lived in a house just opposite the campus (the house has now disap-
peared and a college clubhouse stands in its place), and he could,
therefore, hear the campus sounds very clearly. On one day he was
prevented from attending his class by a temporary illness, and he
heard the boys outside cheering his absence. The next time he met
one of the class, he said that he had been very much touched to see
how glad they were to learn he was ill. And then the rude young bar-
barian said, of course intending to be funny, "We would have
cheered twice that loud if you had been dead."

Speaking of this sort of thing reminds me of something I am going
to interpolate here, though it belongs to many years later, but as illustrating the attitude of students toward a beloved and admired
professor. After Mr. Wilson had become president of Princeton University, he still continued, unlike most college presidents, to lecture
to certain classes, but of course he had to travel a great deal as president of the university, with the result that he missed a great many of
these lectures. One autumn I happened to be in the post office at
Princeton, just after the adjournment of the first session of the president's class of that term, and two students came to the post office
directly from the lecture room. I heard one of them say: "Did you
ever in your life hear anything to equal that?" The other one said: "I
never did. He lives up to his reputation. Believe me, he is a world's

wonder." And then said the other: "And do you know, the best part of it is that he cuts half the lectures."

At Wesleyan, Mr. Wilson's associations with the members of the faculty were very delightful. There was a club, the name of which I cannot now remember,[25] which used to hold periodical meetings at which papers were read and discussions held, and all members of the club seemed to regard those club evenings as thoroughly delightful. His most constant companion was Professor Winchester. They used to play lawn tennis together a great deal. For some of the older professors he had a very great respect, particularly for Dr. Van Benschoten, the venerable and distinguished mathematician.[26] Mr. Wilson used to say that he doubted if there was a college faculty in America in which there was so little "dead wood" as in the Wesleyan faculty. As a simple matter of fact, Wesleyan was in those days, and probably still is, one of the best educational institutions in America. Mr. Wilson was to realize very vividly that the standard of scholarship and of attention to college duties at Wesleyan was very much higher than at Princeton in the 1890s, at which time perhaps because of overexaggerated college athletics or to whatever other reason it may be ascribed, Princeton, like so many of our greater eastern universities, had come to grow very lax in scholarship—all of which has a sequel in the great Princeton quarrel which I shall have occasion later to rehearse in these notes.

It was in the spring of 1890 that Professor Johnston,[27] professor of politics at Princeton, died, and I suppose there was not a moment's hesitation on the part of the trustees in calling to the successorship Professor Woodrow Wilson, of Wesleyan University. So, in the summer of 1890, the family moved to Princeton and took up a residence in the old square frame house on Library Place, next to which, a few years later, they purchased a plot of ground and built their own home. I think it might be said that every stone of this building and every shrub in the garden was sanctified by love. The president remarked to Admiral Grayson: "You cannot imagine the pride which I enjoyed when I looked upon this house and realized that it was my possession." Every detail was worked out by Mr. and Mrs. Wilson themselves. They built the house in a style which had their special admiration and affection—the old English quartered style.

The twelve years of life in Princeton preceding his election to the presidency of Princeton seem to me to constitute the happiest period of life which Mr. and Mrs. Wilson had together, for the simple

11. Faculty of Wesleyan University, ca. 1889. Wilson is in front row, third from left; Winchester is in third row, standing to the right

reason that they were undisturbed then by all the violent things that belonged to subsequent life as president of Princeton University and political life. They were never separated, except on the brief intervals on which he would go out on his lecture trips. I feel perfectly certain that if the first Mrs. Wilson could speak, she would say that the contentment of that period surpassed anything that she had ever experienced either before or since.

He quickly made his impression on the undergraduate life of Princeton, both in the lecture room and outside. Here, for the first time in his career, he was able to teach the things that he most loved, and his courses in jurisprudence became the most conspicuous thing in Princeton intellectual life. They were elective courses, but they were elected by nearly the entire junior and senior classes, to which the lectures were open, so that instead of a class, he, of course, had a large audience consisting of many hundreds, which he addressed twice a week on the subject concerning which he had most original ideas. He became the idol of the students; was elected year after year the most popular professor; and was known to them in all of their student councils. He became the faculty adviser in athletic matters and was a frequent attendant at football and baseball practice. I omitted to mention, by the way, that he had been a very active adviser of football at Wesleyan. It was a rather curious circumstance that Wesleyan University even as late as 1890 belonged to the great Eastern League, which consisted of five colleges—Harvard, Yale, Princeton, the University of Pennsylvania, and Wesleyan. Of course, this little college had no chance of winning the championship against these great competitors, but it is evidence of how well football was played at Wesleyan that it had for years been a member of this great combination. A few years later it had to drop out because the odds were too great against it. But Mr. Wilson was intensely interested in football, attended practice regularly, was a faculty adviser, and was in all of the councils on strategy of the game before the great games were played. In Princeton he had the same relationship as at Wesleyan, and in the 1890s the Princeton team was a thing to be wondered at. It was in the 1890s that the famous Poe family, of Baltimore, figured so conspicuously in the football history of Princeton.[28]

There is a chapter of Princeton history which never has been clearly written, simply because the people who figured in it were too modest to make any special and personal claims. I am referring to the introduction of the honor system into Princeton. It was really Mrs. Wilson herself who was the first promulgator of the honor system in this college, a system for which Princeton was supposed to be peculiarly preeminent among the eastern colleges for many years. In practically all the eastern and northern colleges, as contradistinguished from the southern colleges, there was the ethical or nonethical idea that to cheat on examinations was perfectly legitimate, and men would frankly copy each other's examination papers and get all the assistance they could from each other during examination, even though they had clear notions of honor about other things. It was one of those vicious traditions which is so hard for human nature to rid itself of. Mrs. Wilson had been shocked at Wesleyan by what she had learned about classroom cheating. And when she got to Princeton and found that the same thing prevailed there, where there were so many southern lads who were supposed to have higher notions of honor, she became a good deal agitated. In those days the Wilsons in their simple manner kept a sort of open house for students who used to drop in informally in the afternoons and evenings. Mrs. Wilson began to talk to a group of these young men about the viciousness of this cheating and began to tell them how she understood that in many southern colleges cheating on examination was regarded as dishonorable as any other form of cheating would be. Several of these lads became interested. Among them was young Brodnax, of North Carolina,[29] afterwards a devoted missionary. And these youngsters began to agitate the question among their fellows. Then it was that Mr. Wilson systematically supported their attempts to formulate some plan for suppressing the cheating evil, and before a great while the Princeton honor system was devised, a system by which every student signed a pledge on his examination paper, giving his word of honor as a gentleman that in this examination he had neither given nor received aid. Infractions were punished not by the faculty but by the student honor committee, who would try alleged offenders, and if they were found guilty would dismiss them from the college, the faculty doing nothing more than simply corroborating the act of dismissal. It was purely an act of student self-government. By the time I went to the Princeton faculty in 1899, this so-called Princeton System, namely, the honor system, was regarded as one of the most precious heritages and traditions of Princeton life, though, of course, the youngsters then in college did not know how very short the tradition was, that it reached back only some six or eight years. And, of course, none of them knew that the unostentatious wife of the professor of jurisprudence was the person who was primarily responsible for the introduction of the system in their lives.

Within a year or two after he had become professor at Princeton, overtures began to be made to Mr. Wilson to become president now of this college, now of that. I remember encountering him by mere accident one night at the old Grand Union Hotel on 42nd Street in New York in, I think, the autumn of 1892. My companion and I asked him what he was doing. "Why," he said, "I am here to try to keep from being made a college president." He was there to meet the trustees of some small college—I don't remember which now—who wanted to offer him the presidency.[30] I know that no offer or overture of offer interested him unless it was the suggestion that came to him to become president of the University of Virginia. For many years, I suppose ever since Thomas Jefferson founded the university, the University of Virginia had been without a president, had been governed by a committee of the faculty, but they began to agitate at the university for a president. And young Mr. Wilson was frequently mentioned for that position. I am not sure but that the agitation formulated itself almost into an offer. It would have done so undoubtedly had he himself not checked it. I think he really did tell them rather seriously at one time that this might be an interesting move, but he was thoroughly devoted to Princeton, and it was not easy to wean him away.[31]

As I look back now on all that has been said by Princeton enemies about his lack of college patriotism, I should be indignant if I did not have to smile when I realize how deeply his affections were rooted in Princeton and everything that concerned Princeton. As a matter of fact, Mr. Wilson, with all his breadth of view, has some very powerful partisan instincts. He is a good partisan, and he was a most doughty Princeton partisan in everything that concerned the welfare of Princeton, whether in athletics or in more intellectual contests with other colleges.

Mr. Wilson arranged as soon as possible to separate the duties of his chair and to get called to the Princeton faculty a professor of economics, and thus relieve himself permanently of teaching a subject in which he had never had any special interest. The new chair was formed in 1892, and its first occupant was young W. M. Daniels,[32] then a teacher at Wesleyan, who remained in the Princeton faculty and was one of the stoutest supporters of President Wilson in all the controversies of later days. Afterwards he was appointed by Mr. Wilson to the Interstate Commerce Commission.

I do not recall the time, but there should be no difficulty in getting the dates from some source, when a group of wealthy Princeton alumni, chiefly the Garretts of Baltimore, formed a special chair of jurisprudence for Mr. Wilson to occupy.[33] It was probably made with the purpose of making Princeton just as attractive as possible to him so that he would stay there.

As indicated in my narrative elsewhere, Mr. Wilson was chosen by the colleagues of his faculty to deliver the great sesquicentennial address in 1896, on which occasion the College of New Jersey became formally and officially Princeton University, and on which occasion something else was done which nobody realized the significance of then, but which was to have a profound influence upon the future, namely, there was provided on paper the establishment of a graduate school, and a dean of the graduate school was appointed— Professor Andrew F. West.[34] Old Dr. McCosh had been president of Princeton for twenty years—from 1868 to 1888—and he had then been succeeded by Dr. Francis L. Patton,[35] a man who Mr. Wilson himself still says is one of the most brilliant men that he has ever known. But as a president he was as incompetent as he was brilliant as a philosopher—a man who should never have allowed himself to be inveigled into accepting an executive office, as he had no executive qualities whatsoever. Not only did executive duties rather annoy him, but he took a rather flippant view of his whole administrative duty. I myself once heard Dr. Patton unconsciously sum up his whole attitude toward the serious things of college life in a faculty meeting many years later, when the more serious-minded were agitating for educational reform, which agitations were being resisted by Dr. Patton. It was then that I heard him say, with that incomparable waggishness of tone which he knew how to adopt, that "There seems to be a law, I will not call it of predestination, we might say a law of divine permission, whereby every year a certain number of young men should leave Princeton University knowing less than when they entered."

By 1896 it was pretty clearly recognized that this brilliant man could never guide the newly formulated university into a great career, and so, quite deliberately, the graduate school was constitutionally arranged so that it could be governed independently from the college presidency. They wanted to give the graduate school a chance to develop without any hampering from a reactionary president. And they naturally supposed that they had made the best and wisest choice for the deanship when they put Professor Andrew West in this office. Up to this time, and indeed for a good many years later, Professor West and Professor Wilson were cordial, personal friends. Professor West is a very fascinating man, a man in whose life there has been a great tragedy, his wife having gone insane after the birth of their child and having lived on. So far as I know, she is alive today in an insane asylum. His devotion has been of a sort that must make his worst enemy melt when he thinks of it. He has a great deal of scholarship, a great literary gift, a great wit. At least until he began to grow into such a political intriguer as he turned out to be, there was no better entertainment to be had than an evening's conversation with Professor West. Because he was forced to live a sort of bachelor life, his home was the center for the unmarried men of the faculty. W. M. Daniels, for instance, was perfectly devoted to West until the great breach came in later years. Professor West was given a year's leave of absence, sent to Europe to study European universities, and he was expected to come back with a formulated plan for the Princeton graduate school. Apropos of this, by the way, Dr. Patton made one of his characteristic remarks when he said that Professor West would go to Oxford, spend a year there, and come back and solemnly tell the world what everybody else had already known for a long time. This was the germ of the graduate school—and, though nobody was conscious of it at the time, it was the preface to the great controversy that occurred more than ten years later.

Early in his serious thinking, Mr. Wilson believed in a considerable degree of centralization, called himself a federalist, paid his devoir to Alexander Hamilton.[36] It was long before he rightly appreciated Thomas Jefferson. He was a student of law at the University of Virginia, was eyewitness to the excellence of Jefferson's planning and building of the university; by lifting his eyes could see beautiful Monticello, where "Mr. Jefferson" (nearly all Virginians to this day speak of "Mister" Jefferson as of a revered neighbor) lived; whether or not he made the pious pilgrimage to that gracious mansion, I do not know. The proximity to the sage's haunts was insufficient to make of young Wilson the idolizer of "Mr. Jefferson" which most University of Virginia students used to be. I don't know if changing times may or may not have altered this disposition. Wilson trafficked too much in ideas to fall subject to the witchery of a great, almost remembered presence. For many years Wilson remained a Hamiltonian, down even to his early years as president of Princeton. He deeply admired Oliver's book on Hamilton,[37] which always seemed to me an exceedingly unfair book, written on a too familiar formula, that of exalting his subject by minimizing the qualities of his subject's adversary. But Wilson's long-lasting objection to Jefferson lay deeper than the influence of any book about Hamilton. He long thought Jefferson too much of a political theorist, too immersed in an abstract something called "the Rights of Man," too ardent an advocate of French revolutionary doctrinaire philosophy.

He admired Edmund Burke above all political writers, admired him for many traits, expounded in his long essay, "The Interpreter of English Liberty,"[38] wherein he succinctly states one quality of Burke's which turned him instinctively to the great English-Irish statesman: "There is no page of abstract reasoning to be found in Burke."

In his younger days, whatever you may think about his later international visions, Wilson was a realist. This quality, which I had long discerned in him, was emphasized when I had opportunity of comparing President Wilson with Mr. Bryan. Bryan, who had engaged in practical politics for some twenty years, was the theorist; Wilson, with two or three years of political practice, was the man of facts. He had had a philosophy of politics since he was a Princeton sophomore, but no political metaphysics, no empiricisms, no disposition to experiment with untried and unproven ventures in matters governmental.

And so it came about, in the earlier 1890s, when this country was nearer a revolution than many suspected, Wilson reacted strongly against theories of the Middle West, of Kansas and Nebraska; reacted against the Farmers' Alliance, Populism, labor doctrinaires; against Jerry Simpson,[39] and, in especial, against William Jennings Bryan.

He was a convinced Cleveland man in the second Cleveland administration[40] when the lines of party division were being drawn tight, believed in Mr. Cleveland's tariff reform ideas, the Cleveland gold-standard position, the Cleveland strong-arm methods with Governor John A. Altgeld of Illinois and the Pullman car strikers who were retarding railway transit and transportation, and the stouthearted Cleveland's ignoring of Altgeld's protest against federal interposition in state of Illinois affairs.

I can see now, in memory, his face aglow, his eyes shining, as he came one morning to the breakfast table, a New York newspaper in his hand, exclaiming: "Here is great news! Mr. Cleveland has issued a pronunciamento, declaring the railways between the East and Chicago military and post roads, and has ordered out the army to enforce the decree."

A few days, or hours, later we witnessed artillery trains rumbling up Broadway in New York, and Wilson rejoiced, for here was a demonstration of the power of government against anarchy.

In the hot campaign, later, over "free silver," Mr. Wilson took, I think, no active part, but Princeton juniors and seniors heard not a few digressions from the set lecture on the heresy, the mad heresy, which if permitted its course would bring woe to the country. He returned, in 1896, from a recuperative journey to England, and had scarcely greeted his family, when he turned and asked if the so-called Democratic party had gone crazy in the nominating convention, and expressed withering contempt for Bryan's "Cross of Gold" speech.

Frankest of men, usually, Mr. Wilson kept his own counsel as to how he voted in November. It seems incredible that he could have voted for Bryan in 1896. I have no proof, but a strong suspicion, that Wilson kept "regular" in that momentous election by voting for Palmer and Buckner.[41]

But Mr. Wilson's first *personal* impression of Bryan was very favorable to the man, though not in the least to his ideas. He saw him first four years later during the 1900 campaign in this manner. Mr. Bryan had spoken at Trenton one afternoon and was to speak that evening either at Newark or Jersey City. A small group of insistent young Democrats among the Princeton students had arranged beforehand to have Mr. Bryan stop at Princeton Junction and deliver a brief address. A special train was run over the three-mile spur and was loaded down with students and some of the faculty, as well as some townspeople. A little stand about two feet high had been built just off the station platform, and when Mr. Bryan's train arrived he and his escort pushed their way through the compact little crowd, and a student, the president of the Students' Democratic Club (which was a very small organization, by the way), introduced Mr. Bryan in a very brief speech, the concluding words of which were: "I introduce you to the next president of the United States."

12. William Jennings Bryan, next to the podium

Mr. Bryan mounted the platform and his first words were: "You don't have to believe everything that a presiding officer tells you in his speech of introduction. I may not be the next president of the United States, and I may never be president of the United States, but I have some things that I want to say to you young college men which are more important than the question as to what personality is to sit in the presidential chair." With extraordinary simplicity and directness, and without any of the ornate oratory which in those days was associated with him, he told these young men that he realized that the college men of America did not believe in him; that he knew he was speaking to an audience not favorable to him and to his ideas; but that there were things which they and their fathers ought to think about without any prejudice at all. The simple speech which he made had for its theme the thesis that the government of the United States had slipped away from the masses of the people and come into the hands of a privileged few, and that this was bad for any country. After all these years can anybody deny the truth of what Mr. Bryan told those young men? It was as true as the law and the gospel.

In fact, it was on this rock that Roosevelt planted himself years later and did whatever good he did for the country—good so much mixed up with evil. As Bryan himself said later, Roosevelt had stolen his clothes when he was in swimming. That work of arousing the United States to understand that it was ceasing to be a self-governing country was a work begun by Mr. Bryan, let people say whatever they choose about some of his wrong fixed ideas.

I had gone down to the junction with one of my friends, not knowing that Mr. Wilson was there at all. In returning to Princeton on the train I chatted with my friend, John Finley,[42] then a member of the Princeton faculty, afterwards president of the College of the City of New York. Finley and I sharply disagreed about Bryan. I insisted that whatever erroneous ideas the man might have, he was fundamentally sincere. And this Finley stoutly denied. Before the train reached Princeton, I encountered Mr. Wilson, and he at once expressed himself as most agreeably surprised and deeply impressed by Bryan. And he said precisely what I had been saying to Finley—that this was a sincere man with a fundamental conviction. Both of us were really touched by the simplicity, the lack of egotism, the earnestness with which Mr. Bryan had addressed a group of men who he knew were hostile to him.

I am writing this on the fourteenth of August 1919—a long time after the event, but it was only last Sunday that Mr. Wilson, in family conversation, referred again to this episode at Princeton Junction, and with real feeling described the qualities which he saw in Mr. Bryan this first time that he ever saw him.

I may add here another incident belonging to much later years. I was living in Texas when the break came and Mr. Bryan resigned from the cabinet.[43] On my next visit to Washington, I spent an evening with Mr. and Mrs. McAdoo,[44] and Mr. McAdoo was talking in rather a heated manner about Mr. Bryan. The next morning at the breakfast table (I was staying at the White House)—Mr. Wilson and I were alone at the breakfast table—I said to him: "Mac tells me that Bryan is insincere. That's very hard for me to believe." The president looked up from his plate and fixed his eyes steadily on mine and said, with that quiet emphasis so characteristic of him: "Mr. Bryan is absolutely sincere." He added: "That sometimes makes him dangerous." It seems to me that it is only just that when the biography of Mr. Wilson is written there shall be written into it this unswerving confidence he has had in the fundamental sincerity of Mr. Bryan through all the years. He got the impression first in Princeton Junction in 1900 and he holds it today in 1919.

Shortly prior to the 1900 presidential campaign, a war had been fought with Spain over Cuba and Governor General Weyler's atrocities.[45] Wilson was aflame with enthusiasm, would have enlisted but for the fact that he had a wife and three little girls entirely dependent on him. He was quite Americanized now, lamented the assassination of McKinley, ardently admired his successor, Theodore Roosevelt, in the early part of Roosevelt's first administration.[46]

But that short war between the United States and Spain brought before our people a new problem, and a new political issue, so-called Imperialism. The question was what to do with the islands which Spain had lost—leave them as ready prey for the possession of other governments, or take them over temporarily or permanently. Professor Woodrow Wilson thought earnestly over the problem, in the light of American history, and became, still a Democrat, a convinced "Imperialist."[47]

The years between 1896 and 1899 were busy literary years. His college work was arranged so as to give him a good deal of unoccupied time for writing. He did all his college lecturing on Mondays and Tuesdays and had the remainder of the week for his own literary production. He once told Mrs. Wilson that he was always ashamed to tell professors from other colleges how little he did in Princeton. But I am sure that everybody felt that it was to the advantage of Princeton that Mr. Wilson should have abundant leisure for his productive work. He was a member of the more important committees of the faculty. He had already published *Congressional Government, The State, Division and Reunion*, and *An Old Master and Other Essays*. If I remember correctly, it was in 1896 that he published the volume entitled *Mere Literature*, and he was now busy writing for *Harper's Magazine* the articles which were subsequently collected in the volume entitled *George Washington*. Following this came from Harpers the invitation to write, also first for a magazine, afterwards to be published in book form, his *History of the American People*. He himself has said frequently that he did not write this history because he considered himself an historian, but that he wrote in order that he might learn some history. That is, of course, a modest way of expressing it, for certainly he had known enough history to write that admirable little volume, *Division and Reunion*, which I rather think is generally praised even by the professional historians who are somewhat inclined to speak lightly of the *History of the American People*. I suppose the truth of the matter is that Mr. Wilson was not allowed enough time to write the *History of the American People* as it should have been written. His ideal was Green's *Short History of the English People*. But probably the result was not as absolutely successful as were some of Mr. Wilson's other books.

Now, as a matter of fact, all that Mr. Wilson wrote was regarded by him merely as preparation for the book which he intended to write when he should feel that he was ripe for the task. It is an example of his controlled and systematic mind that he was deliberately waiting to begin his *magnum opus* until he should feel that he was fully prepared both in years and in learning for the task. He once told me that he would not be ready for that book until he was forty-five years of age. In the family circle, this prospective work was always referred to as "POP" which, being interpreted, meant "The Philosophy of Politics." He said that he had not found his real title, but this was as near as he had yet come to it, but whether or not this would be the title under which the book would appear must be left to the future. He whimsically added that Montesquieu had stolen his title when the great Frenchman of the eighteenth century gave to his book the title *The Spirit of the Laws*.

It has often interested me to realize that in this deliberate preparation for his master work, Mr. Wilson was like that great artist, Robert Louis Stevenson, who considered all that he ever wrote as merely his apprenticeship to the literary profession and his preparation for the great novel which he intended to write. But Robert Louis Stevenson died before the time came for the great novel, and Mr. Wilson was elected to the presidency of Princeton when he was forty-five years of age—just the time when he was getting ready to write his great work. Of course, we all hope and believe that it is yet to come when he retires from the presidency of the United States, and equally, of course, it will be a very much greater work than even he used to anticipate, because of the vast experience which he has had in actual politics.

Social Disposition and Habits

❧

WITH ALL of Mr. Wilson's activity of mind and career, and with all of his constant insistence that the college is a part of the great world and not an isolated and remote thing, it must still be remembered that he was for many years a college professor, leading the rather uneventful life of a college town. He was forty-five years old before he became president of Princeton University. Previous to that he had been a teacher in colleges, all of which were situated in rather small towns. Bryn Mawr and Princeton were only villages; Middletown, Connecticut, a quiet New England town of not more than 10,000 inhabitants, in which the college unit of two or three hundred professors and students formed a community of its own. He had entirely committed himself to the life and habits and pursuits of his profession. In these colleges of liberal arts, situated in small towns, the things of the mind are things of very great moment. An idea is as interesting as an event in the lives of men of more active business. The professors at Bryn Mawr, Middletown, and Princeton prior to 1900, at any rate, lived modest lives. Their social pursuits were very simple: little dinners of a few friends attended by the professors and their wives; an occasional meeting of a literary or scientific or philosophic club, at which "papers" were read and discussed. The purchase of a new book gave to a simple professor of those days something of the thrill that a hunter has when he purchases a new firearm.

In these simple surroundings, Mr. Wilson really formed his life habits. They were not the habits of a recluse, neither were they the habits of a gregarious animal. They were the habits of sweet and natural intercourse among a few chosen friends and quiet surroundings, with conversation generally on a fairly high plane—by which guarded statement I mean to say the conversation was not pedantic, not strained, not self-conscious, often involved little details of family or village life, jokes, and anecdotes, and was well within the region of the things of the mind. A rather beautiful atmosphere it is, too, in spite of all that is said in favor of the busy bustle of active affairs—an atmosphere of singular purity, both of thought and conduct. Of course, when one is thinking about it one naturally thinks of the ideal which Wordsworth expressed in the famous phrase, "plain living and high thinking."

It very aptly describes the atmosphere in which Mr. Wilson formed the habits of his life. To people living in these conditions, clubs and fraternal societies and things of that sort do not seem necessary in their own domestic circles and in their own friendly intercourses with the groups to which they belong. They find all the satisfaction that they need for the social instinct, which is, after all, the fundamental, legitimate reason for the existence of clubs, fraternal orders, etc. These professors just did not need them, and not needing them, they did not have them. There was in Princeton a little club called the Nassau Club, founded some years after Mr. Wilson went to Princeton as a professor. In those early days it was a very modest affair, occupying two or three rooms on the first floor of old University Hall, which was one of the dormitories—a reading room where there were a few daily papers and a generous collection of the better type of magazines; another room in which there were two or three billiard and pool tables. That was about all there was to the club. Some members of the faculty used this club a good deal; some not so much. Mr. Wilson was among the latter class. Though not a man of independent means, books and magazines he had always regarded as among the necessities of life, and therefore he and his wife had about all the magazine literature at home that he found time to read. And so he was not dependent on the Nassau Club reading room. Occasionally he would drop in after a lecture in the afternoon and browse in the magazines. Occasionally he would go to the club for a game of billiards, of which he was quite fond; and he was considerably better than the average player, and yet even for that pastime he did not go often to the club.

The simple fact of the matter is that the pleasantest evening Mr. Wilson could arrange for himself was an evening at home with his wife and such guests as were visiting in that very hospitable home, for it should be remarked that there was no more hospitable house in Princeton. Relatives of his own or of Mrs. Wilson, or friends from some part or other of the country, were continually arriving for visits, sometimes of two or three days, sometimes extending over several weeks. I fancy it would be safe to say that, during his entire professorship at Princeton, he and Mrs. Wilson did not sit down to a third of their meals alone, that at least two thirds of the time there were guests at the table. The talk around the table was always genial, natural, frequently humorous, and, as I have already indicated, apt at any moment to drift into fine and lofty things. Some people seem to think that the term "intellectual" is a cold and forbidding term. I cannot conceive that anybody with any brains at all in his head could have felt that the naturalness of the Wilson table was other than a genial, happy, sweet thing. Certainly there are very few tables at which more good anecdotes could have been heard, and probably few tables at which more puns, good and bad, were perpetrated, particularly if Dr. Joseph Wilson was there, because he was a more chronic punster even than his son. But at that table there was never any shamefacedness about talking about books. In fact, more than once it was suggested that there ought to be a revolving bookcase in the dining room, because so often questions arose which led to a demand for the encyclopedia or the *Century Dictionary* or the *Century Biography of Names*, and one of the little girls would be dispatched to the study or the library to fetch the volume.

I might remark, while speaking of these table manners, that whether breakfast, lunch, or dinner, there was always amiable conversation. People did not come to that breakfast table cross. I can truthfully say I never heard a cross or an ill-natured remark made at the Wilson table.

In those days nobody ever would have thought of calling Woodrow Wilson "severe" or cold or aloof or forbidding or self-centered. He had in his little circle the reputation and the deserved reputation of geniality. In every college faculty there are a few pedants, and undoubtedly the pedants among Mr. Wilson's associates would have charged him chiefly with being frivolous, so ready was he with a joke or an anecdote or a pun. His humor was never sharp or cynical, sarcastic or cruel; in fact, I have never known a man to joke so much whose jokes were so generally kindly.

Such, roughly described, is something of the atmosphere in which Mr. Wilson formed the habits of his life, and when he entered the broader field as president of Princeton, which, of course, led up to the governorship of New Jersey and the presidency of the United States, his habits were too entirely formed for him to break them unless there was some very strong reason for breaking them. As president of Princeton, as governor of New Jersey, he traveled far and wide, making many speeches, meeting many men of prominence, and certainly having keen enjoyment in his contact with men of position and influence. But none of this altered his fundamental tastes. When he sought his own private pleasure in a social way, he still sought it primarily at his own fireside with a few friends whose intellectual tastes were sympathetic with his own, and where there could be bred the type of conversation which he most loved. That is as true of life in the White House as it was of life in the cottage on Library Place in which he lived while professor at Princeton.

This that I have been insisting on, namely, the formation of a life habit, is one explanation of the fact that he has not been the type of president who continually invites in public men to lunch or dinner with him—not even the members of his cabinet. There is, however, an additional reason for that procedure, for which he has been a good deal criticized, namely, a reason of self-protection. It is characteristic of the president's mind that he concentrates his thought entirely on matters of business when business is before him and as entirely dismisses it when he goes to his table or for a ride in his automobile or for a game of golf. Mental relaxation is as necessary to him as physical exercise, and he has found it impossible to get the salt of mental relaxation at the table which he needs if he has as his guests men whose interests or duties lead them to talk of public affairs. Those who know the president well personally continually have to tell their personal friends that they are not the people through whom public business can be transacted with the president. Speaking for myself, I have had to say a great many times in reply to letters or in conversation to people who wanted me to ask the president for some appointment, or use what they mistakenly supposed was the influence I had with him for some desired end, that I had no influence whatsoever, no part in public affairs, and that the president would very deeply resent it if I should attempt anything of the sort, and that, furthermore, when they suggested that this was something that I could easily mention to him casually at the lunch table when I was at the White House or on the golf course, so far from that being the case, it was exactly and precisely what I could not do; that if I should begin to talk public affairs at his lunch table or on the golf course or in the automobile in a country ride, I should very soon find that I should not be invited to participate in any more of those pastimes; that one reason why I hoped I was welcome was because the president knew that I was one of the three or four or half-dozen people who were certainly not going to bother him with public affairs at all at the time when his mental and nervous rest and his very digestion depended on his being relieved from all consideration of public affairs.

Mr. Wilson soon found in his life as president that his associates in the government almost inevitably and invariably at the luncheon table or on the golf course would bring up some political matter, especially some matter of appointment, and so in self-protection he had to form the rule of seeking his social life with those people whose relationships to him were nonpolitical. This instinct of his goes back to the days of his college presidency. I have spoken of him as an infrequent visitor to the Nassau Club during the days of his professorship in Princeton, but even these sporadic visits practically ceased altogether after he had been president of the university for a year or so. I remember hearing him say that he could no longer enjoy a game of billiards at the club because invariably, as soon as he was well started on his game, some member of the faculty would ask if he might speak to him a minute about some departmental matter and lead him away to a corner to hold a business conference, when the president had gone to the club purely and simply for the purpose of escaping business responsibility and getting a little mental relaxation. So this is the second reason why the president's circle of intimate associations has been rather small while he was president of the United States.

There is a third reason. The president has steadfastly refused to play any favorites among his political associates, especially among the members of the cabinet. He would not ask the secretary of this department or that frequently to the house because inevitably suspicions would arise that this particular member of the cabinet was pulling a strong oar with him to the disadvantage of some of his cabinet associates. Dr. Grayson has said that the president told him that he would not permit a member of the cabinet at a cabinet meeting to lead him off into a corner to hold a private conversation with him while the other members of the cabinet sat around and waited for the meeting to begin or to proceed. What the cabinet officer had to say to the president could be said in the open, since public business was the business of all concerned at the table.

I frequently heard Mr. Wilson say that he used to cross the Atlantic Ocean on the slower boats of the less conspicuous lines because he could not afford the smart boats of the more famous lines. But that, what was a mere necessity, was also a great advantage, because in later years, when he did make a few trips on some of the fashionable lines, he realized how much better company and conversation there was on the smaller boats, because on those smaller boats there were so many more intellectual people. I can testify from personal experience that he was the genial center of the smoking room on two voyages across the Atlantic, for he and I went together for his second and my first trip abroad in 1899. We crossed on the old *Furnessia* of the Anchor Line. There were several college professors, including Professor James Seth, the philosopher, who, after a period of teaching in American universities, was returning to Scotland and a professorship in the University of Edinburgh, his own alma mater. In company with Professor Seth were two younger men, men of my own age, one Mr. Alexander Meiklejohn, now president of Amherst College, and the other, one of the most entertaining of brilliant conversationalists, Professor Lefevre,[1] who had been at Cornell and was subsequently at the University of Virginia. Those three, together with Mr. Wilson and myself, formed a quintette which made the journey across pleasant to remember in spite of atrociously bad weather and a mishap to the vessel—a broken shaft, which delayed us considerably. In addition to our group, there were numbers of other congenial Americans, and at least one very picturesque figure, a Mr. Fitzpatrick from New York, whose eccentric and humorous behavior, both on ship and ashore (we encountered him once or twice) are still remembered by Mr. Wilson and recited among his favorite anecdotes. Though Mr. Wilson did not smoke himself and never has smoked, he spent every evening—and the whole evening—with those of us who were smokers in the little smoking room which was situated on the deck of the *Furnessia*, a crude little room, with leather benches running around the side of it, like the waiting room of a station. We were all made happy in the evenings by the conversation that went on within this room, in which conversation Mr. Wilson was always a leader, ready to talk, ready to hear others talk, and geniality itself.

Mr. Wilson was as kind and thoughtful and considerate as he was genial. His going to Europe that summer was rather at my sister's solicitation than on his own account, and I honestly believe as much for my sake as for his own. A year or so before, one of my old friends and associates in the faculty of the University of Vermont, where I had taught several years previous, told me that he had received a letter from Mr. Wilson, whom he had never met, stating that I had often spoken in the family circle of this friend and the congenial relationship that existed between us and had happened to mention that the friend frequently went to Europe, and that in this letter Mr. Wilson had asked that this gentleman pardon the liberty he was taking in suggesting that he invite me to accompany him on his next trip, saying that he and Mrs. Wilson had been a good deal concerned about the unsatisfactory state of my health and felt that a trip abroad would be of great advantage; that they had not been able to persuade me to take it alone.

In 1899, just prior to my entrance into the Princeton faculty, Mrs. Wilson was very insistent that I ought to get the European experience, and finally, by her urging, Mr. Wilson and I took the trip together. As it turned out a few months later, when I submitted to an operation,[2] I had been suffering for six years from appendicitis and had been pretty badly run down. Mr. Wilson's gentleness and consideration on this tour was something I cannot speak of even now without emotion. One thing he insisted on the ship was that I take the lower berth and that he take the upper, swearing that he rested better above than below, thereby perjuring himself, for I know he did not. We had taken our bicycles to Europe—two new Columbia machines—for the purpose of having a bicycle tour. As a matter of fact, we generally traveled on the train, with the bicycles in the luggage van. And I often thought how beautifully considerate he was in this matter. He loved his bicycle, loved the rides along the fine British roads, and had looked forward to the rides from Edinburgh to southern England all by wheel. But my vitality was very low, and again and again, when after breakfast at some inn in the morning I would say: "You know, there is a perfectly good train going to our destination today. What do you think of just putting our bicycles aboard and taking the train"? He would laugh and say: "All right, if you feel that way about it." And that was the way we did the major part of our traveling. Finally, in an attempt at reciprocal generosity, I begged him to spend the last three weeks alone on his bicycle, while I went down into Surrey and spent the time with an American friend who had a little box there. That Mr. Wilson did, he going to Ireland and riding his bicycle there.

It will be impossible to speak adequately of the sweetness, gentleness, geniality, and camaraderie of the man, not only with me, but with everybody he met that summer in Great Britain. He had an instinctive liking for the British people, though I think I remember dictating in these notes in an earlier chapter that he had come back from his first journey in 1896 with the statement that he liked England very much, but that the journey abroad had made him a better American. However, he had by instinct that breadth of mind which has seemed so hard for many of our fellow countrymen to get, which enabled him to be a thoroughgoing, absolute, devoted, patriotic American, and, at the same time, have sympathy and relish for the peoples of other lands.

We landed at Glasgow and from there went to Edinburgh. We had two or three most delightful days there, taking afternoon tea and dinner at the home of Professor Seth—I have already spoken of him in these notes—and his mother in a typical British home, almost a country home, right under Ben Arthur. I remember Mr. Wilson laughing and saying it looked as if I were not going back to America, so completely in love had I fallen with that region.

We took the trip through the Scottish lakes, then went down through the Burns country, over to Carlisle, entering on our bicycles, a contrast to the later visit he paid to Carlisle when president of the United States and a leading figure of the world. We then went into the lake district, which is the part of Great Britain he loves most of all, and to which he returned again and again in subsequent years. I rather think I have stated somewhere in these notes that Mrs. Wilson used to urge him in his subsequent journeys to Europe to spend more time on the continent. One day she said to him: "Why do you always go to the English lake country? Why not go to France, Italy, etc.?" And he replied: "Are you never going to understand me and how I do not need to do a variety of things, but how I love most to do the thing I love best again and again? There is no spot in the world in which I am so completely at rest and peace as in the lake country." Here we talked with many of the natives, and here, I am glad to remember, we really did use our bicycles continually. We were held up in Keswick for three days by a torrential rain. I remember the boy's delight with which Mr. Wilson came to my room one night after I had gone to bed, while he had been lingering in the smoking room hob-nobbing with commercial travelers and other folks, and telling me he had just met a man who had a great talent for narrative or lies, whichever interpretation we chose to put on what he had been relat-ing. This man had been telling some very strong stories about the rains, among other things that all the ducks were being drowned by rain.

One morning at the breakfast table the sun began to show through the clouds and Mr. Wilson said: "Well, I think we will get away on our bicycles this morning." I looked at him in astonishment and said: "After all this rain? Why, we will have to wait two or three days longer to let the roads dry." He laughed and said: "You don't know English roads. You will find them as dry as if it had not been raining at all." And of course he was right.

We drove down to Grasmere, visiting a little church in the Words-worth haunts, and particularly Dove Cottage, where Wordsworth and his sister had lived, and to which Wordsworth had brought his bride. We went to the arbor which is described by Wordsworth in the famous poem on Dove Cottage,[3] a poem which I have heard Mr. Wilson read again and again, always with tears in his eyes, it being among the things that for a time at least he loved most in the poetry of Wordsworth. The whole region delighted him out of measure, partly for its own beauty, partly for its associations with the serene poet who has meant so much to him.

At Ambleside I had one of my attacks of pain, which I was to learn a few months later was really an attack of appendicitis. I had not gone to bed but was reclining on a lounge. Mr. Wilson was standing at the window looking down the street. Presently he chuckled and called me to the window and pointed out a policeman who was walking up the street with an abnormally long stride. He said: "That is the only person I have ever seen who walks just like you." And always after that he described my stride as my "Amblestride."

We went over to Durham, where we had a most interesting two days. Sunday we attended service in the great cathedral and walked about the village. On Monday court was to convene, and Mr. Wilson told me that he had just learned that Justice Grantham[4] was going to preside at court and that this was a most happy circumstance, as he himself felt it would be an opportunity to attend a session of the En-glish courts sitting under one of the most distinguished justices of England. He suggested that I could amuse myself in any way I chose, but if I cared to go to court with him he would be very glad to have me do so. It was just exactly what I did want to do. We went in the morning but found the courtroom too crowded for us to get in. They told us, however, that the morning session was a very short one; that if we would come back immediately after lunch they would see to it that we had seats. This we did, and both of us were very much impressed by the solicitous kindness of the court policemen. As soon as we appeared, we were greeted by one of them, who passed us on to another, saying: "These are the American gentlemen who were here this morning. Be sure that you find them good seats." A murder trial was in progress, and Mr. Wilson watched the swift and sure proceedings of British criminal practice with the eager eye of an expert. It was all over within about four hours—the impaneling of the jury, the taking of testimony, the pleading of the advocates, the charge of the judge, the return of the verdict, which, in this case, was a verdict of "not guilty." Judge Grantham practically instructed the jury as to the verdict which they should bring in. He himself analyzed the case in a most clear way; showed how the death in question could have occurred by mere accident, and how the testimony against the prisoner was not such as to warrant the bringing in of a sentence of guilty. The jury did not leave the box. Mr. Wilson remarked at some length on the contrast between that kind of procedure and the abuse of justice in some of our American courts, where delays and pettyfogging prolong such trials over days and weeks. He said: "Mark you, if that man had been found guilty he would have been hanged in a week. British justice is as swift as ours is slow."

We visited the East Coast cathedral towns and went to Cambridge and Oxford. It was vacation time at both universities, but the summer session was on at Oxford and Mr. Wilson visited the classes of Professor Dicey.[5] After that I went on to London; he to Ireland. We met in Glasgow for the return voyage, returning on the *City of Rome*, which, by the way, was another act of his considerateness, for we had engaged passage back on the *Furnessia*, which had brought us over, and the *Furnessia* was not to sail until some ten days later. Mr. Wilson would have been glad to have had that additional time in England, but I complained that the *Furnessia* was a most uncomfortable boat, and I thought it much nicer to go back on a large boat, the *City of Rome* being very much larger than the *Furnessia*. And he, without protest, had consented to the change.

As it turned out, it was a very unfortunate change, for the *City of*

Rome had a very serious accident. It went up on an iceberg in a fog and was so seriously damaged, though we did not know it then, that when they got her back to Great Britain on the return voyage and lifted her into dock for repairs, she fell into two parts, showing that she had broken her backbone when she climbed up on the iceberg. The accident occurred at late dinner time. Mr. Wilson had finished his meal and had gone on deck. I had lingered in the dining room and was talking to the two people who remained at our table—Dr. Christie,[6] of Allegheny, Pennsylvania, and a young college woman who was returning to America under his chaperonage. It was a pretty savage experience, about which I will not enter into any detail, except to say that everybody in the salon behaved very well indeed, though the ship turned almost over on her side when she ran up on the shelf. The *City of Rome* had a cutter bow, enabling her to slide up on the shelf like a sled. The shelf broke and let us back into the water, but more on our side than on our keel. Nobody left the dining room immediately, there being a general tendency not to create a panic. Gradually, however, people began to go out one by one, wading through broken crockery above the ankles. As soon as it seemed decent, I left the dining room very anxious to join Mr. Wilson on the deck. I found him chatting with a Presbyterian preacher from New York, Dr. Cuthbert Hall,[7] and the moment I saw him I felt a sort of ease and calm because of his own perfect calmness and possessions. He and Dr. Hall were chatting in the most natural way as if going up on icebergs was a daily experience and an event of no concern whatsoever. And this was Mr. Wilson's attitude through the whole thing on a ship on which, while the general behavior was most excellent, it was perfectly evident that there was a degree of suppressed panic.

Mr. Wilson suggested that night that we just take off our coats instead of going to bed. Still nobody knew what condition the ship really was in. We had hardly settled down in our berths when there was a grinding noise, it being perfectly evident that the ship had scraped another iceberg. The gangways of the vessel were filled with pretty excited people this time, for a second experience was a little too much for jangled nerves, but again Mr. Wilson was smilingly calm and said that, whatever it was, evidently it was not going to do us very much harm, and we settled back in our berths. The next day the fog had cleared and we were sailing very slowly and under a heavy list, but still the people were not entirely recovered from the shock of the experience, and I said to him, as he was reclining easily in his deck chair reading: "You seem more completely at ease than anybody on the boat." "Well," he said, "nothing is to be gained by worry, and besides, we are all right now."

I have often thought of Mr. Wilson in that accident and have speculated on what some of his thoughts must have been. Of course, he must have faced the possibility of going down, for that was too obvious a possibility to be ignored by anybody; in fact, I fancy that for ten or fifteen minutes there wasn't anybody on the boat who did not expect to go down. Of what was he thinking? One thing, of course, I know. He was thinking about his wife and his little girls. But I have often wondered if there did not flash through his mind some thought of the unfinished career. He was without vanity, conscious of his own great powers. He knew, he must have known, that if a long life were granted him he was to make a distinguished career, either as a scholar or as an administrator. He was forty-three years old. In that calm, deliberative way of his, he had decided that at forty-five he was going to begin his great book, his *magnum opus*—the book which I have referred to in earlier notes—the book which we used to call "POP." He had been developing deliberately, waiting until he felt he was fully ripe to lay his hand to the great literary task of his life. And what there was beyond that, who could guess? But he must have had some thoughts sometimes about it. And here he was at forty-three, with all this undone and a very genuine threat that within a very few minutes he might be down under the brine. But there was nothing in his face or demeanor to indicate anxiety, apprehension, or regret. He was smiling and chatting just as normally as at his own table.

Mr. Wilson has told Dr. Grayson that while the experience with the iceberg was an unpleasant one, he was glad to have had it happen because it proved to him that he would not be a coward in a crisis.

Ellen Axson Wilson and Woodrow Wilson

◆

W HEN THEY were living in Mid-
dletown, Connecticut, Mr. Wilson said to me one day as we were
walking across a bridge that spanned a beautiful New England
stream and paused to look at the water and the trees: "Ellen ought to
be here. I have never known anybody in my life with such a passion
for beauty as she has."

This quality of Mrs. Wilson's was one which undoubtedly had a
strong influence on Mr. Wilson himself. His father was the strongest
educational influence on his life, and Dr. Wilson had a decided literary talent, but it was of the somewhat robust eighteenth-century
type, which is to say, not primarily aesthetic in its appreciation. In
fact, Dr. Wilson was more like Samuel Johnson than any man I have
ever known in the flesh—a man of books, but also of intimate contact with life; an extraordinary power for conversation and a robust
personality. From him unquestionably Woodrow Wilson derived by
inheritance and training a very considerable portion of his great literary power.

But Mrs. Wilson had just that refinement of literary appreciation
which we call "aesthetic." Her artistic gifts were really very great, and
she had fully made up her mind to be a professional portrait painter.
Her opportunities for training in the little southern town in which
she lived were, of course, very meager, but she worked extremely
hard. And when she was perhaps twenty-two years of age she really
contrived to earn a tidy sum of money each year by crayon portraits.
Though the idea of crayon portraits suggests a horrible form of art,
she was able in that unsympathetic medium to get some really very
fine effects. Of course, she was not going to rest there, and so she
purposed to go at least to New York, if possible later to Europe, and
educate herself as an artist in oils. This was a career which she had
fully determined upon when it was all changed by the destiny that

brought Woodrow Wilson definitely into her life. Even after her engagement to him, she did go to New York for one year and studied at
the Art Students League, making extraordinary progress as a portrait
painter. But, of course, she regarded this now merely as an interlude
in what she realized was to be her real life, namely, the wife of this
man who she told me the night of her engagement was "the greatest
man in the world."

They were married after about a year's engagement; in fact, would
have been married earlier had Mr. Wilson not been in the midst of
his course at Johns Hopkins University. They were married in June
1885, and in the following autumn they went to Bryn Mawr College,
which had just been founded, where a small faculty of young men
were collected by, as she was then, Dean Thomas. As it turned out,
this constituted one of the most remarkable faculties ever connected
with an American college, because these men were all young, practically unknown, and practically every one of them became a distinguished man in his specialty.

The first daughter was born a little less than a year after their marriage, and the other two children followed at brief intervals.[1] In these
circumstances, it was impossible for Mrs. Wilson to pursue her art.
No woman ever gave herself up more completely to marriage and
wifedom and motherhood than did Mrs. Wilson. I may remark that
she was the amazement of her very practical uncle in Savannah[2] (her
father and mother were both dead), who was devoted to her, but
never believed that she had any turn whatsoever for practicality.
However, when she, as one of the first steps in her married life, attended Mrs. Rohrer's Cooking School in Philadelphia and learned
to be a perfect queen of cooks, her uncle's astonishment knew no
bounds.

This is merely characteristic of this early married life—she gave
herself up completely to practical things. She, who was a reader of
poetry and a painter of pictures, now collected, as her most valuable
library, books on cooking and the rearing of babies.

Until the girls were well on into their teens, Mrs. Wilson scarcely
touched a paint brush, with one notable exception. When there
came to the recently established Princeton Art Museum Bouguereau's Madonna for a brief period of exhibition,[3] she, who scarcely
ever saw good pictures in this interval—for this busy mother with
very limited financial resources, even trips to New York had to be few
and for very practical purposes—welcomed the advent of this rather

13. Ellen Louise Axson, ca. 1885

famous French picture as a thirsty person welcomes an oasis in the desert. After she looked at it several times she decided that she must have it for a possession, and so she got out her easel and paint brushes and went to the museum and copied it. I remember Mr. Wilson saying, when it was completed and hung in the little house in Princeton, that one of his colleagues came in one day and seeing it on the wall said: "Great Scott, have you fallen heir to a fortune that you are able to buy a French masterpiece?" His friend thought this was the original. I also remember Mr. Wilson saying: "As a matter of fact, the copy is better than the original."

Thus, Mrs. Wilson practically painted nothing until her children were grown, when one summer, being in not very good health (she had suffered one of the severest bereavements of her life—the death by accident of her young brother, who had been more like a son than a brother),[4] Mr. Wilson, solicitous about her condition, decided to take her up to Old Lyme, Connecticut. He felt that not only because the country was beautiful, but because she would have artistic associates there,[5] it would be a good place for her to recuperate. And then there happened a rather extraordinary thing. Just as she had been unable to look at the Bouguereau painting without copying it, just so she was unable to associate with landscape painters (and they were the best landscape painters in America) without wanting to do something even in a very modest way in their own style. So she, a woman well past her fortieth birthday, who had not painted for years, and whose previous painting had been all in portraiture, suddenly turned into a landscape painter. Her health was soon restored, and in subsequent summers they returned to Lyme primarily for the purpose of giving her an opportunity to continue her studies. The famous painters at Lyme considered that her progress was almost phenomenal. Each summer she did work so much better than the preceding summer that she came to have a sort of disgust for all the work of previous summers. Perhaps one of the few things she was ever proud of that belonged to her own career as separate from her husband's career was that she was able to sell some of these landscapes for good money, which she gave to a mountain school in Georgia,[6] in which she was very much interested.

When Mr. Wilson was lying ill in the White House in 1919, a kinsman was talking with him in his bedroom, when his eye fell upon a landscape on the wall near the bed. Mr. Wilson had acquired many fine pictures by many fine American artists, and this kinsman remarked that he was unable to identify the painter of the particular picture at which he was looking. "Who did that?" he asked. "Why Ellen did it," said Mr. Wilson. The kinsman remarked on the beauty and finish of the work, and Mr. Wilson said in effect that there were very few people in America who could paint better than Ellen could. Many of these landscape pictures by Mrs. Wilson hung in the White House and later in the S Street house, the house to which Mr. Wilson retired on March 4, 1921.

Of course, Mrs. Wilson could not have given Woodrow Wilson anything that was not innate in himself, and equally of course he has by nature an affinity for good painting, as he has for good music, but unquestionably it was Mrs. Wilson's influence which enabled him to discriminate and become so sure a judge of good painting. Their influence on each other was of course reciprocated. She learned from him to love the more solid kinds of literature, such as Burke and Bagehot, prime favorites of his. He learned from her a deeper appreciation of poetry and painting. She from the outset of their married life became an eager reader of books in history, political economy, and political philosophy. And in this, as in everything else, she was intelligent and discriminating; she learned how to distinguish between excellent and inferior political writers. She carried this development so far that when he was preparing to write his book, *The State*, she, having learned German for the purpose, read and made digests of a great many very dull German treatises on government in order to save him the time and energy for his more creative type of work.

Of course, he never had a literary project that he did not discuss with her from its first inception. And she would listen, suggest, object, and criticize in a way that he unquestionably found extremely helpful. I do not think she ever undertook to act specifically as a critic of his literary style. I fancy that from the start she felt that that was too perfect a thing for her to meddle with—a style, by the way, he had been trained in by his father in the strictest manner. But Mrs. Wilson did criticize very freely his judgments, and he always would seek her objections as well as her praise, esteeming her, as I heard him say many times, his best critic.

An interesting thing occurred in this connection. After they had been married perhaps a score of years he said to me one day: "Ellen used to be the best critic I ever had but she isn't any longer, for the simple reason that she and I have become so much like one person that she sees everything now just as I see it, and there is no longer any correction of her mind on mine." I remember at the same time he said that he was practically without a critic now. He did not know if there was anyone to whom he could turn for honest, suggestive, and constructive criticism. This phenomenon may be taken as an illustration of the extraordinary unity of mind and spirit that came to exist between this man and wife. Her loss of power as his critic was not due to any timidity, for all who knew Mrs. Wilson well recognized this characteristic, that, though she was the gentlest woman, she was at the same time one of the firmest, and though she was the most adoring of wives, there was in her an uncompromising quality which would have made it impossible for her to say to him that something he did was done well if she thought it was not done well. I never knew a person who declined more completely to compromise her judgment than did Mrs. Wilson. In fact, I remember Mr. Wilson once reading with great relish aloud from one of Chesterton's essays, and applying what he read to his wife, who, of course, was present while he was reading. It was the passage somewhere in Chesterton in which he says that only foolish people think that love is blind, and in his whimsical way goes on to say, in effect, that a man's friend likes him and leaves him as he is, but his wife loves him and therefore is always trying to change him into somebody else, and he adds that women have an almost morbid lucidity about the men they love, the thinness of their excuses or the thickness of their heads. The point of all this is that Mr. Wilson laughingly applied it to this devoted wife's attitude toward him, and correctly so.

So the point I am making in all this is that Mrs. Wilson ceased to be a good critic of her husband's literary product, not because she was afraid to tell her husband what she thought about his work, but because, as he himself said, their minds had practically coalesced into one.

Her pride in him as a literary man was absolutely without limit. I do not suppose in their early days she ever thought of him as being other than a literary man. She had such reverence for literature that a great literary career seemed to her to be in and of itself sufficient even for his greatness. And she had not a shadow of doubt that he was destined to be one of the most famous men in world literature.

I remember so well her pride when the young husband—he was then professor at Wesleyan University—was selected by the editor of the "Epochs of American History" series to write the volume of American history covered by the period of Civil War and Reconstruction; or, as he termed in the title which he gave to the book, *Division and Reunion,* a book which, by the way, many of his literary admirers consider one of the finest pieces of historical writing that he has ever done.

An uncle of Mrs. Wilson's[7] came to pay her a brief visit shortly after this invitation had been received and accepted, and I can remember how Mrs. Wilson at once got out some of the existing volumes in the series, turned to the pages which contained the announcements of all the volumes, and read the distinguished names of contributors to the series, calling her uncle's attention to the fact that her husband was invited to enter this company. She showed by her entire manner that she felt that on the whole this was rather more flattering to the company than to her husband. I remember how Mr. Wilson, sitting like a schoolboy, rather embarrassed by the whole thing, nudged me and said: "Ellen is too absurd."

It will be hard to say what early event in Mr. Wilson's career first made a pronounced impression, because, of course, he had the gift of genius to make his impression felt from the start on at least a chosen few. When he published *Congressional Government*, his first book, he was twenty-seven years old. The book was reviewed by Professor Bryce, now Lord Bryce, who said that though it seemed extravagant praise, he must say that this young American had made a study of the American Constitution which could be compared only to Bagehot's classical study of the English Constitution. This was, indeed, praise and was naturally most gratifying to the young author; and so in successive stages in his career, recognition came now from this source and now from that group of people. I remember that, as early as the Chicago Exposition in 1893, Mr. Wilson was invited to Chicago to deliver an educational address, and I think it is perfectly safe to say that the first cartoon of him appeared in that connection in a Chicago paper.[8] Some local artist had drawn pictures of various people at this educational conference, and, among them, the young Princeton professor, who, for some reason I do not understand, was represented as a little boy in knee breeches, flying a balloon.

Invitations came to him very frequently in his young years to deliver very important addresses here and there, but I suppose it is safe to say that the first occasion in which he got something like national recognition was when he delivered the sesquicentennial address at Princeton University in 1896. It was a very great occasion—one of the greatest academic occasions in the history of America. Famous scholars from all over the world were in attendance, and it was Professor Wilson who had been selected by his colleagues of the faculty to deliver the most important address of the occasion—the address on the university itself. I remember, by the way, receiving a letter from my sister in which she spoke with jubilation of this distinction that had come to him, and she said that it was personally so gratifying to them both because he had been then six years a member of

the Princeton faculty, and it was the first intimation he had received
from the fellow members of his faculty of their recognition of his superior powers. He was selected as their spokesman to speak to what
was literally a representation of the educational world at large. Char-
acteristically, he chose as his theme not a purely academic topic but
a topic which linked Princeton College with the world of affairs and
the nation's destiny. The title of his address was "Princeton in the
Nation's Service."[9] It is an essay which has been read far and wide
and has had a wide influence not only upon the development of
Princeton but upon the attitude of American educators at large. It
was in effect an announcement that America could not tolerate a
purely cloistered type of education, an academe withdrawn from the
world of affairs, but that the college must stand in the midst of affairs, influencing the destiny of the nation. This was the occasion. Of
course, he prepared the address with great care and read it verbatim
from manuscript. I was, unhappily, unable to attend this famous
celebration. I was not then a member of the Princeton faculty, but I
ran down to Princeton to visit the family, perhaps a fortnight later,
and I remember so well Mr. Wilson saying to me apropos of this
address: "You know, I sometimes wonder if I have a touch of the
mountebank in me." He then went on to say that he had written the
address in full and brought it to a conclusion, and, of course, the first
thing he then did was to read it to his wife. She was thrilled and delighted, but she said: "It does not end well. It ends too abruptly. It
needs something to lift it and to lift your audience up to the highest
plane of vision. It needs a great final paragraph somewhat in the
manner of Milton's *Areopagitica*, and that great passage in which he
says: 'Methinks, I see her as an eagle mewing her mighty youth and
kindling her undazzled eyes at the full midday beam.'"

Mr. Wilson recognized at once the validity of the criticism and the
suggestion. He at once caught her point and proceeded to write that
concluding paragraph, which, as any one man sees now who turns
to the essay, has the true, great Miltonic movement of manner—a
superb passage of eloquence.[10] It was characteristic of the man who
combines in so interesting a way the most masculine qualities with
an almost feminine sensitiveness that he should have thought and
said that he felt just a little bit like a mountebank in that he was so
easily able to take this suggestion given to him by his wife and frame
the sort of paragraph which she in a sense had ordered him to frame
on the model which she had suggested, and then turn out this fin-

ished product, which incidentally is the most famous passage in the address.

Just as Mrs. Wilson was entirely too honest not to tell her husband exactly what she thought, so he was entirely too honest to pretend to share a literary enthusiasm of his wife's unless he really did share it. As a matter of fact, when I pause to consider, I think he really did learn to love most of the authors whom she loved most. Even Browning, who was one of her great enthusiasms, Mr. Wilson learned to love very much. And I say "*even Browning*," because Browning's mind and Mr. Wilson's are not at all alike. Mr. Wilson is characterized, of course, by clarity in everything; Browning by obscurity. There were many things in Browning that he did not like and did not profess to care for, but he and Mrs. Wilson read Browning enough together for him to become very fond of some of the Browning poems, though I remember, by the way, that he never shared her enthusiasm for *Andrea Del Sarto*—and for the very characteristic reason that he felt it was too depressing. He acknowledged it to be a great piece of art, but built up on a man's acknowledged failure, the man being too supine to take his own career in his hands.

All this introduction is just by way of saying that though Mr. Wilson shared, I think, most of his wife's greatest literary enthusiasms, he perhaps shared none so completely as her enthusiasm for Wordsworth. I have known some of the best of the Wordsworthian scholars and critics, and, naturally, in my profession I have been a good deal of a student of Wordsworth myself, but I must say that Mrs. Wilson was in my opinion the most illuminating commentator on Wordsworth that I ever listened to. She understood him apparently by intuition. I do not want to analyze too closely, but it occurs to me at the moment that in two sides of Wordsworth's nature I find things that represent Mr. and Mrs. Wilson. The serene austerity of Wordsworth corresponds to a certain quality that we recognize in Mr. Wilson. With all his human quality, there is that calm serenity which can on occasion become austerity. In the mysticism of Wordsworth, I find something that corresponds more nearly to a quality of Mrs. Wilson's, who, with all her common sense, carried idealism sometimes to a point of sheer mysticism.

It is, of course, characteristic of Mr. Wilson that he loves to do the same thing over and over again. He loves to take the same rides, the same walks; other people want variety; not he. So it came about that his favorite spot in all the world for recreation was the Wordsworth lake country. Of course, primarily because of its own natural charm, but undoubtedly, secondarily, because of the Wordsworth association, he loved this place. And with that same quality of loving to do the same thing over and over again, he loved to read the same poems of Wordsworth again and again. Not always the more famous poems were they either. I am not sure that I ever heard him read the *Ode on the Intimations of Immortality*, but I have heard him read, perhaps a score of times, the simple lines which Wordsworth wrote on his and his sister's bower;[11] and even now as I sit and think about it, I can hear his rich and expressive tones, I have never heard anything more beautiful than his reading of that simple poem. And, again, in simple lines like those in which the poet addresses Hartley Coleridge, Mr. Wilson found a rare delight. I have heard him read that poem aloud again and again. There is something in the dignity of the Wordsworthian style, the severe exclusion of everything that is ornate and spasmodic, that corresponds to Mr. Wilson's own serene literary style. There is a real kinship between the literary genius of Wordsworth and the literary genius of Woodrow Wilson. And what I am saying all through here is that he probably learned his first lessons in appreciation of Wordsworth from his wife.

A humorous incident occurred in connection with his wife's love of Wordsworth. Governor Wilson of New Jersey had been nominated for the presidency of the United States. He was living in the little cottage in Cleveland Lane in Princeton, there being no official governor's house in New Jersey except a summer home at Sea Girt. He was at home very little, however, for, of course, his duties as governor and his activities in the presidential campaign kept him very much occupied. It was in this autumn that a distinguished French literary critic, a Wordsworthian scholar, M. Legouis,[12] was announced for a lecture in McCosh Hall on Wordsworth. On the evening of this lecture, I went to the cottage to find if my sister did not wish to go with me and hear the lecture. M. Legouis' book on the youth of Wordsworth[13] was a favorite book with my sister. When I arrived, to my astonishment I found that not only was she expecting to go but that her husband was going with her. I did not even know that he was in Princeton on that particular night, and certainly this was the only lecture that he attended during his presidential campaign. It is an evidence of how devoted he was to Wordsworth. He wanted to hear this famous critic speak of Wordsworth, so he said that he was going to the lecture and suggested that I go along with both of them.

I did not begin this story at the beginning. I ought to have prefaced it by a paragraph which relates to rather large public things. Theodore Roosevelt had been shot in Milwaukee,[14] and Colonel House,[15] without consulting Mr. Wilson, had telegraphed down to Texas to Captain Bill McDonald, a famous ranger, to meet him in New York. The telegram had been forwarded to Captain Bill, who was away from home at the time. The captain telegraphed back, "I'm acomin,'" borrowed a shirt—he had his revolver with him—and took the next train for New York, thinking that Colonel House was in trouble. When he arrived, Colonel House said: "Captain, Colonel Roosevelt has been shot, as you know, and I do not think it is right for Woodrow Wilson to be traveling around the country unprotected. So I determined to ask you to come up here, and when I had you on the spot I would open up with the governor the proposal that you travel with him from now on until the election." Of course, Colonel House knew that he could count on Captain Bill to do his duty, and he also knew that Captain Bill, when he had to shoot, practically always hit the mark. The captain at once consented. Mr. Wilson himself ultimately consented, and there grew up a close friendship between these two.

Now I turn to the evening of the Wordsworth lecture. We were sitting at the dinner table and talking about going to the lecture when one of the girls, Jessie, said: "Father, you are going to take the captain with you, are you not?" Mr. Wilson looked at me and said: "Surely that is not necessary." I replied: "I haven't the faintest idea what you are talking about." "Why," he said, "Captain McDonald, whom Colonel House insists on having for my chaperon, reached Princeton this afternoon and is staying at the Nassau Inn; and Jessie here is hinting that if I want to go to the lecture I must take him with me." Jessie knew her father well enough to know the appeal which he could not resist, namely, the sanctity of a promise. "You know, Father," she said, "that you promised Colonel House that you would take Captain McDonald with you wherever you went." Mr. Wilson said: "So I did, and I suppose I have got to take him, but it seems very ridiculous that I have got to go with a guard to the very hall where I have been lecturing myself for several years past as professor and president in the college." So it was determined, and so we went. When we got to the Nassau Inn, I got out and inquired for Captain McDonald. He appeared and there never was a man who more completely satisfied expectations than he. Subsequently, after the president made him marshal in Texas, and he had perhaps grown a little lazy and prosperous, he took on flesh. But at this time he was lean as a hound, hard as nails, brown, blue-eyed, mild of manner, grave in demeanor, with a voice so low that when he talked across the table, it was a little difficult to understand everything he said; but he had shot more men in his career than I am able to account for—"always," as Mrs. Wilson said, with great satisfaction, "always on the side of the law."

Captain McDonald had had a great many experiences in his rather long and varied life. But it is safe to say that he never had the experience before of going to a lecture on the poet Wordsworth. We rode up to McCosh Hall, the four of us, in a queer village vehicle, the seats facing each other; and when we got out to go in, I said: "Captain, I am afraid you are going to have a pretty yellow time of it tonight." "Oh," he said, "I don't mind." We went into the hall, and the seating arrangement was such that we could not get four seats together, but Mr. and Mrs. Wilson sat in one row, and Captain McDonald and I immediately behind them. Just after we had entered, M. Legouis began to read his address. I think it is a safe proposition that if Mr. Wilson, Mrs. Wilson, or I could get nothing whatever out of a lecture on Wordsworth, there wasn't anything in that lecture. It was the sort of phenomenon that people grow fairly well accustomed to in college life—of a distinguished author absolutely incapable of making a public address. M. Legouis read a collection of detached notes on Wordsworth and Rousseau, but without any connection at all and without the slightest human interest. Insofar as he had a theme at all, it was the influence of Rousseau's educational ideas on Wordsworth's *Prelude*, and, of course, the name Rousseau occurred again and again in the course of the address. The lecture lasted for about an hour and a half, and only courtesy kept us in our seats.

When we left the hall in the order in which we had sat, Mr. and Mrs. Wilson ahead, and Captain McDonald and I behind, I said: "Well, Captain, it was even worse than I feared it was going to be." "Well," he said, "I didn't find it very interestin' either. I sort of wished he would talk French. I wouldn't have understood it, but it would have been kind of pretty to hear him talk French." Incidentally, M. Legouis' English was perfect. We climbed into the little wagonette, and Mrs. Wilson, with characteristic sweetness, said: "I am so sorry, Captain McDonald, that you had this tedious evening, but you must not think that any of us liked that performance. There really wasn't anything in it." And Captain McDonald, with that beautiful, crude Texas chivalry of his, said: "Well, ma'am, I don't really mind. I didn't know much what he was talking about, but it was all right.

What was that book he kept talking about so—Trousseau?" This was the most complete evidence of just how intelligently Captain Mc-Donald had followed the lecture.

While speaking of Captain Bill and Mrs. Wilson, I think I must record another anecdote. Though the captain lived at the little hotel, Mrs. Wilson, of course, frequently had him up to dinner, and he was always the guest of honor, sitting at her right. He had to be persuaded to talk, and, as I have already said, he talked in tones so low that you really had to strain to hear him, but all he said was so worthwhile that you did not mind the strain. Mrs. Wilson was very fond of hearing him talk, and, of course, had a natural instinct for wanting to guide the conversation in a way that would give him an opportunity to talk. One night when I myself happened to be present at the table, the conversation got on the Mexicans, with whom, of course, Captain Bill McDonald, Texas ranger, had a varied experience. He told a rather long story, very long for Captain Bill, who was not a wordy man usually, about an encounter he and two or three other rangers had with a band of Mexicans very much more numerous than their own band. I have entirely forgotten how the story went; I only remember that the point was that Captain Bill was illustrating the proposition that the Mexicans are by nature treacherous. And this particular story hinged upon an ambuscade in which this very much larger band had very treacherously undertaken to surprise him and his two or three companions. As I say, he told the story at great length to illustrate this one point. When he had illustrated it, the story for him ended. But all of us had a natural curiosity to know what really had happened afterward, and Mrs. Wilson expressed the desire of all of us when she said to the captain: "Do tell us how it all ended." And the captain, with perfect gravity, and in that soft, modulated voice of his, said: "Well, ma'am, they had mighty bad luck." It required a deal of questioning to ascertain just how bad it was. As I remember now, nearly all were killed outright and the rest so wounded that they never recovered.

Mrs. Wilson was a singularly selfless person—but anything but negative.[16]

She merged her life in Mr. Wilson's, but she never lost her personality or independence of opinion. Her love for her husband was worship, but without illusion about his lesser qualities, and perfect frankness in telling him (with great sweetness) when she thought he was in error.

When her father died, she thought she should break the engagement, though to do so was to break her own heart. Only his ardent importunity overrode her scruples.

She was firm with him. When he wanted to cut short his studies at Hopkins, find a teaching position, and was all for immediate marriage (in 1884) she flatly declined, insisted that for his career's sake he must spend another year at Hopkins.

When they were married in 1885, she abandoned everything to him. She educated him in love of beauty (especially pure literature and painting). He educated her in interest for public affairs and political philosophy.

Mr. Wilson said repeatedly that he never knew anybody to whom beauty meant so much as to Ellen. When he and I would be riding our bicycles (in Great Britain, around Princeton) he would pause at a clear-flowing stream under overhanging boughs, or before a mountain translucent with a setting sun, or some other natural object, and say, "I wish Ellen were here; how she would love this." For she deepened immeasurably his love of nature.

He also said that she had courage which seemed to make her unconscious of danger—told how they were riding in a carriage when the horses got out of hand and ran away. He was uneasy but she turned to him quietly and asked, "Is there anything to be afraid of?"

Once in the Middletown days, he and I were discussing a little trip together, she urging it. We vacillated. She said, "*Now* you *must* go, for you are both getting paralysis of will."

Unexcited she was, once when a burglar (he proved to be a lunatic) haunted for several nights the house in Bryn Mawr; once when their first (rented) home in Princeton caught fire, and *he* was a bit excited.

She sheltered him from interruptions of his work as much as possible, planned small masculine dinners for him that would stimulate him, packed him off by sheer will on short pleasure trips (theaters) to New York—never dreaming of accompanying him, for their funds were limited. She planned for feminine company for his entertainment, guests in house. When his interest in Mrs. Peck (Hulbert)[17] became pronounced (and that was scarcely "beer and skittles" for her), she took two of her daughters and visited Mr. and Mrs. Peck (in the Berkshires, I think) to give countenance of her approval of the friendship. She had Mrs. P. as house guest at Prospect, in the White House.

His and her mutual love was an idyll at least from 1885 to 1902, when he became president of Princeton. Possibly deepening responsibility may have taken a little of the bloom off the pure romance of it, never off the real love.

If she had been capable of selfishness, she would undoubtedly have preferred the quiet home life in Library Place, but she was thrilled by the honor to *him*. The election came suddenly, you know. I was leaving Princeton one morning on a university errand. She knew it, sent a messenger, bidding me to come to her at once before the train departed. Her face glowed, her eyes danced as she told me the news.

Which reminds me to say that I fear you a little overemphasize her seriousness and intensity. When she was a young woman, and a young middle-aged woman, she was gleeful, her face would brighten, her eyes sparkle, her laughter ripple over a good joke— though she herself was not greatly given to anecdotes, not at all to puns. Her humor was character humor, pronounced power of "hitting off" (not by mimicry but by description) some quaint character. Her smile was famous—even the newspapers remarked on that.

She had frank and natural reverence but abhorred cant.

Her truthfulness was almost disconcerting. I don't believe she was capable of a hair's breadth of deflection from truth.

She was compassionate, less given to reforms than to quietly performed acts of mercy—an old washerwoman, a sick gardener &c.

After she met Woodrow Wilson there was but one *man* in the realm of her consciousness. But she "mothered" boys, young men, and women. "I am so sorry for women," she said once apropos of some struggling young woman's attempt to get on in the world. I recall her successful efforts to organize and engineer a concert for a young woman who had very little claim upon her attention. She was quick to plan and execute schemes for getting business or professional openings for young men, and her eyes would glisten with joy when she would tell of some young man's success. It seemed *personal* to her—as if some great thing had come to *her*.

She was an enormous worker—took little exercise (except to walk with her husband) for exercise's sake. But she was healthy and so busy about the house, among friends, that *this* was exercise. She was quick to think, equally quick to act. The thought and the act seemed simultaneous. I was somewhat procrastinating. It was Dr. Woodrow Wilson's idea that I might make a good teacher of English, and he wrote to me suggesting that I come to Wesleyan, where, so he said, there was "the best teacher of English in the land, Professor Winchester." I signified a purpose to follow his advice, but continued to work on a newspaper in Athens, Georgia, for a little while. Meanwhile I had been informed that during the summer I should have to make up two years of German under a private tutor in order to enter senior class at Wesleyan. Still I stayed with my newspaper. Whereupon arrived a letter from Mrs. Wilson: "What on earth are you waiting for, with all this German to be learned? Come on next train. You are like the farmer who had so much work to do that he went fishing." She was always emphatic in a decision.

She conceived and quickly executed a plan for Mary Hoyt to go to college at Bryn Mawr—living with them, the Wilsons.

She conceived and set in motion plans for the boasted "honor system" in examinations at Princeton. Her principles were adamant. Her young sister, a mere child, wanted a certain book. Mrs. Wilson didn't think it good for a child. Said to me, "It hurt to deny Madge (now known as Margaret Elliott) that book. She couldn't understand. But what's the use of having principles if you don't act on them?" I recited the incident to Mr. Wilson, remarking, "*I* would have bought that book for Madge, but not *she*." He replied, "Yes, when Ellen sees a principle, nothing under heaven can swerve her from it."

She was a vast reader, in pure literature and in philosophy. Mastered Kant, Hegel, Fichte, &c. Hibben said she understood Hegel better than most professors of philosophy.

Her intellectual curiosity was insatiable, her spiritual search scarcely less. She remained a Presbyterian to the end, but she wanted grounds of assurance more satisfying than the dogmas she had learned in childhood, and so she read *and* pondered, and discussed.

She read new books as well as old—all she could lay her hands on.

No need to repeat here the reading she did in politics and history and the digests she made to help her husband—in Middletown and in Washington—doubtless also in Princeton, though I don't recall instances.

He read her everything he wrote. She listened attentively (had great power of concentration), criticized, suggested changes—you know what he told Dr. Grayson and me about the "hit" of his speeches being germinated by her suggestions.

She went to the bottom of all the Princeton controversies. I doubt if she ever knew what hatred was until these arose. She really hated some of the Princeton opponents, had scurvy nicknames for them—

the only one I can remember was her name for Cooper Procter of Cincinnati[18]—always called him the "soap-fat man."

She was as uncompromising as her husband. Doubtless it would have been better if she had advised mollification and less fighting— but she didn't—a principle at stake.

How much she had to do with the final decision to enter practical politics, I don't know. They were in Lyme that summer, and I did not join them there. But he certainly *discussed* everything with her.

She did some political turns—had Bryan for dinner,[19] got Colonel Harvey invited down for a speech to some club,[20] &c.

In the house in Cleveland Lane, she used to discuss measures with the visiting politicians. She advised (or agreed) that Bryan must be in the cabinet. Ultimately she was a strong proponent for Tumulty as secretary—met and argued out her husband's objections—social and religious.[21]

And now a very important point. I was in California during the Baltimore convention.[22] Almost as soon as I returned (when all events were fresh in everybody's mind) Tumulty told me—and with convincing circumstantial detail—that it was she who prevented Governor Wilson from sending to Baltimore a message of withdrawal of his candidacy. McCombs had collapsed. The Texas delegation and others were sitting tight and fighting hard. But long-distance telephone conversations had convinced Governor Wilson that the time had arrived to withdraw. Even Tumulty (at Sea Girt) had wilted (according to his own account). Governor Wilson wrote out a message of withdrawal, showed it to Mrs. Wilson. She immediately flashed back: "What do you gain by doing this? You must *not* send it." After some argument, he deferred to her opinion. As Tumulty told me the story, it never occurred to me to doubt it—nor, unfortunately, to confirm it. If it is true, and nothing but documentary evidence to the contrary could convince me that it was untrue (it was like her, and what earthly reason had Tumulty to manufacture the story, with all sorts of detail, for me?), then she quite literally as well as spiritually made him president.

And yet she didn't want this thing for herself, though Tumulty once said she was "one of the best politicians" he knew.

Everything for him, nothing for herself.

To me she had said (earlier) that he seemed physically strong enough now for the burden, "and we must do nothing to check this great career."

Yet she had debated the matter in her own mind. She witnessed in New York an impressive performance of *Macbeth*—said, "It makes one pause to consider whether a wife should encourage her husband to have everything to which his ambition prompts him." But having considered, she went on to promote his cause in every way she could.

Yet, to me, the most affecting picture of her in Washington is that given me by Representative Walsh[23] of New Jersey, who, going into the Congressional Library, recognized her alone studying the murals. "Why, Mrs. Wilson!" he exclaimed, approaching her. With her finger to her lips, she said softly, "Sh! please don't call attention to me here. I have slipped away from the White House just to enjoy pictures a little while."

It is thirty-one years today, Labor Day, that she and little Edward Axson and I were in an art gallery (downtown in New York)—she trying to make even the child Edward and me understand a little of the rudiments of fine painting. A Labor Day parade passed. Little Edward very naturally was more interested in that than in pictures and wandered to the window. Mrs. Wilson somewhat impatiently exclaimed at his dereliction.

She loved children devotedly (I have said elsewhere that her love for her own children seemed to deepen her love for all children). She grieved over the death of the little Cleveland girl,[24] she tried to understand the child-mind but also tried to develop it—provided Christmas and birthday toys and books for her little girls, but was always trying to lead them, by easy stages, to appreciation of what is *fine* in thought and letters—read to them all the Andrew Lang fairy book collections—but also Homer in a paraphrase. Browning's poem *Development* has some bearing here.

It is really difficult to generalize about Wilson's "cultural" reading, isn't it?[25]

Though this is a minor phase of his career, it is one of the difficult phases—and yet must be handled.

It seems to me that the difficulty lies, partly, in the fact that, after all, greatly cultivated man though he was, *his general reading was desultory, spasmodic and his judgments sometimes arbitrary.* Added to which he did not read "merely literary fellers" *whole.* For instance, I recall his enthusiasm for Swinburne's *Tristram*, especially the passage describing Isolt's unafraidness of the sea, but he never knew or cared to know much about Swinburne's complete product (he disliked, and properly I think, Swinburne's unbalanced vehement critical essays). He (at one time) loved a few of Matthew Arnold's poems, such as *Dover Beach* and *Rugby Chapel*, but I don't think he ever read the comparatively small body of Arnold's poetry entire (there was no reason why he should), and spoke contemptuously of Arnold's literary and theological criticism (perhaps justly). Though Wordsworth was a favorite, I don't think he read *far* in Wordsworth, am practically sure he never read *The Prelude* (to say nothing of the other longer poems). (It was a beautiful experience to hear him read aloud some of his favorite Wordsworth poems, sometimes they were minor poems, like the lines to Hartley Coleridge, frequently *Character of the Happy Warrior.*) Keats was a prime favorite (one couldn't count the times he read aloud the *Grecian Urn*), but by the time I came to know him the love of Shelley had (I think) rather faded. In fact, until I read your *ms.* I had not known of the Shelley period. I *have* heard him read aloud a few of the Shelley lyrics. Even when he was in the White House, he read one night the *Ode to the West Wind* and closed the book, smiling with admiration, and remarked only "the imagery is incredible." (It reminded me of the man who looked at a camel and said "there ain't no such animal"—Shelley's imagery was "incredible," even though printed in a book.)

He loathed Byron. He certainly came to cherish *some* of Browning's poems (*Epistle of Karshish* was one). With beautiful modesty he said toward the end of his professorship at Princeton that he wanted to read each night a play of Shakespeare's to catch if possible a little of the magic of his phrasing. But I think that, like his keeping of diaries, was never carried out systematically. You know, of course, that *Henry V* was one of his favorite Shakespeare plays.

He, as you know, loved to *re*read the same things—as he loved to repeat other experiences, auto rides, visits to lake country, &c. I think in general literature it was "non multa sed multum" with him. We used to remark on his rereading of *Lorna Doone* several times as interesting precisely because he did *not* read much fiction.

You also know that he was a slow reader of general literature—took a long time to get through a book. He exclaimed in Middletown, "I wonder if I am the slowest reader in the world!"

I don't think his reading in the English novelists was "deep."

I recall that shortly after his first marriage, he and Mrs. Wilson read together some of the 18th-century novelists. Later he read a good deal of Jane Austen. In his last illness, Mrs. Edith Wilson read much fiction aloud to him (through the autumn of 1920 I had the honor of being what he called "official reader"—he had formerly read a good deal of Stanley Weyman and called upon me to reread to him many of Weyman's romances). From his father he inherited a strong taste for Walter Scott.

In the essays, one of the favorites of earlier days was Charles Lamb (a natural affinity with Lamb's antique flavor). But I don't think he read a great deal of Lamb's contemporaries. Of course, he had an extravagant affection for Birrell's essays (have you ever seen the inscription in his presentation copy of the first series of *Obiter Dicta* to Ellen Axson?). It wasn't his business to be a discriminating critic of literary critics, and possibly he set an overvaluation on Bagehot's essays on literature. In the midst of his struggles as president of Princeton he found much to his taste in G. K. Chesterton—especially in Chesterton's reiterated paradox that the only way to preserve the great past is by a continual process of renewal—Chesterton's simile of the old white post which must be constantly repainted, *renewed*, to keep the old post white, was a favorite metaphor with Wilson in conversation and impromptu speeches—I don't know how much it got into *published* addresses.

I am glad you make the point that Ellen Axson "widened his horizons" in literature and other arts. It was a debt which he acknowledged gratefully and unceasingly. I think there was a time when she was practically the only person to whose judgments in taste his proud independent mind *deferred* (though he was always respectful toward Professor Winchester's judgments—even in his last days I heard him refer more than once to the art with which Professor Winchester blended biography and criticism in his literary lectures. "He did not sketch the author's life and then assay his writings, but merged the two"—this he said after 1920, when of course this had become the usual procedure of critics).

Returning to the influence of Ellen Axson—it brought into activity his innate but previously undeveloped, perhaps unrecognized, passion for beauty in *all* art forms—and in nature. In this somewhat evasive matter that we are discussing it seems to me that the outstanding points (some of them) are the quickening of his appreciation for beauty through the influence of Ellen Axson; the desultory and yet penetrating nature of his reading; a strong *personal* approach to literature (not the detached catholicity of the professional critic); his constant rereading of the things he loved; his devotion to things akin to his own mental and aesthetic predilections; and his chariness of fresh adventures into "new" books; and his "non multa sed multum."

Have you discussed how fond Wilson was of Miss [Mary Noailles] Murfree's novels (he who read so few novels). Of course, *the* novel he loved most (in the early years) was *Lorna Doone*—he reread it several times. But "Charles Egbert Craddock"[26] was a delight to him in Middletown days and early Princeton (professor) days. Used the mountain dialect in his playful conversation—until he said that if he wasn't careful he would form the *habit* of ungrammatical speech. He was delighted to find vestiges of 16th- and 17th-century English in the mountain speech—"survigorous," for instance, analyzed the author's descriptive method—answered the objection that her descriptions were too long with the theory that mountaineers speak slowly and that in the interstices of speech there was time to gaze far and long on the landscape—that, in short, the deliberate narrative and descriptive method suited the *genre.*

The poets from whom he read were favorites: the least known, Edward Rowland Sill, he came to know (his small volumes, I mean) in Middletown and constantly reread from the volumes aloud. He continued this habit in the White House, reading most often from that thick anthology of poetry edited by Burton (?). His favorite was of course Wordsworth; Browning another (I rather think Mrs. Wilson taught him to love both). As you know, he never wearied of doing the same thing over and over again (Chesterton says that's a quality of God's and of little children; children keep saying, "Do it again" when we ride them "pick-a-back"; God goes on with unfaded delight making the same kind of leaves on the same kind of trees. That's Chesterton—also by the way a prime favorite of Mr. Wilson's). Well, he would read repeatedly the same poems, not always highly significant poems; for instance, he rejoiced with joy undiminished in Wordsworth's *Lines to Hartley Coleridge* and the poem Wordsworth wrote when leaving tiny Dove Cottage to be married.[27] More significant (for him, it would seem) was John Burroughs' poem (*Waiting,* I think): "I know mine own will come to me"; Matthew Arnold's *The Future* and *Rugby Chapel* were favorites. He passionately loved Keats' *Ode on a Grecian Urn.* He disliked Byron, but loved some of Shelley (among the Shelley poems was *Ode to the West Wind*). Among his *favorite* favorites were Wordsworth's *Character of the Happy Warrior* and Henry the Fifth's speech before the Battle of Agincourt in Shakespeare's play—both in character with Wilson. I should say that his reading was intensive rather than extensive. He didn't devour whole shelves of books, like Theodore Roosevelt. Of course, I am not now referring to his reading in history and political philosophy—though even there he would continually read aloud the same passages from Burke and Bagehot—in earlier years from Augustine Birrell.

He read nonsense verse, Lear, Gilbert, &c. ad infinitum.

President of Princeton University

❧

I

T WAS in the autumn of 1899 that I became a member of the Princeton faculty and practically a permanent member of the household, though I had my own bachelor quarters and my own club. It is pleasant now to remember that both Mr. and Mrs. Wilson urged me to live in their house, but I naturally had the feeling that I wanted to be independent. I speak now of my going to Princeton because I am about to tell the story of the great Princeton controversy, and I want to begin it by saying something of my own impressions of Princeton in 1899, which I am sure were mine, and I am not sure just how definitely they were Mr. Wilson's impressions, since he had been growing up among circumstances upon which I came somewhat suddenly. Since 1890 I had been a constant visitor to Princeton, but, of course, it was not until I actually entered the faculty that I became thoroughly familiar with the spirit of the place. And I had not been two months in the faculty before I saw that Princeton was selling its birthright; was in great peril of losing the simplicity of a country college town, and becoming merely a fashionable suburb for New York City. The change since 1890 was to me very apparent. At that time there was a village in which the life was as simple as in any New England college town. There were a few old estates of antebellum tradition, but most of these were falling into disrepair. Gradually, however, people of wealth began to move to Princeton and take up these old estates or buy new places and build on them country mansions. The village streets began to fill up with smart looking traps and horses. The automobile was still somewhat of a rarity.

Now, these wealthy people who moved to Princeton were good people, and not one of them consciously sought to splurge or make a show of his wealth. They merely brought to the simple village the standards of life which were perfectly natural to them.[1] But when they entertained college professors and their wives they naturally entertained them on a scale which professors and their wives could not reciprocate without putting themselves to severe financial strains. I remember hearing Mr. and Mrs. Wilson both say that they never knew what the word "informal" meant when they were invited to dine informally. Previously it had meant that you went in whatever clothes you had been wearing during the day. But now they went to an informal dinner to find men and women in full evening attire. I also remember Mrs. Wilson quoting one of her friends, who said in effect: "Really, you know, some of these people (referring to the newcomers) have a standard which prevents them from understanding our lives at all. One of them was saying recently to one of his friends that the Princeton professors ought to receive more salary, for, said he, 'some of those fellows have to think twice before they break a five-dollar bill.' And Mrs. Wilson's friend said: 'As a matter of fact, we have to think twice before we break a ten-cent piece.'"

These wealthy people were nearly all Princeton graduates, who brought their families there; and they were absolutely unconscious of being a demoralizing influence in the community. But I became quickly convinced that they were a very demoralizing influence, and events more than justified what I said and what some of my friends said back in the autumn of 1899.

Now I think it important to try to discriminate. The students themselves still appeared as ordinary American youths—many of them, of course, sons of wealth—but purposely avoiding the show of wealth. They dressed in what was in those days called the "horse style," that is to say, extravagantly ordinary sort of dress. Nobody, in other words, dressed up at all. But I think we were just at the turn of the tide. I remember one incident which seems to me to be significant. There was a club of students banded together for intellectual purposes, and the members used to invite older men sometimes from the faculty, sometimes from New York City or elsewhere, to address them informally in some student's room. I had the good luck to attend these meetings frequently, not merely when I was the speaker, but as an invited guest when others were speaking. For a year or so we used to assemble in the clothes that we had been wearing all day, but I remember my astonishment when I went one rainy night in clothes much the worse for dampness and lack of tailor's pressing and found several of the boys in evening clothes. And it soon became the habit for everybody to put on evening clothes when attending one of these sessions. This is a very small matter in itself, but it is significant of something that was going on, namely, a bringing into the simple, spontaneous life of a village and country college the ways of the city and of fashion. A few began to bring saddle horses to Princeton; a few others began to bring automobiles, then coming into general use.

I am satisfied that in 1890 it would have been impossible from any outward show to have known whether the Princeton student was the son of a millionaire or the son of a blacksmith. But the distinctions began to come about in just the inoffensive ways that I am now re-counting. And what impresses me about the whole thing is that no-body had any deliberate intent of undermining the democracy of Princeton. It was the very naturalness of the things that occurred that made them so insidious. Subtly, slowly, the tone of the *monde* was beginning to make itself felt, where a few years before everything had been as simple as a village schoolhouse in the Middle West. Un-dergraduate clubs were increasing in number. Again, I was not aware of any snobbish motive in creating these clubs. Young men who had not been invited to membership in the clubs which already existed merely banded themselves together to form clubs of their own, but the club life was growing and becoming one of the very pronounced features of Princeton.

I have purposely related all this with the use of the first personal pronoun, because I want it understood as my impression. I really do not know how much Mr. Wilson shared the impression at that time. Remember, he had been in the midst of all this—I had come into it from the outside. What I do feel perfectly clear about, and what I want to make clear in these notes, is that when the great fight came it was in Mr. Wilson's mind, first, a fight for what he believed to be a sound educational principle, and that only secondarily did it resolve itself into a fight for democracy. As Mr. Wilson looks back on it now, he himself undoubtedly feels that from the start he was fighting for democracy, but I must believe that I, who saw it all more objectively than he could, am correct when I say that the first object of his con-tention was educational, and that not until he fully realized what were the forces that were opposing his educational reform did he perceive that what he had really entered upon was a fight for essen-tial principles of democracy. And in saying this I must think I am saying something very important, because, if I am correct, we see how absolutely wrong are those who to this day contend that Mr.

Wilson used his presidency of Princeton University to promote his political ambitions. I believe that he was as absolutely committed to his career as president of the college as it is possible for a man to commit himself to any career, and that he never dreamed that he would pass from this to active politics.

Now, I have something very interesting to record, namely, that in 1897, two years before I became connected with the Princeton faculty, on one of my numerous visits to the family in Princeton, Mr. Wilson had outlined to me what he himself would do if he were the autocrat of Princeton. He would institute three fundamental reforms: first, he would reform the curriculum; second, he would reform the method of teaching; and, third, he would reform the plan of college life.

With regard to the first point, he felt that the Princeton curriculum lacked coherence and was haphazard. While the elective system was by no means so liberal as at Harvard, while Greek and Latin still held their place as requirements for the Bachelor of Arts degree, there was still a great deal of the hodgepodge in the arrangement of studies by the men in the junior and senior classes. Besides the degree of Bachelor of Arts, Princeton gave only one other nonprofessional degree, namely, the degree of Bachelor of Science. And the Bachelor of Science degree came to be a catchall for men who wanted to get some sort of degree from Princeton but did not want to do the hard work necessary for a Bachelor of Arts degree. Therefore, men were taking the B.S. degree from Princeton who knew very little about science or about anything else, but who were merely taking the line of least resistance, electing all the "snap courses" they could find, and making up their cards accordingly.

Now, Mr. Wilson was insisting as his first point that it was the business of the faculty, and not of the students themselves, to arrange coherent systems of study—such groupings of studies as would give a young man a well-rounded education.

With regard to the second point, Mr. Wilson realized that Princeton, like so many other American colleges, was overworking the lecture system. He, himself the most popular lecturer of Princeton, had abundant opportunity to see how little a man might know about a subject and yet be able to pass an examination in the subject. Day after day the boys would attend lectures, be marked as present by the monitors, and do no work whatsoever until a few weeks before the final examination, when they would buy syllabi of the courses, which were prepared by the more intelligent and industrious students and sold at a fixed price. Many a student had passed through Princeton who never read his textbooks at all but merely read the digests made of those textbooks and of the lectures, and was able to pass his examination on this scrapped knowledge, which knowledge, of course, it goes without saying, he proceeded promptly to forget the moment he passed the examination. I am satisfied that many a student going down the steps of Dickinson Hall began the process of forgetting everything that he had just said on his paper; he did not want his mind littered up with extraneous matter.

Now, Mr. Wilson told me back in the middle of the 1890s that his second reform would be an introduction of something corresponding to the Oxford tutorial system—an employment of young scholars, who would "read" with the students, only, if I remember correctly, he told me even as far back as the time of this conversation that he thought the Oxford tutorial system was too disconnected from the courses themselves, that his idea would be to make the tutors a coherent part of each course in which he gave instruction. I am trying to make these notes just as honest as I can, and so I must say that it is barely possible that in this last observation I may have read back into the original conversation the thing that Mr. Wilson really did advocate when he became president of Princeton. But up to this last point everything was exactly as I have stated it.

With regard to the third point, Mr. Wilson said that an education should really involve the student's life and not merely the random hours which he happened to spend in a classroom; that, therefore, there should be some arrangement by which the student would spend his whole college life in an intellectual atmosphere, and that he believed this could best be accomplished by some adaptation of the English plan of dividing the university into "colleges," thus grouping the undergraduates of all classes together with young and unmarried instructors into a family life. He probably in this conversation to which I am referring instanced the peculiar need of this sort of thing in Princeton, because of the singular Princeton system of deliberately separating the members of the freshman and sophomore classes from the members of the junior and senior classes, and building between them an impassable barrier and wall.

This needs a word of explanation. Princeton has no fraternities. There is a history that goes with that remark, but I shall not take time to tell of it now. But back in the early 1880s, one or two eating clubs began to grow into established clubs for juniors and seniors. Out of this there developed the system of Princeton upper-class clubs, to which only members of the junior and senior classes were eligible. Naturally, freshmen and sophomores looked with eager hopes to election in one or another of these clubs. But any open canvas for election was the height of bad form. Therefore, with the extreme ways of youth there grew up a situation in which it was not good form for an underclassman to be on any social terms with the upperclassmen, else he might be suspected of "boot-licking" for club election. So far did this go that no freshman or sophomore ever walked down Prospect Avenue, the street on which the clubs were all situated. Thus is explained what I mean by this impassable barrier between the members of the lower and upper classes.

Now, Mr. Wilson contended that this separation was an obstacle to something that was very important in the education of a young man, namely, its continual association with minds only a little older. He said, and many of us can verify his saying from our own experience, that in college life, nothing is so influential on the mind of a freshman or a sophomore as association with a junior or senior— a man a little bit older than himself, a little bit more experienced, a little bit more learned. There is probably no hero worship to surpass the hero worship of a college freshman for a college senior. Yet Princeton had built up a system by which all association of this sort was absolutely prohibited.

These were the points which Mr. Wilson several years later, when he became president of Princeton, undertook to put into operation, and I keep insisting that the whole program was purely educational. When Mr. Wilson told me these things, I am satisfied he had not the slightest expectation of being in a position to put them into effect, for there was no reason to suppose that President Patton, who was only a few years older than Mr. Wilson, would retire from the presidency until Mr. Wilson himself should have been too old to be elected president. However, the Fates were preparing for Mr. Wilson's succession to Dr. Patton much more rapidly than any one guessed.

If my memory serves me correctly, it was in the spring of 1901 that Professor William Magie,[2] familiarly known as "Billy," introduced a motion in faculty to have appointed a committee of inquiry into the condition of scholarship in Princeton.[3] I remember so well Dr. Patton's asking from the chair what this motion meant, and Mr. Magie replied, with heat, that it meant that they wanted to find out "what was the cause of the utterly rotten condition of education in Princeton—and what was the remedy." It simply meant that there were earnest men in Princeton who were unwilling to let Princeton drift on in the way it was going; men who realized that it was not sufficient to offer education to young people, but that you had to use some means of making them take what you offer them. In other words, it was a general protest against the attitude in some German universities, which gives a man absolute freedom to be educated or not, according to his fancy. Now, it was precisely this attitude that Dr. Patton began to oppose. He opposed it first humorously.

Once in faculty meeting during these debates, I heard Dr. Patton say: "I consider the student has had a privilege in being permitted to listen to Professor Woodrow Wilson's lectures, and I do not think that Professor Wilson should be required to follow the student about the campus with a spoon and force knowledge down his throat. The student has had an opportunity to hear the lectures, and he can take them or leave them as he pleases."

On the same occasion, Dr. Patton said, in a tone of unusual earnestness: "Gentlemen, whether we like it or not, we shall have to recognize that Princeton is a rich man's college and that rich men frequently do not come to college to study." But subsequently, with a fighting force which I had not suspected him capable of, and which to this day I do not entirely understand, Dr. Patton opposed this movement. The committee was appointed, inquiries and investigations were made, and reports from the committee began to come in. It presently became evident that something fundamental was going to happen in Princeton. The debates grew so warm, and the faculty meetings were so largely attended, that it was no longer possible for the little old-fashioned faculty room to hold the participants. So we adjourned to a large room in the School of Science building, where the debates began to take on the character of a parliamentary crisis.

My story has now reached the academic year of 1901–1902. But, as I say, I think it began in the spring of the preceding academic year. I must say there was some immensely good debating on both sides, particularly from Dr. Patton in opposition because of his brilliancy, and from Professor Ormond,[4] who was advocating the reforms not because of his brilliancy but because of the depth of his conviction that reforms were very necessary. Professor Magie and Professor

Harry Fine[5] were leaders in the fight for the reform. It is rather curious to reflect now that Mr. Wilson took no active part in the debates. It was a time when he was away from Princeton a great deal. But when he was there and attended, he sat and listened. We all waited expectantly for the time when he would rise to speak. Some of my colleagues said to me that they hoped that we would have the benefit of Mr. Wilson's views. But he never spoke, and I now find that my memory is not clear as to precisely what it was that brought our debates to a close. Perhaps it was some matter of commitment to a committee for future report. But I do not remember. I just remember the debates ceased but that the questions at issue continued to rage violently outside of the faculty meetings.

Afterwards, when Mr. Wilson had been president of Princeton, there were heard suggestions of accusation that he had kept silent as part of a shrewd and canny game. He heard these charges himself, laughed at them heartily. There was, of course, nothing in them. I have to offer my own explanation of his silence, but I think it is a true explanation, namely, that he felt that, earnest as was the committee, sincere as was the desire for reform, the program that was offered was not going far enough. I feel quite confident that I am giving a correct analysis when I say that he was watching the procedure and making up his own mind as to when and how he should take a decided position, when it would probably be a position of what in the time of Charles I they used to call "*thorough*." In other words, I am satisfied that he believed that the axe had to be laid at the root of the tree, and that nothing else than a complete reconstitution of the college would meet the real issue. But before the time was ripe for him to take a position in this matter the debates, as I have already indicated, came to a conclusion for some reason which I do not now recall.

Meanwhile, the matter got outside of the faculty into the board of trustees. And there was a general feeling that Dr. Patton was getting to the end of his career and usefulness, though I do not think anybody expected any sudden resignation; in fact, I know that when it came it was like a bolt from the blue, and I may add that it came under pressure.[6] At the June 1902 meeting of the board of trustees his resignation was asked for. He made his own terms of resignation, terms favorable to himself, and he himself recommended as his successor Woodrow Wilson, though whether this recommendation was anything more than a formality I do not know. By this time all the Princeton world knew that if there were to be a new president, it would be Woodrow Wilson. He was the inevitable.

To inject the personal, as I so often do in these notes, I remember so well how the news of it came to me. I was to leave Princeton before commencement day to conduct some entrance examinations in a preparatory school at a distance; and my sister knew that I was leaving about noon of a certain day. Perhaps two hours before my train left, I received a message from her asking me to run up to the house before leaving town. I did so. She met me in the front garden and told me that she wanted me to know something that had just occurred. She did not want me to have to get it from the newspapers. That it was this: "Dr. Patton has resigned and Woodrow has been elected president of the college." We chatted for a few minutes and then went indoors, where we found him in his study. When I congratulated him, he showed what he had seldom shown in life, namely, a moment almost of timidity, for, he said in effect, that there was so much to be done and he was not sure whether the money was promptly forthcoming to do the things that must be done. As I remember his attitude now of modesty, almost of hesitancy, I feel quite convinced that, whatever may have been his inmost thoughts about the possibility of becoming president of Princeton, the actual thing had come to him with a great suddenness and found him mentally not quite prepared.

The following autumn he was inaugurated president at one of the most impressive college functions which up to that time had been held in America. There were distinguished people from many parts of the country, not merely representatives from nearly all of the colleges, but men of affairs, including, I remember, Mr. J. Pierpont Morgan, who was in the audience and whom I saw for the first and only time.

Mr. Cleveland, on retiring from the presidency of the United States in 1897, had made Princeton his home and had subsequently been elected a member of the board of trustees, and on the occasion of Mr. Wilson's inauguration made an address which astonished and gratified us all, showing in Mr. Cleveland a grasp of educational problems which we had not suspected, though I am forced to say, in this connection, that Mr. Cleveland's subsequent attitude was as disappointing as his present attitude was pleasing.

14. Woodrow Wilson, Princeton University president, 1902

Dr. Patton acted his part well, made a brief address, in which he said in effect that it was a gratification to him to hand the presidency down to one in whom he had such complete confidence as Mr. Wilson. Mr. Wilson then read his inaugural address, which was received by all as a contribution to the literature of education. Mr. Wilson reorganized his committees, appointed Harry Fine dean of the faculty, and "Billy" Magie clerk of the faculty, and several months were spent, as it were, in getting the deck ready for action. Then he began to inaugurate reforms precisely along the lines of the program which many years before he had outlined to me in conversation as a desirable set of reforms.

First, the curriculum was revised. An intelligent group system of studies was introduced, and a new degree created, namely, Litt.B. (Bachelor of Letters), leaving the B.S. degree for those who really wished to be educated in science. The B.A. degree kept the Greek and Latin requirements. The Litt.B. degree was so arranged that men could procure it without any Greek at all, with merely a modicum of Latin, and with natural science on only a moderate scale, while they could make up the bulk of their studies of such things as history, politics, economics, and literature. But every possible attempt was made to safeguard this degree and to prevent it from becoming a "snap." Of course, this reform which I have summarized was not accomplished without prolonged debates, and I remember very well that when President Wilson, acting as chairman of the committee on curriculum, made his final report to the faculty for adoption,[7] he prefaced the report by saying that the admirable thing about it was that it was no one man's idea but was made up out of the common counsel of many—a thing that had been arrived at by much thought, much debate, much consideration, and, of course, as always happens, some compromise, but that in the circumstances he believed it was the best plan that the Princeton faculty could devise for offering an opportunity of sound education to undergraduates.

One of the meetings of the general faculty developed the first irritation I had seen in Mr. Wilson and brought to my ears the first echoes of subterranean criticism I had heard of him. Professor Cornwall,[8] one of the elder and mildest members of the faculty, asked for an explanation of a point. I don't know what was the matter with Mr. Wilson. It seemed so unlike him, but his answer was so sharp that all of us were startled and Professor Cornwall said meekly, "I only wanted to understand." "Well, now you understand," retorted Mr. Wilson acidly. Later in the afternoon, I was at the Nassau Club and overheard some very angry comment. Then one member of the faculty came to me and spoke with indignation of the incident, and added that a member of the board of trustees had said that President Wilson was growing so autocratic that he (the member of the board) "gave him" two (or maybe it was three) years more before his resignation would be asked for.

The new curriculum meant harder study at Princeton, and this acted back on the preparatory schools, which had to stiffen their own courses very much in order to fit their boys to enter Princeton. It began to be hard to enter Princeton, and moderately hard to stay in. The students themselves took a humorously complaining view of the new regime, realizing that they had to work much harder than their older brothers had worked a few years before.

It is probably not generally known that the first application to Mr. Wilson of the famous whiskey sign, "Wilson, That's All," was made by a student in Princeton in a cartoon published in the illustrated *Princeton Tiger*. The caption of the picture was "Princeton in 1910" and represented the Princeton front campus and old Nassau Hall absolutely deserted except for one lonely figure sitting on the steps of Nassau Hall. And the legend underneath was "Wilson, That's All."[9]

It was in 1905 that President Wilson completed his second great reform, which was nothing else than a total reform of teaching methods at Princeton, with the introduction of the so-called preceptorial system, an adaptation of the Oxford tutorial system to the genius of an American college. The preceptors were something more than mere tutors, having the rank of assistant professor, and constituting a coherent part of the course. The conception was that a course in Princeton was given not by one man, but by a group of men. There was the professor in charge, who delivered the lectures, but the course of reading to accompany the lectures was determined on in council between the professor in charge and the preceptors in that course. Assuming that the course was a three-hour-a-week course, and this was the normal course under the new system at Princeton, the students attended lectures in a body two periods a week. Then, on the third period, they broke up into small groups and reported to the various preceptors, preferably in groups of not more than five undergraduates, and preferably in the preceptor's own room, amid his library, and here they discussed the books which were to be read in connection with the lecture course and which constituted the real heart and foundation of the course.

The effect on intellectual life at Princeton was, I think, perhaps the most extraordinary mental phenomenon I have ever witnessed. In two years, life and conversation among the undergraduates had taken on an entirely different tone. These young men were really being brought into intimate contact with the things of the mind and being taught how to read intelligently, how to discuss what they read, how to form their own ideas more intelligently. It was nothing less than an intellectual awakening. And, indeed, this introduction of the preceptorial system was a very notable thing in the educational life of America. Probably nothing since the founding of Johns Hopkins University had attracted such far and wide attention to things purely educational as the establishment of this system. Even people who were skeptical about it had to admit that it was a very interesting departure. In a thoughtful article on Princeton in *The Independent*, the writer said in effect: "I am convinced that the preceptorial system is the best system. I am withholding my judgment, but one thing is certain—Princeton is the one college in America which definitely knows what it is headed for." And he concluded: "Keep your eye on Princeton."

The public eye was very much on Princeton. The selection of the preceptors—there were fifty of them—was made with great care, and a really extraordinary body of youngish men, ranging perhaps from twenty-seven or twenty-eight years to thirty-seven or thirty-eight, were brought to Princeton. They came with a zest and enthusiasm equal to their scholarship. It was not only for the students themselves but for us of the faculty an intellectual awakening; and every time I meet one of my old colleagues now and fall to talking about these times, we always agree that that was a "golden age"—a brief while when we all seemed engaged in one enterprise under a great leader, who was marshaling us to a definite object. I wish it might have lasted longer, but the next chapter brought chaos and confusion. The preceptorial system was criticized primarily on the ground that it was too expensive a system for most colleges to adopt, but I think it was President Arthur T. Hadley of Yale who made the very interesting observation that no other college could successfully adopt the preceptorial system immediately, because Princeton had already got all the best preceptors in the country. The term "preceptor" was used simply to avoid the word "tutor," which in America does not carry enough dignity, and everything was wanted to give dignity to this system.

Nobody was prouder of the preceptorial system than the alumni, whose own attitude was very, very funny indeed. They were glad they had escaped from Princeton before so much hard work was required of undergraduates, but they were very proud to know that their college was coming to be recognized as perhaps the most important college in America.

In accomplishing these two reforms, Mr. Wilson had had the hearty support of the board of trustees and the enthusiastic admiration of most of the body of alumni. It is true there had been one or two rather silly ripples of criticism—one concerning an iron fence, which he had built around Prospect, the president's dwelling,[10] which up to this time had been simply a part of the general campus. Princeton was growing more populous, Sunday excursions were coming from Trenton by way of two trolley lines recently built, and the Sunday excursionists were sometimes camping on one of the porches of the house to eat their lunch, and in various ways the house had little of that privacy which a man naturally desires for himself and his family. It is a little hard to explain now just why the erection of a fence around a home should have brought a storm of protest, as it did,[11] but there was probably provocation for a little opposition to Mr. Wilson in the fact that among his reforms he had included a stricter college discipline. Princeton had been running rather wild in discipline, as in other things, and the discipline committee proceeded to make young Princeton students understand that if they willfully broke the laws of the college they had to suffer accordingly. Influential friends would appeal to the president for a decision and reversal of the discipline committee's verdict, and when the president proved to be quite as obdurate as the dean and the committee, they did not always like it.

Furthermore, Mr. Wilson had adopted a somewhat stronghanded method with regard to a few members of the faculty, who he felt were incompetent to hold their places. One case became conspicuous and notorious because the gentleman involved was extremely popular with the undergraduates.[12] But Mr. Wilson had made up his mind that this gentleman was not the sort of material that he wanted in his faculty simply because he did not believe that his scholarship was sound. Mr. Wilson handled the case with great firmness and tried to handle it with equal kindness. The trustees had given this professor a year's leave of absence, which leave was to be spent in Europe. The average college president, I am sure, would have allowed the man to go to Europe and then inform him by letter that his services would not be needed beyond the following year. But this was not Mr. Wilson's method. He sent for him and told him with great courtesy that, while personally there was absolutely nothing against him, he (Mr. Wilson) did not feel that he (the professor) was capable of doing the sort of work which he (Mr. Wilson) desired should be done in the college, and it was only just to tell him before he should go on his vacation that at the end of another year his services would no longer be needed at Princeton, but that he wanted to afford this gentleman every facility for securing a position where his talents would be more in accord with the genius of some other place, and he (Mr. Wilson) would do everything he could to assist him.

This professor was very fiery, and there immediately ensued a very violent scene, accompanied by threats of exposure, etc. The threats were immediately fulfilled. The student body was quickly informed that a case of persecution had arisen, and they grew pretty hot over it. I had a visit one night from a student who was a correspondent of one of the New York papers. He came in great anger to tell me that the next day's papers were going to contain an exposure of the whole matter and wanted to know if I had anything to say. I told him exactly what Mr. Wilson's attitude was toward the gentleman and gave him an unimpassioned account of the reasons why Mr. Wilson did not think this gentleman was competent for his position. Rather to my surprise, the student was convinced and, before leaving the room, he told me the articles would all be suppressed. And so the matter never got into the papers. Notwithstanding flurries of this sort, it is safe to say that Mr. Wilson remained high in the regard of most of the Princeton constituency.[13]

It was in the college year of 1907–1908 that Mr. Wilson began to ripen his recommendations for the third great reform—the reform of college life. I remember his telling me that when he first introduced his proposal before the trustees, one of the trustees laughed and whistled and wanted to know what was coming next. But nobody seemed to take any real offense at the proposal, which in brief was this—to reorganize the college life into groups, in which there should be representatives from all four of the classes, plus representatives from the faculty, these to live in commons together with their dining rooms, living rooms, etc., thus to form a living community of intellectual companionship, in which the younger men should continually be under the influence of men slightly older, and which education should be a continued and daily process rather than merely a matter of attendance on lectures and classes.

Of course, all the world knows by this time that Woodrow Wilson's mind is essentially a constructive mind, never ready to stop with half measures. To his mind, it was a perfectly clear proposition that this third reform was necessary in order to complete the effect of the other reforms and to make Princeton really an educational influence in the lives of young men. And that, I am insisting all through these notes, was his primary object—education, nothing less and nothing more at this time. I was constantly in the house during the discussion of these matters, and I never heard Mr. Wilson at this time make any attack whatsoever upon the Princeton clubs as such. They were merely more or less of an obstacle in the way of the larger result which he wished to accomplish. And so he proposed in effect that some of the clubs themselves might be used as residential homes for these groups into which he was proposing to organize college life. This whole thing came to be known as the "quad system," simply because the proposal involved a proposal that building in the future in Princeton should be in quadrangular form for the purpose of accommodating the physical conditions to the mode of life which he was now proposing.

From now on almost every statement that I make will be a statement which will be disputed by somebody, but I can only tell the story as I know it and as I firmly believe is so. The first disputed statement is what happened at the meeting of the board of trustees in June 1907. My clear and convinced answer is that what happened was nothing less than the endorsement by the entire board of trustees, minus one member, of the plan proposed by the president. They did not vote that Princeton should immediately be changed into a "quad system," and Mr. Wilson had not asked that they immediately vote for that. A change so sweeping as this must necessarily be brought about by degrees and with much forethought and careful consideration of ways and means. What the trustees voted was an endorsement of the idea and the authorization of the president to proceed with his plans and bring in subsequently definite recommendations as to details and ways and means and all the rest of it.[14] The one dissenting vote did not come from one of the leaders of the board—not from Mr. Pyne, or Mr. Russell[15]—but from Mr. Joe Shea, of Pittsburgh, one of the younger members of the board. And I know, from his close, personal friend, that he himself voted Nay, not because he thought President Wilson's recommendations were wrong, but because he thought the whole thing was too precipitate; that there ought to be more time for consideration. Rightly or wrongly, he unquestionably voted in accordance with his conscience, and he is perhaps the only man of the subsequent opposition whose conduct was consistent throughout.

The immediately ensuing summer brought a storm from the alumni, particularly from those of New York and Philadelphia. I may say here that I think there was never a time in the fight when Mr. Wilson could not have carried the great majority of the alumni west of Pittsburgh, but the opposition to him in the East, especially in Philadelphia and New York, was strong, quickly became violent, ultimately insane. Nothing that he has encountered in his subsequent political career has been more characterized by fierce hatred than the attitude of many of the eastern alumni. What they saw was an abolition of their clubs and an abolition of the social privileges which they themselves had enjoyed in Princeton, and which they were determined that their sons and younger brothers should have in turn.

Now, what was it that Mr. Wilson saw? This: that he had been permitted almost without opposition to revise a curriculum, revise a disciplinary system, revise a whole method of teaching, but the moment he touched that which concerned the social privileges and the vested rights of these men, they were ready to fight him to the death. It was in the clear recognition of this that what had been inaugurated as a purely educational reform suddenly transformed itself into a fight for democracy. When Mr. Wilson realized the character of the forces that were opposing him, all of the democracy that was in him latent, as well as conscious, leaped into flame. He had always been a democrat, but now he had become a fighting democrat, and when the story of this great democrat is told in great detail we must go back to Princeton in 1907 for the epochal moment of its development.

Now I must revert back for a moment to the picture of Princeton in 1899 as I have drawn it from my own point of view. These undemocratic things were here as seeds rather than as full-grown plants. I repeat what I said before: the change that was taking place was insidious, and I repeat once more that I am not at all sure that

Mr. Wilson felt in 1899 that there was anything in Princeton consciously to be resisted. I am pretty sure that he did not feel so, or he would have begun to resist it. But when he found that this subtle thing had grown into something that could present a solid phalanx of opposition to what he considered a desirable and rational educational reform, then he knew that he was really fighting for democracy. Fierce and untrue things were said about his attitude toward the clubs. It was asserted that he charged that they were hot beds of immorality, and all sorts of lies like that. I can testify that Mr. Wilson never said one single thing to the derogation of the morals of the clubs. There was nothing he could say. By law and by the voluntary agreement of the clubs themselves, no liquor was ever served within the clubs, except at the dinner which all of the clubs held one night of the commencement period; and there was never a charge of anything verging on sexual immorality in any of the clubs, never any gambling that I ever heard of. These things were carefully guarded by the men themselves.

Mr. Wilson had, I repeat, first seen in the clubs a rather inconvenient obstacle to the immediate accomplishment of what he considered a better social organization for the college, but now, when he found how the clubs were made the center of opposition, he saw that they had in themselves potentialities of evil for the future simply as an influence which ultimately would destroy the democracy of Princeton, and so he fought them.

There is another phase of the matter. Mr. Wilson saw that the clubs were purely an extracollegiate institution, something formed by students and alumni, something in which the college authorities had no direct part; they were really the absorbing matter of interest in the lives and minds of the undergraduates. They and athletics were the really important things to the Princeton undergraduates, and Mr. Wilson was contending that the college had to be reorganized so that the important thing in the minds of all was the college itself. Hence, that famous speech which he made on one occasion in which he said that the side shows had run away with the big show in the main tent, and that as for him he did not care to be ringmaster in the main tent when everything that was interesting was occurring in the side shows. If there is a sober educator in America who does not believe that Mr. Wilson put his finger on the very nerve of the trouble with American higher education, I don't know where to meet that man. Every honest man who knows the American college knows that the athletic and social life has completely run away with the educational life, and this thing Mr. Wilson wanted to reform. That was how the famous "quad" fight was precipitated.

There is a personal side to this which interests me very greatly—I mean personal to Mr. Wilson. All the world knows him for a fighter who fights to win, and, of course, he fought to win in the "quad" struggle, and yet perhaps this is the only struggle he ever engaged in in which he seemed to foresee defeat from the beginning. I remember trying to persuade him that the opposition would pass and that people would come to their senses, and I remember his saying in reply: "No, it never will, because these people are not fighting me out of reason; they are fighting me on the basis of their privilege, and privilege never yields." I do not know just when it was, but as the fight waxed and waned and things seemed to grow very dark at one time, I remember taking a walk with him one afternoon, when he told me that it seemed to him quite hopeless to go on in the presidency of Princeton; that he could not be interested in merely being the titular head of a college formed on lines which he could not believe in; and that he was thinking very seriously of giving up the educational life altogether and taking his family to Virginia and starting life all over again as a practicing lawyer. I told him that it seemed to me horrible that at this stage of his career that he should have to start life all over again like that. But he said he believed he could make a living for the family at law, and that he would be in this a free man, as he was not at Princeton.

Before anything had been brought to a head in the "quad" fight, there was precipitated the second chapter of the struggle, growing out of the fight over a graduate residential college. In the autumn of 1905, a graduate resident hall was opened in an old mansion in Bayard Lane—the house of Professor Raymond,[16] who had retired and gone to live in Washington. Professor Raymond's estate had been named Merwick, and this name was kept as the title of the graduate hall, where graduate students lived in commons. Across the street was Dean West's residence—a house, by the way, built by President Cleveland for the occupancy of Dr. John Finley on President Cleveland's own grounds. Dr. Finley had gone to New York to be president of the College of the City of New York, and Dean West was probably Mr. Cleveland's most intimate friend in Princeton now that Dr. Finley had moved away (in fact, President Cleveland's estate was named Westlands in honor of Dean West, who had secured the property for him when President Cleveland had signified his desire to retire to Princeton to live after the completion of his presidency). Professor Howard Crosby Butler was resident professor at Merwick and came to be referred to, at first humorously and afterwards quite as a matter of fact, as the "master of Merwick." The first year or two at Merwick forms a delightful memory. There was an academic charm about the place which there is no gainsay. I myself was frequently a visitor in the evenings at dinner. There was at least one dinner each week to which guests were invited. We all wore academic gowns, and there was a quiet air of elegance, for which undoubtedly Dean West's ideas and Professor Butler's personal influence were responsible. Butler was a master host. On these guest evenings there was usually some form of intellectual entertainment following the dinner. A paper was read by some visiting member of the faculty and discussed by the students themselves.

It was understood, of course, that Merwick was only a temporary arrangement; that as soon as possible a graduate hall would be built, and the location of that hall became a bone of contention. Mrs. Swann died about this time and left a bequest for a graduate hall.[17] It must be remembered that in 1905 relationships were entirely cordial between President Wilson and Dean West. But gradually the ideas of the two men diverged, and, as I was saying a moment ago, the first conflict came over the location of the building. Dean West became more and more impressed with the charm of isolation for the hall and wanted the permanent building placed on the grounds of Merwick, whereas Mr. Wilson insisted that the building should be on the college campus, at the center of college life. Always he had that idea of unity and of more advanced students being in constant and easy association with younger students; that there should be no aloofness anywhere.

It is at this point that the conception of the graduate college and the conception of the quad system coalesce. In both matters, Mr. Wilson was thinking, as he always thinks, of things in the whole, and in both matters he was thinking of education as a life process and a matter of daily contacts, and not merely a matter of lectures and recitations and quizzes. He wanted to draw Princeton into one organic whole, of which the newly entered freshman and the graduate student about to take his doctor of philosophy degree were all constituent parts. He insisted that these graduate students should not live aloof from the college life, but should be a fertilizing element in the intellectual life of the whole student body. Gradually, the issue began to define itself as an issue of plain living and common associations and unity, on the one hand, as against academic aloofness and an undue emphasis on the elegancies and graces of life on the other hand.

At this point I want to interpolate the account of a little episode which I think is important, for it illustrates what so much that I am putting into these notes illustrates, namely, that Mr. Wilson's ideas were not whims, but grew out of long and deep-seated convictions, fundamental to his conception of the meaning of education and university life. The episode was this:

A year or two before he became president of the university, Jacob A. Riis, author of *How the Other Half Lives*, lectured one evening in Alexander Hall on his own life work, with lantern-slide illustrations. It was really a great occasion, and all of us were deeply impressed. Men emotionally inclined, like our good friend, George Harper,[18] were impressed, almost religiously. Shortly afterward, there was a faculty gathering at one of the weekly meetings at Whig Hall—the usual sort of occasion when members of the faculty were called upon for informal speeches. Several of these speeches made reference to Mr. Riis' recent visit. And George Harper (one of the finest souls in the world and a devoted friend of President Wilson's) said, with deep feeling, that Mr. Riis' visit made him discontented with college life; that it seemed to him selfish and self-indulgent to be pursuing the mere academic life, sheltered and apart from the great, seething mass of humanity, with their pains, their sufferings, and their aspirations. I am perfectly free to confess that I echoed something of Mr. Harper's feeling, certainly in thought, quite possibly in words, though I do not remember what I did say in my own speech. I happen to remember much more clearly the speeches of other men, namely Mr. Harper's and Mr. Wilson's. Mr. Wilson was one of the last to be called on that evening, and he struck a new note. He said he was entirely out of sympathy with the things that were being said, and with the point of view expressed by his friend Harper; that he also had been greatly impressed by Mr. Riis and by what Mr. Riis had done, and he also realized the necessity for people to devote their lives to just that kind of work, but he said in effect: "It is an entirely wrong conception of the college to assume that we are aloof and sheltered. We right here in the college are a part of this seething life of humanity; and there is an obligation not to withdraw from the college and its assumed protection, but to make the college itself and all its life and all its energy a part of the redemptive processes of humanity." He said that for his own part he could not conceive of a vital college which was not a vital part of the national life and reaching down in its influence into those very slums which Mr. Riis had described so movingly. That is the Wilson point of view about a college. That was what Wilson meant when he made his address in 1896, "Princeton in the Nation's Service." And that was what he meant in the fight against the removed and aloof graduate college which Mr. West was counseling.

Mr. Wilson feels the charms of Oxford and Cambridge just as much as Mr. West has ever felt them. I know whereof I speak, for I visited Oxford and Cambridge with Mr. Wilson back in 1899, and I know how he loved the quiet gardens and the cloisters and the peace and the comeliness and the dignity and the beauty of these old world universities. But Mr. Wilson could never give his consent to purchase these things at the cost of separating the college from the national life or to separating any part of the college life from the whole of the college life.

Not until after the quad controversy had set Princeton on fire did the graduate college question become acute. It was in the autumn of 1907 that the lines were distinctly drawn in the faculty and in the board of trustees between Wilson and his adherents and those in the opposition. Dean West became one of the leaders of the opposition. Dr. Henry van Dyke[19] associated himself with the opposition, as did Professor Magie, who, as noted above, precipitated the whole crisis with a motion which he made in faculty back in 1901.

Saddest of all, Professor John Grier Hibben decided to go with the opposition. I cannot write at length about this. It was too acute, too personal. Professor Hibben had been Mr. Wilson's *alter ego*—the one man who knew Mr. Wilson's mind in everything, far more intimate with him in the councils of the college than I, his kinsman, or anybody else. Mr. Wilson had relied on Mr. Hibben as he had never before relied on anybody and never since. My own friendship with Mr. Hibben has remained unbroken. I must allow him the right of judgment, but I must think that had I been in his place I could not have gone to the opposition. In fact, I have often thought of the matter in connection with myself. Suppose I had been convinced that Mr. Wilson was wrong, instead of believing, as I did believe, that he was absolutely right in his fundamental conception—though perhaps making some mistakes in tactics—what should I have done? Of course, no man can yield his convictions to anybody else, not even to the greatest man in the world, but I am very clear what I should have done. I should have gone to Mr. Wilson and said: "This thing is very tragic. I cannot be convinced of your position, but, of course, I cannot oppose you. Neither can I adopt the impossible attitude of neutrality. There is but one thing to do. I must leave the faculty and leave Princeton; and now you must help me to find another job." I have thought of this a thousand times, and I am sure that is what I should have done, and I so much wish that Jack Hibben had done just that. Perhaps he never would have become president of Princeton, as he now is, but certainly he would have kept the confidence and the affection of a man whose confidence and affection he has unfortunately lost forever. I have felt great sympathy for Mr. Hibben in recent years. He is so very anxious to patch up, if not heal, his relationship with Mr. Wilson, for undoubtedly he had a very strong personal affection for Mr. Wilson. But I had to tell him two years ago in a very frank talk: "You must understand that Mr. Wilson is irreconcilable on this point. These wounds have gone too deep for any healing. What occurs in politics seems to roll off of him like water off a duck's back; but this Princeton controversy, involving the deepest affections of his life, have made an indelible impression, and he will never change."

The trustees took up the fight over the graduate college on pretty much the same lines of cleavage as they had been waging the fight on the quad system, and certainly the opposition conducted their battle with consummate political adroitness. I have heard President Wilson say that people have wondered that a mere college president could meet and deal with politicians, but that all he had ever seen in the politics of New Jersey or in the politics of the United States had never equaled what he learned about politics in his dealings with the Princeton trustees. He said: "Those fellows could give lessons to professional politicians." And, by the way, the only people that I have ever heard him place above the Princeton trustees as politicians were some of the people he met with in Paris in his dealing with world affairs. He once said: "I feel when I get away from here that I shall draw a long breath like a man who has been shut in a room with foul air and gets out where the air is fresh and sweet again. The atmosphere of intrigue here is almost unbearable." When he said it, I wanted to ask him if these men had really surpassed the Princeton trustees, but he was so earnest that I did not like to inject an element of levity.

One of the trustees once made one of those apparently common-sense remarks, which was very effective, when he said that he could not understand why there should be all this fighting about the "location of a boardinghouse." It is one of those specious remarks which catches the fancy. It does seem in a way as though it were a matter of merely locating a boardinghouse, and that it was not very important whether this house were in one part of the village or half a mile away. But the location was the emblem of the idea held by different factions. The simple fact of the matter is that, insofar as President Wilson and Dean West were concerned, there was a temperamental difference absolutely irreconcilable. And it is a curious thing, too—one of life's paradoxes—that the man who was contending for the aloof idea of the graduate college was much more of a mixer than was the man who was contending for the "social" position of the graduate college. Dean West is by nature a more "social" sort of person than the president in the sense that he likes to mix and talk with people, whereas the president has a certain reserve well known to everybody. But West had the distinctly aloof and academic conception of education; Wilson, the distinctly democratic conception of education; and the two men could never be reconciled. And, of course, as always happens in these cases, they grew steadily further apart. I have often thought of them in the figure of two men standing in absolute contact with each other, back, let us say, in 1902, when Mr. Wilson became president, but the contact was back to back; that is to say, they were facing in opposite directions, and the more they moved, the further the distance between them.

There came a new figure on the scene, Mr. Procter, of Cincinnati, who, I have been told, had been prepared for Princeton through private lessons given him by Dean West. Mr. Procter appeared in May 1909 with a gift of money for the graduate college, to be given on two conditions: first, that the trustees would raise an equivalent sum of money, and, second, that the graduate college be built off-campus. Subsequently, he offered for this as a "compromise" (I remember how my dear sister laughed at the compromise) that the college be built on the grounds of the golf course, where the buildings were ultimately erected.

I give my own interpretation of Mr. Procter, which may be unjust, but I do not think so. It is founded on a knowledge of his acts, not on personal acquaintanceship. I have never met him; never want to meet him. And perhaps because I am judging him merely by his acts, without any surrounding atmosphere of personality, I may be too severe. When I think of Dean West, I must remember the things that I know of West personally—his geniality, his extraordinary kindness to individuals. I cannot forget that Dean West one summer took poor dying Walter Wyckoff[20] out to his little cottage and brought him and his wife[21] and baby to his (West's) own home and kept him there, where the rooms were more spacious and the piazza more comfortable for a dying man to breathe on. It is no simple matter to bring a dying man and his family into your household, but West did it. He did it without any mawkishness. I used to call on Wyckoff and was always impressed with the fact that there was no sickly sentimentalism in West's attitude. He would laugh and chat and tease poor Mrs. Wyckoff just to arouse her from her misery. And here Wyckoff did die. The kindness of West is beyond all question, and this I can never forget. It makes it seem all the more pitiful that he should be the political intriguer that he is.

But with regard to Procter I know nothing except the way he behaved. I think very few Princeton men knew anything about Procter until he appeared on the scene of the controversy as a sort of *deus ex machina*. Certainly, I, who am not a Princeton graduate, had never heard of him before, as I had heard of so many other prominent Princeton alumni. My interpretation is that after his graduation from Princeton he had given little or no thought to the place; was too busy out in Cincinnati turning soap fat into millions and attempting to act the dominant part in his community. But, meanwhile, Princeton had become fashionable—since 1900 let us say—and association with it meant the sort of pleasing sensation which a snob covets. Procter had money; was arrogant by nature; liked the things which were beginning to be so prominent at Princeton—display and social advantage. So with his money he sought to settle the dispute in a thoroughly characteristic way—by purchase. To assume that there was anything he could not buy was unbelievable to his mind.

Well, he got a shock; he found there was something he could not buy. He could not buy Wilson and his principles. Mr. Wilson entered upon a campaign to have Procter's money returned to him, with or without thanks. And now I have to recall a very painful thing, but I am making these notes very frank and I wish the book might be equally frank. The members of the trustees who took the idealistic point of view with Wilson that a principle was something too precious to be compromised by the acceptance of money gifts were many of them themselves hardheaded men of business, like Cleveland Dodge of New York, Cyrus McCormick of Chicago, and Ed Sheldon[22] of New York, etc. And most of the ministers on the board sided with the opposition, with Mr. Pyne and Mr. Russell insisting that Mr. Procter's money must be taken on Mr. Procter's own terms. A notable exception among the ministers was Dr. Melanchton W. Jacobus of the Hartford Theological Seminary, who stood staunch with the Wilson group right through. Among the rich alumni in New York and Philadelphia, there was amazement and horror at the thought of Mr. Procter's beneficent gift being handed back to him, but there can be no doubt that among the great rank and file of the Princeton alumni who lived west of Pittsburgh and the money centers, there was approval of the Wilson idea. These men saw that there are some things that money should not be allowed to buy.

The fight in the board of trustees was hot and almost incredibly bitter. We used to await the stated meetings of the board of trustees almost like a city awaiting the arrival of an army. I remember remarking to my sister one day: "Just to think of it; there were times when I did not even know that the trustees were meeting in Princeton." I told her how one day I went to the university library and, seeing a number of gentlemen going to and fro, I asked "Wilkie" Collins[23] what it all meant. And Collins laughed and told me that it meant nothing more or less than that the board of trustees were holding their meeting. Now, in these troublous times nobody could have any doubt about a meeting of the board. I think the very children in the streets of Princeton knew the times and the crises and the suspense.

But Mr. Wilson won the fight. The board of trustees actually voted to decline Mr. Procter's gift,[24] and plans were formed to locate the graduate building on the campus.

Before recording how victory was turned into defeat, I think I ought to say a word about the faculty. There used to be a saying in college circles that "Harvard is governed by its president; Yale, by its faculty; and Princeton, by its board of trustees." And there is perhaps a certain justice in this. We have seen how the original contest under Dr. Patton back in 1901–1902 suddenly seemed to cease in active faculty meetings and the matter passed into the hands of the board of trustees. There was much the same situation with regard to the quad fight in the faculty. There was never but one faculty vote taken and that was overwhelmingly with Wilson.[25] One of the most gratifying things about it was that nearly all the young preceptors voted on the side of the president, the significance of this being that these young men showed that they were unterrified by what was being said, namely, that the preceptors knew on which side their bread was buttered and would of necessity vote with Mr. Pyne's side, the side from which came the money support for the preceptorial system. But contrary to expectations, these young men showed their mettle and their independence by registering their vote (it was a registered vote, by name) against the side favored by Mr. Pyne. There were some tense meetings of the faculty, particularly the meeting in which Dr. Henry van Dyke brought in a motion hostile to the president, which motion to the astonishment of nearly all of us and to the cruel amazement of Mr. Wilson was seconded by Mr. Hibben. And, by the way, Mr. McClenahan offered another second. Mr. Wilson, presiding, quietly informed Mr. McClenahan that another second was not needed; that Mr. Hibben had already provided the seconding motion; but Mr. McClenahan insisted that he wanted to go on record also as seconding the motion, and so it was done. Mr. Wilson made just one speech in faculty, and then, just as in the fight back in 1901–1902, further formal faculty action ceased and the real fight was transferred to the board of trustees, though there were, of course, constant committee meetings for and against the Wilson plan.

Without Mr. Wilson's consent, and first without his knowledge, a sort of steering committee was formed in the faculty, with Dean Harry Fine as chief. We used to meet frequently at Dean Fine's house to confer on ways and means. Among the members of the self-constituted committee, in addition to Dean Fine, were Professor Harry A. Garfield, subsequently president of Williams College and United States Fuel Administrator; Professor Ormond; Professor W. M. Daniels, now of the Interstate Commerce Commission; Edward Elliott,[26] who had not then married my sister, and several others. Professor Harper would undoubtedly have been a member of this committee, but he was in Europe on leave of absence. There never was a more loyal group of men than those members of the faculty who were associated with the president in this fight. Daniels and Elliott both returned to Princeton in the autumn of 1907. Daniels had been in Europe; Elliott had been away from Princeton. Each came to my room in turn to inquire what it was all about, and each gave me the impression that he was going to be on the other side, but each in turn came back subsequently to tell me that he was for the president and proposed to stick. I remember so well Daniels quoting Daniel Webster, saying, "Sink or swim, live or die, I am with with Wilson." There was a deep-seated conviction that a sincerity of principle was on the side of Wilson. As new and very important men came into the faculty from the outside, like Capps of Chicago and Conklin of the University of Pennsylvania,[27] they aligned themselves with the president. So a large majority of the faculty were with the president. And though there was never any test vote of the students and the alumni, we have always believed this—that the great majority of the alumni, particularly those of the West, were with the president, but that the more aggressive alumni of the near vicinity of New York and Philadelphia were opposed to the president, and that the undergraduates could almost at any time have been aligned with the president.

I think I here ought to record an undergraduate incident. It was in the spring of 1908, when feeling was most intense against the president, that at a *Princetonian* dinner[28]—an annual affair of importance—a dinner at which President Wilson had said in earlier years he felt he owed it to the student body to report back to them on the condition of the college—it was at this dinner that something very impressive and very surprising occurred. The atmosphere was very tense, and many of us feared the president would be hissed when he rose to speak. He was, of course, the last speaker of the evening. Preceding him were Dean West, Dr. Henry van Dyke, and Mr. Charles Scribner of New York. The student committee of arrangement had apparently seen to it that all of the other speakers should be of the opposition. Each of these gentlemen made an appeal to the Princeton spirit against the quad system, and each was very insidious in his veiled references to the president. I was sitting where I could see the president's profile. I could see his jaw tighten; could see that lump rise on the jaw, which indicates the clenched teeth, and which always appears when he is in his most dangerous mood. He was very pale. It was really a very tense occasion when he rose to speak. It is a thousand pities that this speech was not taken down, has not been kept for posterity. After all these years, after I have followed him systematically through the great New Jersey campaign for governor, and after I have heard him speak to the multitudes as president, and after many great addresses that I have heard him deliver before Congress, I still count that speech at the Princeton Inn to the Princeton students at the *Princetonian* banquet as one of the great speeches of his career.

15. Wilson in a grim mood, ca. 1910

It was only twelve minutes long—somebody timed him—but it was twelve minutes of shrapnel shot. His face never relaxed; his eyes never softened; he just poured forth a volume of withering scorn upon the sort of thing that had been going on in the speeches that evening, upon the sort of thing that was going on in the Princeton constituency. I remember how he began. He said: "It is my lonely privilege to find that on Princeton academic occasions I seem always to be the only person who talks about the things of the mind." He then went on to pour scorn upon what the preceding speakers had said about the college as a place of beautiful friendships. Said he: "Do I not know what those friendships mean? Was I not here four years as an undergraduate? Has any man ever known more of the beauty and dearness of college friendship than I?" He then went on to tell these lads, in a way in which I cannot even suggest now after this lapse of years, that friendships, wonderful, beautiful, and endearing as they are, are not the primary things for which the college exists; that the college exists for education and for leadership in national affairs; and that the college which does not insist on an arrangement by which the individual students shall get the utmost of mental growth is a college which is false to its trust. It is a pity that I cannot reproduce this speech, but I remember the ringing note in which it closed. It closed with the first personal pronoun, with magnificent audacity, knowing that his audience was supposed to be hostile. He summoned these young men, for the sake of Princeton and its dignity and its usefulness and its perpetuity, to follow *him*, exclaiming at the end of his speech: "I summon you men to follow me."

It was a great inspiration; it was an invitation and a defiance at the same time. He told them that he, and he *alone*, was offering the way by which Princeton might be redeemed from misuse and applied to a great purpose and a great end. He said himself afterwards that he had never known language to flow from his lips the way it did that night. When he sat down at the end of twelve minutes, the students, who had been like men bewitched into silence during the speech, sprang to their feet practically to a man and began to yell as if they would rend the roof. Many mounted tables, waving their napkins and yelling.

There is a custom at Princeton, when the spontaneous cheering has gone on for a time, for a leader to call for "the locomotive," that is to say, the Princeton concerted college yell, and that always concludes the cheering. But not on this night. Three different times the "locomotive" was called for and given, and three different times the spontaneous cheering went on in increased volume after this usual period of the cheering had been given. It was a scene which no one can ever forget. During it all, I, still sitting where I could see Mr. Wilson's profile, saw that not a muscle had relaxed; it was as if he was not hearing those cheers at all. I have never seen him so stony. It was as if nothing could move him. That night he was almost terrible to behold. I walked to my apartments with Ed Elliott, not then my brother-in-law, and I said: "Ed, what on earth do you make of that demonstration? It cannot be that these students are for the quad plan yet." And Elliott replied: "No, they are not yet for the quad plan, but they know a man when they see him." And that was the answer.

Later on in the fight, I am not at all sure that they would have been for the quad plan at any time that it might have been presented to them, but, of course, this statement will be denied by others. What I am perfectly sure of is that later they were in a position where they could have been won to the quad plan if the faculty and the board of trustees had united to invite them.

But, as I was indicating when I made this long digression, the actual fighting was now purely trustee fighting, and the battle seemed to be won when Mr. Wilson persuaded the trustees to vote to return Mr. Procter's money.

But there came a bolt from the blue. Up in Massachusetts there was an old gentleman named Wyman,[29] practically unknown to any of the Princeton people except to the ubiquitous Dean West. At some time Dean West had visited this old gentleman and had persuaded him that his wealth, which was supposed to be very considerable, could be put to no better use than as a bequest for the graduate school. In the late spring of 1910, old Mr. Wyman, a graduate of the Princeton class somewhere back in the 1840s, rich old recluse, practically forgotten by the world, died. And his will was published. It left everything to the graduate school, to be administered by Dean West. The news of this bequest came first to Mr. Wilson in the morning newspaper. He read it aloud at the breakfast table, and, though I was not present, my sister told me of the scene. She said she had not seem him laugh so in months. As he read each new item, tying the matter up closer and closer, and making West absolute master of the situation, he would just throw his head back and guffaw. It was so complete, so dramatic, so absolutely unexpected. Just as he had defeated a living man, a dead man arose in his path and stopped him. Wilson never tried to fight the Wyman bequest.

I think I ought to mention here that the Wyman bequest, for which Princeton sold its soul, has turned out to be almost nothing in actual money.[30] Whatever the properties were, they realized very little. There is nothing that makes a Princeton man look more sheepish than to talk to him about what the Wyman bequest did for Princeton. But it changed the whole situation. Procter came back with his gift. The graduate college was built. It now stands crowning one of the hills at the golf course, where Mr. Procter said it should be built. Beautiful Gothic buildings they are, and the great tower is named for Mr. Cleveland.

Of Mr. Cleveland's association with this whole fight, I am going to say very little indeed, for there is nothing pleasant to say. We who had admired Mr. Cleveland as the leader of the Democratic forces of America were so utterly disappointed to find that he could not see the democratic implications in the things that Mr. Wilson was fighting for. Mr. Cleveland was certainly not himself in those last years in Princeton. His continual associate was Mr. Andrew West, and Mr. West seems to have had his will and his way with Mr. Cleveland. Mr. Cleveland not only opposed Mr. Wilson; he even opposed him bitterly. Mr. Wilson sought him out once to argue the case with him. Mr. Cleveland heard the argument and said: "There is nobody who can answer you in an argument." And he concluded in effect with the statement that, though he could not meet the arguments, he was unalterably opposed to the Wilson plans. How curious is the circumstance that today the leader of the Princeton undergraduate forces for the things for which Mr. Wilson fought for is young Richard Cleveland, the son.[31] This young man has seen what his father could not see—that the life of the democracy of Princeton was at stake—and he, the most popular member of the undergraduate body, refused membership in any of the clubs and has fought for the things for which Wilson fought and his father opposed. The wheel has come full circle.

The family were to spend the summer of 1910 in Lyme, Connecticut. Shortly after commencement they started one bright June morning on their journey, and I, having seen them off at the train, went back to Prospect to oversee the last details of closing up the house for the summer. In about an hour, to my astonishment, Mr. Wilson appeared. It seemed that he had forgotten some important thing—I do not recall now what it was—and had returned to Princeton from Princeton Junction, sending the family on to New York by the appointed train, he himself to take a later train and meet them there. So he and I sat on the pleasant terrace porch of Prospect that June morning and talked throughout the interval between the two trains. I regard it as a very memorable talk, because I realized for the first time, and I am strongly inclined to believe that he made up his mind for the first time, that the severance of his connection with Princeton was inevitable. I resisted the idea, stubbornly optimistic, believing that in some way, though I could not see how, "everything would come out right in the end." But to his clear vision there seemed no prospect of it. He said that it would never interest him to be the figurehead in an institution whose policies were being determined by others and in opposition to the things in which he most profoundly believed; that the position was growing intolerable; and that he believed that the time was ripe for his resignation. Then he said: "I am sure I can be elected governor of New Jersey. The convention meets in September, and I believe that I had better listen to the people who have been wanting to present my name to it." I personally did not like it. I am free to confess I did not want to see him go into politics. I had seen Princeton break his heart, and I felt that what he had received at Princeton was only the elements of what he would receive from the political world outside. But he made a promise to his wife, which he kept, namely, that he would not let politics hurt him personally the way the Princeton fight had hurt him, because that sort of thing is expected in politics, but not expected from one's personal friends. He has been absolutely faithful to that promise.

The convention met in September and nominated him. He resigned immediately from Princeton, and, by the way, his resignation was about as complete as anything could be. The board met; he handed in his resignation; he took the train for a political meeting; and from that hour he washed his hands as completely of Princeton as it is possible for a man to cleanse himself of anything. The Princeton trustees voted to continue his salary for a few months, I suppose until the end of the first term. The checks came in and Mr. Wilson returned the checks. The college treasurer met me one day and said: "I don't know what in the world to do with those checks; I have orders from the board of trustees to deliver them to the president, and the president sends them back." "Well," I said, "I guess you and the trustees will have to settle that. Certainly, the president will have none of it."

Mr. Wilson wanted to pack up and leave Prospect within three or four days, and preparations were started, but that proved to be quite impracticable, and he was at length persuaded to stay there for a few months, as there was no other president of Princeton and there would be absolutely no use whatever for the house. I suppose, as a matter of fact, that Mrs. Wilson probably made him realize that it was quite impossible to move out everything just at once, but certainly he was very reluctant to seem to accept the slightest favor or courtesy at the hands of the Princeton trustees.

He conducted a most notable campaign, about which I shall hope to say something in another chapter. He was, of course, overwhelmingly elected governor, and in January took office.

Procter, West, and company, and the shade of Wyman, had successfully launched him on his career, which was to lead to the presidency of the United States and the leadership of world affairs in the world's greatest crisis. Many have claimed the distinction of being "Original Wilson Men," and the agile Colonel Harvey confesses with a sour countenance that he made Wilson president. But the colonel agitates himself unnecessarily. The original Wilson men were purely academic. The real makers of Wilson as president were the Princeton group, but for whose ingenious activities he would have remained indefinitely president of Princeton. As their names will never be inscribed upon his monument, let them be written in the book of his biography: "They builded better than they knew."

I am absolutely convinced of the wisdom of the purposes which Mr. Wilson had in view for Princeton. I and many other people interested in American education believe that Mr. Wilson was the one man in the country who saw how to rescue American education from confusion and give it a lofty and enduring purpose. Of his ideas and of the motives which governed him in his ideas, I could not if I tried find a word of criticism. His methods for getting Princeton to do the things he wanted done, his tactics in the fight, are open to some criticism. I believed at the time, and I still believe, that he could have softened some of the asperities in the struggle and could early in the conflict have made friends for himself and his cause among those who ultimately aligned themselves with the opposition. I believe, in short, he could have been more conciliatory. This is not to say that he could have won the fight by any methods. It is impossible for anybody to be sure about that, one way or another. But I do believe that the rancors of the struggle could have been lessened, and this notwithstanding the fact that some of the people whom he fought were venomous in their spirits.

From the beginning of his presidency of Princeton, Mr. Wilson had been too much inclined to rely on a few, too little inclined to listen at length to what others had to say. There was the impression in the faculty, even while the members of the faculty were practically all his friends, that he was trusting too much in the judgment of Mr. Hibben and not giving enough opportunity to other members of the faculty and other elements to vent their ideas. His concentration on Mr. Hibben really was extraordinary. I remember I began to feel actually embarrassed in faculty meetings at the number of committees on which Mr. Hibben was appointed. If there was to be a new committee to be appointed, you always knew that Hibben would be on it, or a vacancy on an old committee was always to be filled by

Hibben. The policy of this was certainly not good. Without any reflection whatsoever on Mr. Hibben, it was simply human nature for his colleagues to resent passively, if not actively, the assumption that Mr. Hibben was the only person on the faculty who had anything to say to the president which was worth the president's attention.

It is a good psychology to permit even foolish people once in a while to express all their foolishness. It clears their systems and gives them a sense of being a part of things.

I recall on one occasion the unusual spectacle of myself angrily resenting Mr. Wilson. He was laughing at some suggestions for procedure received from an alumnus living at a distance, a man whom I knew well, knew to be loyal and devoted, and I blazed out: "Blank is doing everything he can to help in this fight, and whether what he offers is wise or foolish, he ought to be treated with the respect due to loyalty and conviction."

To this day, even Mr. Wilson's friends wish that he could find it easier to talk with numbers of people. Only the other day a warm admirer of his was asking me if nothing could be done to persuade Mr. Wilson to see more people and talk with them more and hear them talk more. I replied to this with an analysis, saying that this quality in him was partly temperamental, partly a matter of conviction. By temperamental I mean this—that with all his originality, and what some people call his radicalism, he has this strikingly conservative quality, that he does not care for the adventure of new personal experiences; he loves to reread the same books and the same poems; to take the same automobile rides Sunday after Sunday; to go to the same theater—Keith's—each week; and when he used to indulge in vacations he loved to spend his vacations in the same place—in the lake district of England—when it was possible for him to get there. Only a few days ago he said he would rather go back to the lake district now for a vacation than to do anything in the world. By the same token, he loves to talk to the same people rather than to make fresh acquaintances.

So in the Princeton controversy it used to be complained that he did not see enough people and talk with them at length, and, therefore, did not know what was going on. I was satisfied that he did know what was going on, but at the same time, just for the sake of the impression made on others, I did wish that he would see more people. And his loyal lieutenant, Harry Fine, used to wish the same thing.

However, besides the temperamental quality, there is that quality of conviction in this matter, namely, that a great deal of talking confuses rather than clarifies an issue. Who will deny this as a general proposition? The only question is where to draw the line between what is helpful counsel and what becomes confusion of counsel. Mr. Wilson is impatient of a vast deal of talk. What he always desires is to get at the heart and principle of a question or problem—to strip from it all that is unessential—and a vast deal of talk hinders rather than helps this process.

I lived in bachelor quarters in Princeton at the corner of Nassau Street and University Place; in other words, at the central point of the village. And the result was that my rooms became a rendezvous for the Wilson faction. They would drop in at all times of day and at very inconvenient times at night. I was robbed of much sleep that I ought to have had in those busy times. They would come to my rooms from out of town, these quarters being within five minutes' walk of the railway station, and they would talk and talk and talk interminably.

Dean Fine was *the* leader of the group. I think Daniels conceived the idea of our self-constituted steering committee in counter action to the conferences which some of the opposition were holding *sub rosa*, and Daniels was a "bonny fighter." But he and all of us regarded Fine as our leader. All of our group meetings, except the first (which was at Professor Ormond's house) were in the dean's office, and he was our informal chairman. His activity was unceasing, his loyalty unswerving.

All these strong men subordinated their lesser differences of opinion to their leader's major purpose. They believed in Wilson as against the opposition and by degrees assimilated the ideas and purposes of the leader. They illustrated Wilson's power of magnetic leadership of strong men.

These friends of our cause, and friends of Mr. Wilson, were often severely critical of their leader; and particularly on just this point—that he shut himself in and did not see people and did not know what was going on. I used to say: "I agree with you; for the sake of the situation, he does not talk at length to enough people, but I very much question that he does not know what is going on. Now, I suggest to you that you make an appointment with him to see him at his office, during his office hours, in '79 Hall. He will see you there. That is where he wants to talk business, not in his residence." Again and again and again this happened: that the man who acted on this suggestion of mine would come back to my room and say—I remember precisely the language which one of them used—"Well, by God, he does know, doesn't he?" And I replied: "Yes, that's what I told you." "Well, how in the world does he know?" was the question. And I replied: "I don't know how he knows; I only know he knows." Now, of course, the rational explanation of this is that a man like Mr. Wilson makes quick deductions from a little. He lets a few things that he hears construct in his mind many other things which he knows must go with the few things, just as a paleontologist will construct the skeleton of an extinct monster from a few bones. The bones which he finds are evidence to his informed mind of what the other bones must necessarily have been.

But I have a profound conviction which goes beyond this, namely, that in most of the greatest men of the world there is a vein of mysticism. That is what seems still misunderstood about Lincoln. The "Honest Abe" pictures represent only one aspect of Lincoln. So far from being the simplest of men, he was one of the most complex men that ever lived. And while he was the most approachable of men, he was at the same time the loneliest man in all America. Read his biography attentively, and you will find that, while he had many acquaintances, he had no intimates. His soul dwelt abroad and alone. There was depth under depth of mysticism in that plain exterior. And very much of this applies to President Wilson, though, of course, because of a certain exterior reserve which Mr. Lincoln had not, the president does not seem so affable, so genial in his personal contacts.

Now, besides this quality that I have been analyzing, this quality of comparative aloofness, there was in Mr. Wilson during the Princeton controversy a rigidity of attitude. He attempted sharply to classify men as friends or foes, wise or foolish, and to allow very little ground between the classes. There was an uncompromising quality about his judgments and assessments, which was really an inheritance of his father, who was one of the most uncompromising men in his opinions that I ever knew. I have just been saying that the tendency to aloofness is today what it was in the Princeton days, but the quality of rigidity is not so. Perhaps the most notable change which has taken place in Mr. Wilson is the mellowing of his character, of his judgments of men. I never cease to wonder at the gentleness with which he now speaks of men who are opposing him at every point. Though I had realized this change for a number of years, I was almost startled by the extent of it when I saw him in Paris during the trying days of the peace conference—the patience with which he would deal with opposition, the allowance which he would make for other men and their conduct. There was none of this in the Princeton controversy. The simple fact of the matter is that Mr. Wilson learned in that Princeton conflict some great lessons which have been undoubtedly of immense use in the greater battles which he has had to wage since. He has learned patience, and in Princeton he was a very impatient, fiery man. Mr. Wilson has great confidence in a destiny—he with his old, simple Presbyterianism, which to this day he has kept quite unsophisticated.[32] He calls it not destiny, but Providence, and a Providence which governs men's lives and gives them the occasion to turn even their misfortunes into benefit. I am sure this is what he has done with his Princeton experience. It was bitter and painful, and the bitterness of the memory of it has not left him. But the lessons he deduced from it have made him a wiser, more patient, and therefore more skillful political controversialist and leader.

Politics, 1910–1913

 ❧

I WAS FIRST thrown into intimate daily contact with Mr. Wilson in the summer of 1886, though two summers before that I had seen him several times in Rome, Georgia, when he was already engaged to my sister and had been engaged to her for a year. All this is pretty far away from the subject of the governorship of New Jersey, but I am led to speak of these things simply because my mind has reverted to the long, long walks which Mr. Wilson and I used to have together, and to the talks about books and things and politics, theoretical and practical, in one of which talks I heard him make the first reference, and probably the only reference for nearly twenty years, to the fact that he would regard it rather as a pleasant thing to get into active politics.

One of our favorite walks was on the railroad track leading northward to Holland Springs, then a summer resort, now turned into an extensive cotton-mill town. I never journey down on the Southern Railway without looking out for Holland Springs and living over again the walks and talks which I, as a lad of nineteen and twenty, used to have with my brother-in-law. Very little, if anything, has been so important in my own life, for he opened up all kinds of new worlds to me and led me to understand the joys of the things of the mind.

It was on one of these walks to Holland Springs that he was unfolding to me that recurrent idea of his that the British government has an advantage over the government of the United States in that the ministry is directly responsible to the British people. This led him into a good deal of talk about Congress. While he was talking about Congress, I suddenly exclaimed: "Do you know, I should think that you yourself would like to go to the United States Senate some day, wouldn't you?" And he laughingly replied: "You bet I would." Robert Bridges, in his memorial address on President Wilson at Princeton, relates that when Wilson was a Princeton undergraduate he would sometimes conclude a discussion with, "Well, I'll continue that debate with you in the Senate." It was all utterly casual, and he had no more real idea of going into practical politics than I had, which is the extremest form of statement that I can make. I do not recall ever hearing again even a casual and semijocose reference to actual engagement in politics until he had become president of Princeton University, and people outside began to talk about him as possible political timber.

The first time any of this talk became anything like definite was when, at a dinner in New York, Colonel George Harvey in his speech made a personal and informal nomination of Woodrow Wilson to be a future president of the United States.[1] This episode, and it was nothing but an episode, was played up on the front page of the next morning's New York papers, which reached us in Princeton at breakfast time. I was at Prospect when Mr. Wilson returned from New York, and I remember very well meeting him just at the foot of the stairs leading to the living rooms on the second floor. Mrs. Wilson was just coming down the stairs to greet him. The first thing said was by me, laughing: "I see Colonel Harvey has nominated you for the presidency." And he made some laughing assent. Mrs. Wilson, who had just reached the foot of the stairs, said: "Was he joking?" And Mr. Wilson said, in rather slow and uncertain tone: "He did not seem to be." I think that was rather interesting as showing how so aloof anything of this sort was from the minds of Mr. and Mrs. Wilson that their first interchange of comment was whether or not the nominator was joking.

Mr. Wilson is fond of telling to this day how he was sitting at a table in the dining room of the old Everett House on Union Square one day, when Mr. Richard Watson Gilder, the editor of *The Century*, approached his table and said: "I heard a man the other day mention you for the presidency." Mr. Wilson said: "Presidency of what?" Mr. Gilder replied: "Of the United States, that's all. And the man wasn't a fool, either." Mr. Wilson said: "Why, Gilder, I never expect to be president of the United States, but I should rather that it would not have to be explained to me that a man who spoke of me in that connection was not a fool." I rather suspect that this humorous little episode antedated the Harvey dinner, but I don't know.

The first reference that I ever heard made in Princeton to his possible elevation to the presidency was at the Nassau Club, when one evening somebody remarked to our old friend and fellow townsman, "Pete" van Doren, who was one of our town characters: "I see Woodrow is being talked about for the presidency."[2] And Van Doren replied, in a dry, droll way: "Well, why wouldn't it be a good idea to let him try it? He has been talking about governing a good while. Why not give him a chance to see what he can do at it?"

The first political cartoon that I saw of Wilson was hung in the Nassau Club, some member having clipped it from a newspaper and pinned it on the wall. It represented a bicycle race—it must have been in 1904—and represented bicyclers racing for the presidency. A great number of figures appeared in the cartoon, and among those, by no means in the foreground, was Woodrow Wilson.

I find my memory is very much confused about the points concerned with Colonel Harvey's subsequent and unauthorized "grooming" of Wilson for the governorship of New Jersey and the senatorship from New Jersey. Harvey, without permission of Wilson, constituted himself the advocate of Wilson for both of these positions, avowedly proclaiming that one or the other of these offices would fit him ultimately to be president of the United States. Colonel Harvey was very active in 1907 in pushing Mr. Wilson for the senatorship of New Jersey. And Mr. Wilson was reluctant to have his name used in this way. He talked the matter over with me at length one day, and I asked him why he did not go to New York and see Colonel Harvey and tell him frankly that he could not consent to have his name used in this way. Mr. Wilson replied that he did not think it would be wise for him to seek an interview with Colonel Harvey at all. "Then," said I, "why don't you ask one of your friends, possibly Daniels, to go up and lay before Colonel Harvey your opinions and feelings about the unwisdom of this procedure?" He considered a moment, and then quite unexpectedly said to me: "Why don't you go yourself?" "Well," I said, "I should be delighted to do so if you think I could execute the commission to your satisfaction." He said he thought I could. What he wanted was not merely that his own reluctance should be indicated to Colonel Harvey, but that his commissioner should find out what it was Colonel Harvey was really up to; what his motives were. So the appointment was made by letter and telegram, and I called on Colonel Harvey at the Harpers publishing house in Franklin Square. It chanced that this was on the same day[3] that Nell Wilson was being operated on by Dr. William W. Keen in Philadelphia for tubercular glands in her neck—a desperate and pro-

longed operation—during which the father and mother waited in another room. As time passed and no news came from the operating
room, they paced the floor, arm in arm, in anguished anticipation.

I took the train directly from New York down to Philadelphia and
found the mother and father comparatively at ease, as good accounts had been brought to them of the success of the operation,
which had proved much more serious than had been anticipated.
After a while we got our minds back to Colonel Harvey and my errand to New York, and I gave Mr. Wilson a detailed report of the conversation, which it is impossible for me to reproduce now after all
these years. But what I do remember is the impression I got in New
York from Colonel Harvey, and what it was I said to Mr. Wilson about
this impression. Said I: "He talked to me for one hour. He was genial,
interesting, and apparently as frank as candor itself, and yet I knew
all the time, and I know now, that not once in the entire conversation
did he expose his real mind and his motives to me. Not once did he
tell me what it was he was really thinking. I deduced from this the
conclusion that there is a type of politician who thinks that the truth
is dangerous *per se*, and that even though he is talking with a friend
of a friend he must not state the real facts and conditions lest he
should be confronted awkwardly on some other day."

This was the only time that I ever met Colonel Harvey personally.
But when Mr. Wilson went to England in the summer of 1908, Mr.
Wilson left me as a sort of political agent to block any movement that
might be made to nominate him for office in his absence. He was at
that time being talked of for the presidency of the United States on
the ticket with William Jennings Bryan. It was only newspaper talk,
but Mr. Wilson feared that possibly something might happen in the
convention; that there might be a stampede just in order to get the
convention closed and let the delegates go home after the nomination for president. Possibly by some fluke he might be the nominee
for the vice presidency, which he very much did not want. He therefore left with me a written statement, which I was to make public if
necessary, that he could not and would not in any condition or in
any circumstance permit his name to be presented to the convention. Before the date of the convention, I was called up on the long-
distance telephone by Colonel Harvey, who was, I think, not in New
York but in one of the North Jersey cities, and he asked me to meet
him at some appointed place. This I declined to do, pleading engagements which made it impossible. I was keenly aware of my own in-

competence to deal with this shrewd and adroit man if he wanted to bring any pressure to bear to "start something" in Mr. Wilson's absence, and I intended to rely entirely on instructions to use the written statement if necessary.

The convention opened in Denver, and I concluded that Princeton village was too remote for sudden action and that I had better go to some place where the wires were probably in closer communication with convention hall. So I went to Philadelphia and took into my confidence a personal friend on one of the newspapers and asked him to notify me in case any flash came over the wire that Wilson's name was being presented to the convention. I then went to a hotel, left definite instructions at the desk for calling me in my room, and waited through the afternoon, the evening, the night, and a portion of the next day until John W. Kern of Indiana was actually nominated for vice president. It was rather a joke on Mr. Wilson that apparently his precaution was quite unnecessary, for there does not appear to have been any serious mention of him in the convention at all. By the way, the only reference I ever heard of Mr. Bryan's making to Mr. Wilson occupying the second place on the ticket was a newspaper paragraph prior to the convention, when a reporter asked Mr. Bryan: "How does Woodrow Wilson strike you for the vice presidency?" Mr. Bryan replied: "First rate. He strikes me every chance he gets."

Mr. Wilson had no serious thought of political office until 1910, when the crisis came in Princeton affairs and the governorship of New Jersey was opened to him. Mr. Wilson told me how Senator Jim Smith and some of his companions visited him personally at Princeton,[4] and Mr. Wilson asked them, with rather startling bluntness: "Why do you gentlemen want to nominate me for the governorship of New Jersey?" They replied: "Because we think you are the one Democrat who could be elected." "Well," said Mr. Wilson, "this means then that you think that the people of New Jersey would have confidence in me, which means that they would have confidence that I would not be under the control of a group or faction. If I am to be the nominee, I must be what the people suppose I am—a man who cannot be controlled. Therefore, if I accept this nomination you must understand that it is without any obligations, stipulated or implied. If I seem free I must be free to serve the people and not any group or faction." To this these gentlemen assented, though probably with their tongues in their cheeks. They had heard that sort of talk before but could hardly really believe that a man meant it. That Mr. Wilson did mean it they found to their subsequent chagrin.

Of all that happened during the summer prior to the state convention in Trenton, I do not profess to have any acquaintance. Stories have been published about meetings between Colonel Harvey and Mr. Wilson at Lyme or elsewhere during the course of the summer. I am not familiar with any of this. By the way, perhaps I ought to state now that my only associations with Mr. Wilson in a political way have been those two little episodes which I have already described— my visit to Colonel Harvey and my being entrusted with the letter to be presented by telegram to the nominating convention of 1908. As soon as politics became a really serious matter with Mr. Wilson, I naturally had no further connection with him, as, of course, he had to rely on men of more political training and judgment than I have had.

So the next thing that I knew was the convention itself. I went over from Princeton with a group of Princeton acquaintances—not all of them friends of the president. It made me laugh, and it makes me laugh now, to see them and realize now how very enthusiastic some of those Princeton people were to have Mr. Wilson nominated for governor of New Jersey, not because they were especially eager to see him governor, but because they were quite frantic to get him out of the presidency of Princeton. I remember one of these men saying earnestly to me: "You know, I am a Democrat and I am absolutely for Wilson for governor, but I do think this, that when he resigns the presidency of the university, it ought to be an absolute resignation, not contingent at all upon his election. He ought to commit his entire fortunes to the campaign, for if he ties any strings to his resignation from the university, people will think that he does not expect to be elected governor, and that will hurt his political candidacy." I laughed and said: "Don't you worry; if he is nominated governor today you will not be troubled by him as president of the university any longer. And when he resigns, he resigns for good and all." I might mention here, by the way, that the president has very stiff ideas about resignations. He considers that nothing is more fatal than to recall a resignation; and he always accepts resignations. He has sometimes been regarded as a little cruel in that respect, but he goes on the principle that a sincere man will not resign unless he

thinks there are reasons for his resignation, and the fact that he
thinks there are reasons for his resignation constitute reasons; and
that if a man is insincere in his resignation, he is a good riddance.

I went on the stage, back of the crowd, in the Taylor Opera House
[in Trenton], where the convention was held, sat in an obscure corner and watched the proceedings with deepest interest, and I must
say I was deeply impressed by Senator Jim Smith as a personality,
whom I saw for the first and only time. He sat, not on the stage, but
in the front row in the orchestra, and made one of the seconding
speeches to Mr. Wilson's nomination. It was really an admirable
speech. He said in effect that he did not second this nomination because Mr. Wilson was a friend of his; that he did not presume to
claim friendship with a man whose natural life had been lived in
spaces so far above his own environment; that he had no personal
reasons for this nomination, but that he believed that it was high
time that the affairs of the state of New Jersey were taken out of the
hands of the Republicans and put into the hands of people who
would have some regard for the rights of the common people of New
Jersey, which had been willfully disregarded by the Republican machine; and that Mr. Wilson was in his opinion the one Democrat
in New Jersey who had the best chance of being elected. Senator
Smith's bearing was very dignified, and while, of course, there was a
mixture of demagoguery with the truth of his speech, it was all delivered in a way that was very effective.

One of the speeches in opposition to Mr. Wilson at the Trenton
convention was made by Judge John W. Wescott of Camden. I do not
recall much what the judge said beyond a reference to subterranean
connections with Wall Street, which association with Mr. Wilson
seems absurd enough, but it must be remembered that there was a
great deal of ignorance or vagueness about Mr. Wilson. What I particularly remember about Judge Wescott's speech was the fiery quality of it. He was evidently dead in earnest and quite sincere in his
opposition to Mr. Wilson. Admiral Grayson gives a very pertinent sequel to all this, which I myself had not been aware of. I did not know
that Judge Wescott's conversion to Mr. Wilson occurred almost immediately, on the very day, in fact, in which he had made this strong
denunciatory speech. Judge Wescott himself has told Admiral Grayson that his inclination was to leave the hall before Mr. Wilson had
arrived from Princeton to make his speech of acceptance, feeling
that he could not in self-respect remain and listen to a man whom he

so heartily disapproved, but a friend persuaded him that he might as well stay and hear a part of the speech anyway and see what it was like. He and his friend remained more from a sense of curiosity than anything else. They both remained until the speech was finished. When Mr. Wilson had completed his address, both looked at each other and exclaimed: "This is a sincere man. We have misjudged him. He is a great man."

I had known before the campaign was completed that Judge Wescott was a friend of Mr. Wilson's, because I recall once in South Jersey being in an automobile with Mr. Wilson when he was on his way to one of his meetings that we were joined by Judge Wescott. That was the first intimation that I had of the winning over of Judge Wescott to Mr. Wilson's candidacy.

This is the same Judge Wescott who nominated Mr. Wilson for the presidency in the Baltimore convention in 1912. In the course of his nominating speech, Judge Wescott quoted with great effect from a speech which Mr. Wilson had made while president of Princeton. The curious irony of this is worth noting, for the speech from which Judge Wescott quoted was one of the few purely academic speeches of Mr. Wilson that had been printed entire and widely circulated, and it was printed and circulated by the enemies of Mr. Wilson in the college fight in order to do him an injury.

The circumstances were these. Things had gone badly in the Princeton fight, and at one of the darkest periods for Mr. Wilson in the struggle he had to go to an alumni meeting at Pittsburgh in April 1910 in fulfillment of an engagement which had been made sometime before. He told me before starting that he was very reluctant to go because he did not have anything to say. I received a letter from one of my Pittsburgh Princeton friends,[5] which told me that Mr. Wilson had never been so dejected as he was on the occasion of this meeting and afterward, when he had gone with his friend to the suburb, Sewickly, to spend the night. Mr. Wilson told the Princeton alumni in his speech that he did not know why he was there; he was certainly not there as representing the Princeton board of trustees or the Princeton alumni; in fact, he did not represent anything. He then went on to develop that favorite idea of his, that the American college, not merely Princeton, but the American college in general, was out of touch with the great fundamental things of the national life, and he burst into an impassioned passage in which he exclaimed: "The great voice of America does not come from seats of learning. It comes in a murmur from the hills and woods and the farms and factories and the mills, rolling on and gaining volume until it comes to us from the homes of common men. Do these murmurs echo in the corridors of our universities? I have not heard them."

Now this speech from the point of view of the academic enemies of Mr. Wilson was ammunition which they believed could be used to damage him. At their own expense they published the speech, giving it the sinister title, *That Pittsburgh Speech*, and mailed it to great numbers of people. It really must have been an enormous edition that they published, for in subsequent years men occupying mediocre positions in remote colleges have told me that the speech came to them in the mails without explanation.

But the gods were having their revenge when Judge Wescott, in nominating Mr. Wilson for the presidency, quoted the above passage from the despised Pittsburgh speech.

The same friend who had told me how dejected Mr. Wilson was on the occasion of his Pittsburgh visit was in the convention hall at Baltimore when Judge Wescott made his nominating speech, and I shall never forget how he described the occasion to me. His face flushed, his eyes sparkling, he said: "I had often thought in connection with Mr. Wilson's career of that Biblical passage, 'The stone which the builders rejected has become the head of the corner.' " He went on to say that when Judge Wescott began to quote from *That Pittsburgh Speech*, which had been used for the confusion of Mr. Wilson and his friends in the Princeton fight, he, this gentleman, Mr. Wilson's friend and mine, buried his face in his arms and cried like a little child.

Mr. Wilson was nominated [for the governorship] and a message was sent to him to hurry over from Princeton in an automobile and address the convention before it should adjourn. I believe he was playing golf when the messengers found him, though, of course, he was entirely prepared for the call; in fact, he had written the platform himself for the convention. In short, he was already deep in politics. I strongly suspect that he had prepared beforehand the speech[6] which he delivered to the convention, which, of course, is very unusual with him, unless it is a formal written address which he is to read to Congress or on some other formal occasion. This speech was fine and had a tremendous effect upon the convention, but I, who have learned to be so familiar with his speeches, do not by any manner of means rank it as one of his best. It seemed to me to have the mark of preparation on it. I remember it contained a passage on the flag which I thought was not at all in his best style, being, it seemed to me, too much on the level of the oratorical kind of campaign speech. But it is certain that his audience was not so sensitive to discriminate as was I. The speech was an immense hit. As he faced the audience his profile was brought in view of myself and those sitting near me, and I heard one of the "plain people" exclaim to his neighbor: "Gawd, look at his jaw!"

The first speech which Mr. Wilson made in the campaign was a flat failure—the only flat failure that I have ever been aware of in his career. It was made in a hall in Jersey City.[7] I went up on the afternoon train with him from Princeton. He was met at the station by a group of Democrats, who took him in charge. And I, of course, went to the hall alone. I got a seat in the back of the hall and watched with eager interest all that happened. When Mr. Wilson was introduced he was obviously much embarrassed. Perhaps his train of thought had forsaken him entirely. He hesitated, stammered; he started out on one line and abruptly switched to another. Twice I watched him bring in anecdotes that were not related to the thing he was saying, adopting the awkward ruse of some speakers of lugging in an unnecessary word into his speech, and then hanging the joke on that word—the particular word in this instance being *gall*. He went out of his way to say that he hoped that he hadn't more gall than another man. And he then added: "Speaking of gall reminds me" (which of all devices leads to the lugging in of a joke), and he then told a story about a Negro which had been told to him and me together the day before, which had absolutely nothing to do with the things he was discussing. I suffered in this speech, I am sure, far more than he did. But at the end he quite redeemed himself. He had been laboring and he had been not natural, but after he had spoken for about thirty minutes really ineffectively (and that seems a good deal to say of Woodrow Wilson, but it is true), he advanced to the edge of the platform, and with a simplicity that was almost childlike he said: "I have made my first political speech." It was so simply done, so naive, and so charming, that the audience rose back at him with a whoop. It was the first time he had touched them. They instinctively understood what he did not say, but what was implied, namely, "and I do not think my first political speech has been a very great success."

He was to make a second speech in another hall in a distant part of the city. I consulted my watch and found that I would have time to

16. Wilson on the campaign trail

hasten to that hall and hear a little of it before having to take my train back to Princeton—he was not returning to Princeton that night. He, of course, had been whisked across by automobile; I had to make my way by trolley car, and so when I arrived he was in the midst of his speech.[8] It was another Woodrow Wilson. He was absolutely a complete master of the situation. He had the audience in the hollow of his hand. They were laughing, applauding, listening to the serious passages with strained attention, and every now and then you would hear that delighted chuckle from someone, which meant that he had established a personal relationship between himself and his audience. All the clumsiness of the preceding speech was gone, and I think it may be safely said that he never made another failure.

The campaign that followed was beyond all doubt and question the most interesting campaign that Mr. Wilson had conducted—far more interesting than either of the presidential campaigns. I should be quite free to say this myself even if he did not agree to it. But he does agree. I remember that, after the election in 1916, he and Mrs. Edith Wilson and I were riding together in North Jersey, while he was still living at Shadow Lawn, and I said what I have just said here and he agreed heartily. Mrs. Wilson was surprised and said: "What do you mean by that?" And I volunteered and said: "I can tell you what I mean, and I wonder if the president will agree. In the New Jersey campaign for the governorship, he spoke in every county in the state, and in several counties more than once, and he had the feeling that he was addressing the whole people of the state in a series of connected speeches, each leading to the next, so that the result was that these speeches formed a connected whole in which there was one definite thesis, which was that under a democratic government the people themselves must be brought in direct contact with their own affairs; and the measures which he was proposing for his term as governor were simple means to a result to restore a government wrested from the people back to the people. And in explaining this theme he dealt with fundamental principles of self-government, so that the campaign was educational to an extraordinary degree, and probably more educational than any other active political campaign that has ever been in this country, whereas as candidate for president he has had merely to hit the high spots in far distant places, and there has been no connection between the speeches as in the New Jersey campaign." The president agreed that my analysis was correct.

I heard a great many of these speeches during the campaign and followed him wherever I could; and, by the way, it was at a meet-

17. Wilson and Joseph Patrick Tumulty, ca. 1913

ing in South Jersey that I first met Mr. Tumulty.[9] Mr. Wilson had told me after his return from one of his visits to North Jersey: "I met a most delightful young fellow that I want you to know; his name is Tumulty." I did not catch the name at first. Mr. Wilson said: "Just 'Tumult' with a 'y'!" He had gone on to speak of him as a charming fellow personally and one of the ardent young liberals of the Democratic party in New Jersey. At this meeting in South Jersey, I was with Mr. Wilson in the automobile and people were shaking hands with him in great numbers. Presently he called me by name and said: "Here is the man I want you to know." And I shook hands with Mr. Tumulty. We left Mr. Wilson in South Jersey and rode back on the train that night together, sitting, I remember, in a baggage car, and I first came in contact with this eager, ardent mind, and this devoted worshiper of Mr. Wilson. He could talk of nothing but Wilson, though several times I undertook to divert the conversation to other topics, but nothing else interested him.

The adaptation which Mr. Wilson made in his forensic style was very interesting. As professor and college president, he had been not academic in the offensive sense—he was never that—but distinctly classical in his form of address. As political speaker he developed a simplicity which, combined with his natural powers as a teacher and man given to exposition, made him extraordinarily persuasive. Occasionally the fiercer note would come into his speeches. I remember one occasion in the Taylor Opera House at Trenton when he had on his war paint and served notice that if the people of New Jersey did not want the sort of governor that he proposed to be they must not elect him.[10] He was explaining to them that in his conception the governor was not a rubber stamp, but that the governor was at the head of the government, that the governor did not sit back and wait for the legislature to hand him up laws to be signed or vetoed, but that the governor himself had a part in the devising of those laws, that he should advise what laws should be made and what laws should not be made, and use all the influence personally and constitutionally he could exert to lead the legislature to the making of laws; that he personally was responsible to the people for the fulfillment of the platform on which he was standing; and that if he was elected on that platform he was going to see to it that the principles advocated in that platform were enacted into law; that, in short, if he was elected governor, the people of New Jersey were going to have a very active governor. And he said: "Now, if you don't want that sort of governor, don't elect me; and you can't say I didn't give you fair notice."

But while the fighting quality was sufficient in his speeches to the people of New Jersey to know the sort of man they were putting into the gubernatorial chair, the general character of the speeches was that of persuasion, an extraordinary appeal to a reasonable approach to fundamental questions of self-government.

Mr. Wilson is very fond of telling of an episode that occurred in Paterson, New Jersey, when two men in the gallery on opposite sides of the house, each somewhat under the influence of liquor, insisted on carrying on a conversation while he was speaking and exchanging pleasantries and compliments with each other. As is so frequently the case, Mr. Wilson had to go to another hall as soon as he finished in this hall, and Dudley Field Malone[11] was the next speaker. Dudley arose with all his Irish in full heat. He expressed his opinion of the police regulations in a town that permitted the sort of thing to go on that had been just going on while the candidate for the highest office in the state was speaking; and he said that for his own part he did not propose to stand for it; that if the police did not keep order he would undertake to keep it himself, and if anybody had anything to say while he was talking, he (Malone) would make a personal matter of it and they would step outside and settle it in primitive fashion. The police got busy at once, rushing all over the house, stationing themselves at previous points of agitation, and the two previous conversationalists were either put out or subdued. Then Dudley began his speech. From an altogether new and unexpected quarter of the gallery an interruption occurred. A man arose unsteadily on his feet and with a very thick voice asked the privilege of asking a question. The police, under the inspiration of Dudley's previous remarks, started for the intruder to put him out, and there were cries over the house to put him out, but Dudley raised his hand and said: "No, don't put him out; let him ask his question. If it is a rational question, I will try to answer it. I have no objection to a man asking a question." The man in the gallery said: "As a citizen of the city of Paterson, New Jersey, and as a voter of the sovereign state of New Jersey, I should like to ask if the Honorable Rahway Wilson has been here this evening." Mr. Wilson still laughs as he reflects on the impression that he made on this voter of the sovereign state of New Jersey.

The platform on which Mr. Wilson stood, which was written by himself, and on which he so vigorously insisted throughout his campaign, was a brief platform containing only four planks: state control of public utilities, direct primaries, corrupt practices legislation, and workmen's compensation legislation. The interesting thing is that when Mr. Wilson was elected governor, he and the legislature went to work to have these various planks enacted into statutes one by one immediately. Platforms have so often in this country been a thing for the candidates to stand on and then be forgotten, but the promises in this platform to the people of New Jersey were kept absolutely.

One of the first things Mr. Wilson did was dramatic in the sense in which so much that he does is dramatic, that is to say, with no calculated appeal to the theatrical sense, but simply something done so abruptly, so conclusively, that it appeals to the dramatic instinct in us. When Mr. Wilson went to the capitol in Trenton, he found that there was a certain room there in which hitherto the real legislators from New Jersey had assembled. It was not the Senate chamber or the chamber of Representatives. It was a small room in which gathered the representatives of the railways and other large corporation interests. Many of these men were not themselves residents of New Jersey at all, but here they met and here they determined what laws would be beneficial to their corporations, and here they examined the members of the legislature who did their bidding. This was the real lawmaking power of New Jersey, and the members of the legislature elected by the people of New Jersey were simply the errand boys of this group in an upper chamber. Practically the first thing Mr. Wilson did when he reached the capitol as governor was to give orders that that room be locked and the key given to him, and that key he kept in his pocket as a sign and symbol that that branch of the New Jersey legislature had been adjourned for at least three years, that is to say, during the term of his governorship. There was nothing sensational about this. It was just his way of doing things. A more theatrical sort of person would have seen to it that it was all played up in the papers. Mr. Wilson just had the door locked and then demanded the physical key, which he kept with him.

The state of New Jersey has never furnished any gubernatorial mansion except the summer residence at Sea Girt, where the state militia gathers in the summer for encampment and maneuvers. The really beautiful house of the governor here is a frame building, which was the New Jersey House at the St. Louis Exposition, afterwards taken back to Sea Girt and made the governor's mansion.

The Wilsons spent their two summers of the governorship at Sea Girt very happily, the governor playing golf whenever he could get an opportunity, the girls having their friends down to visit them and riding horseback and automobiling about the pleasant country. There is a little anecdote of the Sea Girt life we ought not to allow to perish. The very small son of one of the newspaper correspondents constantly teased his mother for permission to go and call on the governor, which permission the mother never granted, quite naturally. One day at the bathing beach she missed the child, who had been in the surf with some of his little friends and with some older person to act as guardian. Though she could not find him there was no anxiety about his life, because he could not have been drowned without the knowledge of the many spectators around. The only

18. Wilson greeting well-wishers at Sea Girt, New Jersey, ca. 1911

19. Reviewing the New Jersey National Guard at Sea Girt, 1911

question was where on earth the little fellow had wandered to. She started up the road over the beach seeking him, and, meeting an acquaintance, she asked if anything had been seen of the child. "Yes," said this acquaintance, "I just saw him going into the Governor's House in his bathing suit." She hastened on to the house and sent in and had the little fellow brought out, his bathing suit still not entirely dry. After scolding him roundly, her natural curiosity prompted her to ask: "Well, did you see the governor after all?" He said, slowly: "Yes, I did see the governor, and the governor was nice to me. The governor kissed me, and I saw the governor's husband, too."

Of course, a frame house on the North Jersey shore is not adapted to winter residence, and so the governors of New Jersey plan their own winter residences and many of them continue to live in their home towns, going to Trenton daily for business, New Jersey being physically small enough to permit this mode of life. With Mr. Wilson it was, of course, particularly easy, as Princeton is only ten miles from Trenton. However, he had no home of his own. The house which he and Mrs. Wilson had built had long ago been sold and he had, of course, moved out of Prospect. So the first season they lived at the Princeton Inn, and in the autumn of 1911 they rented a cottage[12] recently built by an artist, Mr. Mann,[13] whose wife had died, and who therefore was ready to let this cottage. The income of the Wilsons was so comparatively modest that it is questionable whether or not they would have felt like renting even so small a house as this. But their very dear friends, the Misses Lucy and Mary Smith, of New Orleans,[14] who had spent the summer with them at Sea Girt (as, indeed, they had spent many summers previously with the Wilsons in one place or another), expressed willingness to bear their share of rent and housekeeping expenses if permitted to spend the winter at the North with the Wilsons. And so this arrangement was made. They were so intimate that the girls, and, indeed, Mr. Wilson himself, have always called them "Cousin Lucy" and "Cousin Mary."

Personally, I remember this as one of the happiest seasons of my whole life. I was constantly with the Wilsons, and there was no longer any anxiety about Princeton. I continued a member of the Princeton faculty but felt no responsibility for anything beyond the conduct of my own classes and the part I should play in shaping the affairs of the English Department. The policy of the university was no concern of mine. I belonged to the party that had been licked, and I was not a bit sore about it, neither was I in the least anxious to help the party in power to solve any of its difficulties. That was their affair, not mine. I was perfectly sure that my advice would neither be sought nor heeded if offered. So I was very happy in my work and in my relationships with the students and with the English Department and with my friends of the faculty, and, above all, with the family in the little cottage in Cleveland Lane. There were never better talkers in the world than Cousin Lucy and Cousin Mary. My sister found time to paint pictures again. In fact, one reason for taking Mr. Mann's cottage was that it was fitted with a large north exposure studio, which gave Mrs. Wilson the painting conditions that she needed. The girls were grown up and very happy with their friends. Jessie was in process of getting engaged to Frank Sayre,[15] though I was innocently quite unaware of the fact, for there were so many young men around Jessie that there was nothing to lead me to assume that Frank was a favorite. The governor was necessarily away from home a great deal, but whenever he did return he seemed happier than he had been in years. He was fighting, but he was fighting a winning fight, and he was fighting in the open, which is a very healthy sort of fighting. Talk of the presidency, of course, was growing more and more all the time, and undoubtedly he was giving very serious thought to it. It was in this interval that the acquaintanceship ripened into friendship began with Colonel House,[16] though, by the way, I never met Colonel House in the cottage in Cleveland Lane. He must have been there very little, indeed, if at all. I saw Mr. McAdoo there only once, and of course at that time there was no thought that he would be so closely identified with the family, nor was there any thought of it in the mind of the youngest daughter of the house.[17]

What was perfectly clear was that Mr. Wilson, both in his candidacy for the governorship and in his administration of governorship affairs, was attracting the attention of the whole country, and particularly young men with a vision of a better sort of politics. Young men, earnestly desiring that the people's liberties be made secure, were flocking to his standard. Mr. Wilson's enemies were equally active. The campaign of slanders against him was almost unbelievable. I have forgotten now what day of the week it was, but it was one day of the week, a Tuesday or a Wednesday, that we came to anticipate each week a fresh attack upon him in the newspapers. Each Tuesday (if it was a Tuesday) the papers blazed with some new sensation. Now it was the threat of an exposure of a letter which Mr. Cleveland had written, which was supposed to be very damaging to Mr. Wilson;

now it was the exposure of the fact that Mr. Wilson had applied to the Carnegie Fund for a pension on retiring from teaching; now it was the threat of the publication of a letter which Mr. Wilson had written very damaging to Mr. Bryan; and so it went. The Cleveland letter never appeared, but I assume it is altogether likely that Mr. Cleveland may have written things derogatory to Mr. Wilson. Certainly, in his latter years he was no friend of Mr. Wilson's. The exposure of the Carnegie pension business was planned to injure and it came as near injuring him as anything could, for it was a fact that Mr. Wilson, retiring from the presidency of Princeton on the uncertain enterprises of politics, and having made only such provision for his family as one with a limited professor's and college president's salary could make, had presented his application to the trustees of the Carnegie Fund for the usual pension for a retiring teacher. Certainly there was nothing dishonorable in that. The member of that board of trustees who exposed this application and who is perfectly well known to us,[18] and whose name I keep out of these notes only by the exertion of a strong act of the will, may take what satisfaction he can find in his contemptible conduct. He himself is a college professor, a liar, a hypocrite, and a snake.

The Bryan matter came near being very serious, but its ultimate result was only to destroy the person who had perpetrated the plot. Among the opponents of Wilson's Princeton reforms was Adrian Joline, a New York lawyer and something of a dabbler in literature, also a collector of autographs, a man who had held his head very high in the social and professional and club life of New York. Mr. Joline let the reporters understand that he had a letter which Mr. Wilson had written to him, which, if Mr. Bryan should ever see, would certainly end any chance of Mr. Bryan supporting Mr. Wilson's candidacy for the presidency of the United States. It was the biggest sensation of the hour. Subsequently, the letter was published with an explanation from Mr. Joline that he had kept the letter only for the sake of the signature. It was a brief note in answer, as I recall it, to a note from Mr. Joline, in which Mr. Wilson asked the question: "Is there nothing that can be done to knock Mr. Bryan into a cocked hat?" It had, of course, been written many years before. The time of the publication was ingeniously planned to fall just as Mr. Wilson was to have his first meeting with Mr. Bryan[19] in Washington at the Jackson Day dinner on January 8, 1912. The two men met. Mr. Wilson said: "Mr. Bryan, there is nothing I can say about this episode except that I am

20. Wilson and William Jennings Bryan, ca. 1913

very sorry." And Mr. Bryan said: "Governor, don't let that worry you. Of course, I always knew that you were not for me in my political campaigns, but certainly that is nothing to charge against you." Mr. Wilson said: "Mr. Bryan, all I can say is you are a great, big man." The two men shook hands heartily. Mr. Wilson made his notable address, which entirely captivated Mr. Bryan.[20] All who saw him say that he watched Mr. Wilson as if fascinated, drinking in all he had to say.

What happened at the Baltimore convention all the world knows. So the only person who was hurt by this episode of the letter was the only person who deserved to be hurt by it, namely, Mr. Joline himself. It was said that his humiliation was intense, for in club-land, whose opinion he so much esteemed, Mr. Joline began to be looked at askance, even by men who were unfriendly to Wilson, for it is rather a serious thing to give out private correspondence. It was said that in one of his clubs men were heard to whisper: "Hush, speak softly, Joline is coming," and that the phrase "to Joline" was coined to indicate dishonorable action. The humiliation of the proud man must have been intense, and I have assumed that Mr. Joline's death, which occurred not a great while afterward, was probably hastened by the humiliation of this experience. Indeed, it has been surmised that the Cleveland letter, which was so long about to appear and never did appear, was suppressed because of the Joline episode. Whoever the holder was of that famous letter did not care to get himself in the same kind of mess that poor Joline had got involved in.

Mr. Wilson was asked in October 1911 to go over to Trenton one Sunday afternoon and deliver a brief address at some religious convention; I don't remember what; it was not in a church but in a large hall.[21] He and Professor Henry Jones Ford[22] and I rode over together. Mr. Ford and I went into the gallery, Mr. Wilson went on the platform. Before he was to speak, a hymn was sung, a sentimental hymn, both in words and tune.[23] When Mr. Wilson rose to speak, he startled everybody by making the first part of his address a vigorous assault on the hymn that had just been sung, calling attention to the false and mawkish sentiment of the hymn and asking why people who really believed in religion should undertake to support it with things so meretricious as this hymn; and then, with great scorn in his voice, he quoted certain lines from it. The episode caused a tempest in a teapot. I remember when I went back to Princeton that afternoon, one of our friends, not of the college faculty, said: "It was very dangerous for the governor to say what he did this afternoon, because religious people take their hymns very seriously. His presidential boom is growing, and just some such little incident as that which occurred this afternoon can be used greatly to his damage. It is always a very dangerous thing to trade on people's religious prepossessions." In a way the man was correct in his predictions, for a good deal was said in the papers about Mr. Wilson's sarcastic reference to the hymn. But the episode had rather an odd sequel, and withal rather a pathetic one in the fact that the author of the hymn[24] read in the papers what Mr. Wilson had said and wrote to him saying that he himself realized that the hymn was unworthy.

It was always Mr. Wilson's lifelong habit, whether as professor, president of Princeton, or governor of New Jersey, when he returned from a journey to give his wife, the first thing, a full account of whatever had happened. One Sunday afternoon in the early winter of 1911 I went around to the little house in Cleveland Lane and found that Mr. Wilson had just recently returned from New York and was in the midst of recounting to his wife the circumstances of a dinner of the previous night at which Colonel Harvey and Colonel Henry Watterson were either hosts or guests, I do not remember which.[25] Mr. Wilson had completed the first part of his narrative when I entered, but fortunately I reached the room in time to hear what turned out to be quite the first important thing he had to report about that dinner. Said he: "Colonel Harvey embarrassed me very much last night by a question he asked me. You know, he is a good fellow." And when he said this, he turned his look on me with distinct accusation in his eyes, remembering the opinion I had formed of the untrustworthiness of Colonel Harvey several years before; and when the governor said "he is a good fellow," he meant this for a distinct rebuke to me. He said: "As we were leaving the dining room last night, Colonel Harvey slipped his arm in mine and said: 'Governor, there is a question I want to ask you, to which I want your very frank answer.'" The governor asked what the question was. "I want to know whether or not you find the support of *Harper's Weekly* in any way embarrassing to your candidacy." The governor said: "I very much wish you would not ask me that question, because the answer to it embarrasses me severely. Some of my friends have told me that the support of *Harper's Weekly* is not doing me any good in the West, but I am very sorry you compel me to tell you this." Colonel Harvey said: "I feared you might feel that way about it, and we shall have to soft pedal." That was the whole conversation literally as reported by Mr. Wilson the day after the dinner. And he was as unconscious as a child unborn that any serious significance be attached to it. So unconscious was he that when I asked him a little while later why it was that his name had been taken down from the top of the editorial page of *Harper's Weekly*, he was entirely mystified. I asked if that could have any reference to the conversation between himself and Colonel Harvey. He did not know what to answer; he could simply say that he had not assumed that anything of this sort was to occur as a sequel. Now that is the famous Harvey episode, of which so much has been made, of the ingratitude of Wilson, represented as storming in upon Harvey and insisting that Harvey must immediately cease his advocacy of Wilson, and so on and so on. It was as deliberate a frameup as was ever concocted. Harvey and his friends had come to see that it was not going to be possible to manage Wilson, that he was not going to serve their interests in any way, and they concluded they wanted to shake him, and, if possible, defeat him. I myself have seen letters written to editors of southern papers by editors about other editors, and the chances of drawing them into the plot to defeat Wilson—all emanating from Harvey and from Colonel Watterson, unless we are to assume that Colonel Watterson himself was a dupe in the master hands of Harvey.[26]

The witty Lady Mary Wortly Montague, referring to another Harvey, the litterateur, a philosopher of the 18th century, coined the famous phrase that "humanity is divided into men and women and Harveys." Aptly does the famous witticism apply to the later bearer of the name. Colonel George Harvey is in a class absolutely by himself. He is not to be explained by any of the ordinary principles by which we explain other men. Whether he is just a supreme humorist, to whom all life is one huge joke, and who loves the excitement of playing many different parts in quick succession, I cannot undertake to say. For him personally, I have no touch of that bitterness which I have for the cap-and-gown scoundrel who tried to injure Wilson by exposing the Carnegie pension business. There is in me no trace of either anger or contempt for Colonel Harvey. There is just wonder, just as I would marvel at some mystery of nature that is beyond my comprehension. And I am inclined to think that President Wilson himself has somewhat the same feeling about him.

I shall never forget how on the Monday night preceding the election in 1912 in the little family group in the library in the studio in Cleveland Lane, Governor Wilson said: "I want to read a letter that I have received from Colonel Harvey."[27] He then read one of the most beautiful letters that I have ever read or ever heard read. It began easily, "Dear Governor," and it went on to say that he would be very busy on the morrow getting his paper to press, but that the result of the election was a foregone conclusion, that Mr. Wilson was already overwhelmingly elected president of the United States. He then went on briefly but in exquisite phraseology to extend the writer's hearty congratulations and hopes for future success and happiness. There was no reference to the past; no reference to the future; no indication that he was even conscious that he had been fighting the man to whom he had been writing this letter with all the bitterness of politics and with much of the unscrupulousness of politics; no suggestion that he himself would expect to play any part in Mr. Wilson's future administration. It is inconceivable that so shrewd a man as Colonel Harvey could have assumed that it was possible, the past being what it was, that he could have any favors in the way of appointments from President Wilson. I cannot for a moment believe that that was his motive in writing that letter. It would shock all my sense of the dramatic; it would spoil the whole picture of a serene, unconscioned, phenomenoned Harvey. It is just one of those mysteries that pleases the imagination by baffling it.

The night of the election[28] was, of course, spent in the little house in Cleveland Lane. A great deal was written in the newspapers about what took place—none of it that I ever saw anywhere near the truth. And yet the correspondents could have had the truth, for they were under the roof and could see exactly what was going on. But it is just one more example to my mind that our American journalism is so vitiated by the cheaper form of sentimentalism of what is called "heart interest," sometimes "heart throbs," that newspaper reporters simply cannot write about these simple domestic things in a simple and unaffected way. Except for the fact that the rear room, the study, was occupied by a telegraph ticker, newspaper correspondents, and a few politicians, the scenes in the house were just what they might have been any evening in the home of Professor Woodrow Wilson when he was spending a quiet evening with his family and a few friends were dropping in. Mrs. Wilson and the girls and Helen Bones, who had already joined the family, and I sat around the fireplace, while a few neighbors, among them I remember Mr. and Mrs. Capps, dropped in. Mr. Wilson sat at a little table to one side, occasionally joining in the conversation, at times reading from a book (I do not remember now what the book was—I wish I did); and every now and then looking up to read some figures which were shown him by a newspaperman or politician, who would step in from an adjoining room with new election items. It was impossible that anything could have been quiet. I remember there were very sensational, in the sense of very sentimental, accounts of what he and Mrs. Wilson did when the election was assured. One thing which Mrs. Wilson did was a very simple thing, which I suppose she always did in the great crises and supreme moments of that remarkable career. He had happened to be standing at a time when some figures were brought to him that left the issue no longer any shadow of doubt. She just walked up to him, put one hand on either shoulder, and without saying a word raised her face to his, and he bent over and kissed her quietly. And that was all there was that was dramatic on that eventful evening. I remember Mrs. Wilson herself afterward referring to the ridiculous stories that were published in the papers, laughing, and saying to one of the neighbors: "You know, of course, the fact is that life itself is not very dramatic."

A curious incident occurred in connection with the telegram of congratulation from Colonel Roosevelt. By ten o'clock in the evening, telegrams began to arrive, including one from Mr. Taft, but the Roosevelt telegram appeared merely as a statement to the effect that "you have been chosen by the American people as their president." That was the substance of it—nothing added. Mr. Wilson fingered the telegram thoughtfully and said: "There is no reply that I can make to this, for he simply made a statement of fact. I shall have to leave it unanswered." The singular thing was that the latter half of the message had been omitted in transcription by some curious accident. The next day, when I asked the governor what he had done about the Roosevelt telegram, he said the rest of the telegram had arrived, that it was congratulatory, and that he had replied in kind. But it is singular that this telegram of all others should have been garbled in transmission.

I have always supposed that one reason why Colonel Roosevelt hated Mr. Wilson with such violence and peculiar ferocity was that he was never able to sting Mr. Wilson into making any replies to his attacks upon him. Any tactics of this sort were just the tactics that would infuriate a man of Roosevelt's temperament. He was accustomed to rough-and-tumble fighting, not to being ignored, and Mr. Wilson's plan of going through his campaign blandly ignoring everything that Roosevelt said, discussing principles and never dealing in personalities at all, undoubtedly reduced Roosevelt to a stage of frenzy. When Roosevelt was shot and had to retire from the campaign, Mr. Wilson one evening came into the library in the cottage in Cleveland Lane and said that he had been conferring with some of his advisers and had decided to end his own campaign, for, he said, "Roosevelt lying on his bed will issue every kind of ferocious statement, and it is better just to take the attitude that this episode of the shooting ends the active campaign." I do not remember now just exactly what speeches Mr. Wilson made subsequently, but it will be recalled that the active campaign did practically cease, he issuing a statement in very courteous terms to the effect that he did not care

21. Theodore Roosevelt, ca. 1912

to continue actively campaigning the country while one of his opponents was lying low on a bed of illness. It was a fine stroke of politics.

Temperamentally, of course, the two men were as different as it is
possible for men to be, and yet there was a time when Mr. Wilson
had a rather warm admiration for Roosevelt's qualities—never a time
I fancy when he trusted his judgment; but when Roosevelt first became president through the death of Mr. McKinley, Mr. Wilson was
inclined to believe that he would be a fairly good president. I remember distinctly a conversation with him on the subject. I myself was
always irreconcilably opposed to Roosevelt, heartily disliking everything he was and everything he represented, and I was in a very pessimistic frame of mind when the accident of death brought him into

the chief magistracy. I was expressing myself in very dolorous terms, and Mr. Wilson laughed and said he thought my fears were ungrounded and that he anticipated a fairly good administration from Roosevelt, adding that he took comfort in the thought that John Hay was in the Department of State, as he believed that Hay would exercise a restraining influence upon Roosevelt. At that time Mr. Wilson undoubtedly held the statesmanship of Hay in high regard, though I have reason to believe that since he has come into the presidency himself and has uncovered Hay's tracks, he no longer esteems him very highly as a statesman. What this is founded upon I do not know, but it is a matter of "state secrets," and it is quite evident from things I have heard dropped in conversation between President Wilson and Colonel House that some of the things Mr. Hay did as secretary of state have left serious embarrassments for his successors.

The only time I ever met President Roosevelt personally was when he was a guest of Woodrow Wilson, then president of Princeton University. It was the occasion of the Army-Navy football game in Princeton in the autumn of 1905. Though I was not to be a guest at the formal luncheon, Mr. Wilson asked me to come in and meet President Roosevelt, and I remember distinctly he said heartily: "He is a good fellow." The luncheon party was described to me by all of the family, and it was a very genial, jolly affair, though there occurred one little incident extremely embarrassing to Mr. Wilson. It seems funny now that he who now occupies the presidency himself should have made a serious "break" in etiquette, and it is the more curious that this should have happened when he had taken special advice from Mrs. Cleveland herself as to procedure. He knew, of course, that Colonel Roosevelt should lead Mrs. Wilson into the luncheon room and that he should lead Mrs. Roosevelt, but he was not clear as to in what part of the procession he and Mrs. Roosevelt should walk. Mrs. Cleveland told him that President Roosevelt and Mrs. Wilson would, of course, go in first; then the other guests, and Mr. Wilson and Mrs. Roosevelt would bring up the rear. When luncheon was announced, the president and Mrs. Wilson immediately walked arm in arm to the dining room. Mr. Wilson offered his arm to Mrs. Roosevelt and there they stood, and all the other guests stood. There was obvious embarrassment, but Mr. Wilson was not as quick as he usually is, and though aware that Mrs. Roosevelt was uncomfortable, he did not know what was the matter until one of the other guests, a lady of the presidential party, fluttered up to him excitedly and said: "Mr. Wil-

22. Wilson delivering his acceptance speech, Sea Girt, New Jersey, 1912

son, none of us can move until you and Mrs. Roosevelt pass in to the dining room." I judge that the formal etiquette in this matter must have changed between President Cleveland's administration and President Roosevelt's.

The two men never came very much into contact with each other, though, by the way, I recall at this moment that in the summer of 1901 Colonel Roosevelt, then vice president, invited Mr. Wilson, then Professor Wilson, to his Long Island home to talk with him.[29] I remember I at the time was inclined to be rather cynical about this, thinking that Mr. Roosevelt was not so much interested in getting Mr. Wilson's views on the state of the nation as he was interested in enlisting men of the Wilson type in the candidacy of Theodore Roosevelt for the presidency, which was already beginning to figure pretty conspicuously in the public press.

The only other personal touch as between Roosevelt and Wilson that I recall was a letter from Cleveland Dodge, who was a schoolmate of Roosevelt's and a college classmate of Wilson's, and who wrote Wilson after he was president of the university and while Roosevelt was president of the United States, that he had been visiting President Roosevelt in Washington and that President Roosevelt was rather concerned about some public criticism that President Wilson was reported to have made of the administration.[30]

The two men were certainly quite incompatible in temperament, Roosevelt being noisy, Wilson quiet; Roosevelt sensational, Wilson temperamentally opposed to anything that is sensational. What to this day many of our fellow countrymen do not seem to realize is that Wilson is an immeasurably stronger man than Roosevelt ever was. Roosevelt was always making verbal onslaughts on big business, the special interests, and so on, but the men who conducted those interests came to realize that his bark was much worse than his bite. One of the Wall Street magnates once remarked of Roosevelt: "He is troublesome but not a menace." Whereas, ever since Wilson became known to them, they have realized that he is really dangerous to their plans, because he does a great deal more than he threatens to do. The real fact is that, with all of Roosevelt's noisy energy, he was in no sense so much the man of action as is Wilson himself, who, when he makes his decisions, proceeds to put them into execution without fear or favor.

Just as Mr. Wilson was inclined to take a favorable view of Mr. Roosevelt at the outset of his presidential administration, so he was inclined to take a favorable view of Mr. Taft at the outset of his administration. It was the famous Winona speech of Mr. Taft[31] which led Mr. Wilson to the definite conclusion that Mr. Taft was going to be too good natured to be an effective president. As soon as he read that speech, Mr. Wilson put his finger on what I suppose all the country subsequently came to realize was the weakness of Mr. Taft— that out of sheer good nature and party loyalty he would endorse a party action which in his own individual mind he could not approve. I have heard Mr. Wilson many times quote the witty saying that Mr. Taft was a large body completely surrounded by men who knew exactly what they wanted.

While speaking of these national figures it occurs to me that I might add something to what I have already said about Mr. Bryan and the president in these notes. Only a few days ago a man was asking me why President Wilson selected for his cabinet the men whom he did select. The man who asked this question is a student of American history,[32] and he explained that what he meant by the question was this, that there are two different types of cabinets—that which is made up largely of the president's personal advisers, and that which is made up largely of good executive heads of the various departments. Said this man: "It is quite clear that Mr. Wilson selected his cabinet on the second principle of providing heads of departments rather than personal advisers." And he asked me if I recalled anything about the discussions concerning appointments to the cabinet in the interval between the election in November 1912 and the inauguration in the following March. I replied that it was in this matter of the selection of the cabinet that I came first to realize that Mr. Wilson in the presidency was going to be, and probably necessarily must be, more secretive than he had ever been as president of Princeton, or even as governor of New Jersey. Both as president of Princeton and governor of New Jersey, he had talked quite freely in the family circle about policies and personalities, but he was singularly reticent concerning the men whom he intended to invite to hold cabinet portfolios. Several times in the library of the cottage in Princeton I have heard visitors question about this, that, and the other man as possible cabinet material, but he never gave the slightest intimation of how he regarded their suggestions or objections, or, indeed, anything they said. He would draw them out freely, but he himself maintained a sphinxlike silence concerning his intentions. It was rather assumed by everybody that Mr. Bryan must necessarily be offered a portfolio, and probably that of secretary of state. The nearest thing to a commitment that I ever heard from Mr. Wilson in conversation was some general statement that, of course, the people would expect Mr. Bryan to have a conspicuous place in the administration, and when he said that, he did not indicate that he had any special enthusiasm personally for the appointment of Mr. Bryan as secretary of state. Probably at the time he did not think that Mr. Bryan was specially fitted for this particular office. As all the world knows, Mr. Bryan was offered this portfolio and accepted it.

The first time I ever met Mr. Bryan was in the White House after the inauguration period, when I was merely introduced to him and exchanged the ordinary courtesies. A few weeks later I was on a train going to Chicago to attend a Princeton alumni dinner, and, when the train stopped at some station on the way, I was facing the platform getting a breath of fresh air, and I heard a newspaperman ask one of the railroad men which car William Jennings Bryan was in. Learning that Mr. Bryan was on the train, I did what I perhaps had never done before and don't believe have ever done it since in the case of a public man—I went up to him and reintroduced myself as Mrs. Wilson's brother. He was most cordial and asked me to sit down. I hesitated to do that and returned to my own car. A little later he sent his private secretary in to say that he would be very glad to have me come in and talk with him. Possibly I was very punctilious, but, at any rate, I told the secretary that I very much appreciated the invitation but that I knew Mr. Bryan was a very busy man and I did not like to intrude; that as a matter of fact I had some work which I myself must do and was at that time engaged upon. The secretary came back a little later to say that Mr. Bryan invited me to join him at lunch later in the dining car. This invitation I accepted, and we not only had lunch together but sat at the table for two or three hours after lunch until the train reached Chicago. The impression which I gathered of Mr. Bryan was not only favorable, it was enthusiastic. He was on his way to California to try to persuade the California people to take a more liberal attitude of the Japanese and Chinese.[33] The frankness with which he talked about the whole question was very refreshing. It was as if there were no secrets in the matter; that this was a common concern of the people at large—first of the California people themselves and afterward of the people of the United States. He said—and I remember his actual words—"Though it is not hard to understand how the California people feel about this matter, I feel sure that when they understand what it is the president has in mind and the reasons for the proposals which he makes, they will take a more liberal view of this question." "What the president thinks" was the keynote of all that Mr. Bryan said during those several hours of talk.

I came to realize that in the few weeks in which he had been in personal association with Mr. Wilson, he had come to have for Mr. Wilson not only a great admiration but a great affection; and I made the generalization that day, from which I have never departed, that Mr. Bryan saw in President Wilson a man who had intellectual powers superior to his own, opportunities of training greater than his own, and was able better than he was himself to put into execution the things which he (Mr. Bryan) had been fighting for for twenty years. Here was a man (Wilson) who had the same instinctive feelings about the liberties of the people which Mr. Bryan himself had and who, added to that, had an executive power which Mr. Bryan seemed conscious that he had not. I came to the conclusion then, and from that conclusion I have never swerved, that whatever might be the limitations of Mr. Bryan, he had one of the greatest qualities that a man can have, which, by the way, is unfortunately one of the rarest qualities, namely, magnanimity. For twenty years he had been the leader of the Democratic party, and now he stepped aside to give full recognition to the leadership of Woodrow Wilson. Other men might have done this resignedly, but Bryan did it joyously. That is the great difference. Certainly to Bryan, the cause of the people meant more than his own personal fortunes, and he was not only generously, he was gladly willing to entrust that leadership to another, when he believed that other was fitter than himself to conduct that leadership.

So enthusiastic was I about the impression I got from Mr. Bryan's personal attitude toward the president that the first thing I did when I reached the University Club in Chicago, where I was staying, was to sit down and write a letter to a member of the family telling about the meeting and saying that I could only hope that the friendship and affection of Mr. Bryan were reciprocated by the president. I was in Washington shortly after and found that what I hoped had been fulfilled; that the two men were not only getting on well together, but that they were the closest kind of friends, and that into their friendship had not only entered admiration but actual affection.

The following summer I was in California and heard Secretary Lane[34] talk to a group of intimates at a little San Francisco club, of which he was a member. A most admirable talk it was, by the way—a talk in which he portrayed the president and the various members of the cabinet with the skill of a natural born and trained literary man which he (Secretary Lane) is; and he said, after having described the president with a felicity and insight that astonished me, seeing how comparatively brief a time he had been associated with the president, after describing him: "The first member of the cabinet sitting next to him at the cabinet table is Mr. Bryan, and I can tell you that these two men are so close together that they almost hold hands during cabinet meetings." He went on with great enthusiasm to portray the affectionate relationship which existed between the two.

In some of my visits to the White House during the first two years of the administration, I had many evidences of the personal affection which Mr. Wilson had for Mr. Bryan. He resented bitterly the public attacks on Mr. Bryan and said that the public was exceedingly unjust to him in regard to his Chatauqua lectures. He said that Mr. Bryan had talked to him very confidentially and freely about his financial situation; that he had been able to lay by a fairly comfortable sum of money, but that it was invested in safe securities which paid a very low rate of interest, and that it was costing Mr. Bryan about $30,000 to be secretary of state, and that the salary of a cabinet officer, which is $12,000, in no way enabled him to meet his expenses. Mr. Wilson said that there was no man in Washington who worked harder at his public task than Mr. Bryan did; that his Chatauqua engagements in no way infringed upon his public duties; that Mr. Bryan was a man who did not take his vacations in the ordinary way of out-of-door sports, did not care for that sort of thing; and that there was no reason in the world why Mr. Bryan should not be permitted to spend his vacations in lecturing at Chatauquas according to his custom of years' standing. Mr. Wilson did not say, though I think perhaps he would have assented to this addition, namely, that the so-called lowering of the dignity of the office by Mr. Bryan giving Chatauqua lectures was purely a relative matter dependent upon the man who delivered the lectures. Mr. Bryan was a professional Chatauqua lecturer, and in his case it was not at all as if President Wilson himself had been a cabinet officer and had suddenly turned into a Chatauqua lecturer. That might have seemed like capitalizing the office for the purpose of making an income. But Mr. Bryan was doing as secretary of state precisely what he had been doing for a number of years.

I think it was during the second summer of the administration that a New York newspaper sent a representative to offer Mr. Bryan a sum of money if he would not lecture on the Chatauqua platform, the point of the offer being that if Mr. Bryan needed this money, in addition to his salary as cabinet officer, the New York newspaper was quite willing to provide that money itself and thereby preserve the dignity of the secretaryship of state in contact with the Chatauqua circuit.[35] During that summer, the family being in New Hampshire at a summer cottage, President Wilson had constantly at the luncheon table with him Mr. Tumulty and Mr. Dudley Malone, who was then attached to the Department of State. One day, when I was present at the lunch table and there were no others except the president, Mr. Tumulty, and Mr. Malone, Mr. Tumulty turned to Malone and said: "Dudley, what did Mr. Bryan do when that newspaper correspondent offered him that money not to lecture?" Mr. Malone replied, with a rather sour countenance: "He didn't do anything; he just looked hurt and turned around and walked away." These two hotheaded young statesmen began to express their opinion about what Mr. Bryan ought to have done, how he ought to have kicked the fellow out of the office, have him thrown bodily down the stairs of the building, etc., etc. After they had talked this way for some time, President Wilson, who had been taking no part in the conversation, looked up from his place and said—and the saying deserves to be perpetuated, for it was a memorable one: "Boys, the trouble with Mr. Bryan is that he is a Christian." You stop to analyze; that is a very interesting saying, and that is the point of the whole thing: Mr. Bryan is a Christian. He has dared to try to reply to the ordinary rough-and-tumble affairs of the world, just as it is, the principles of Christianity, in which he so profoundly believes. That phrase "the trouble" is not only amusing; it furnishes matter for thought.

One might carry the analysis a little bit further than this, and it seems to me that this is perhaps the root of it: Mr. Bryan has spent practically all of his life in public affairs. Mr. Wilson had spent most of his life in what people assume is the sheltered, aloof environment of a university. And yet the practical man is Mr. Wilson; the theoretical man is Mr. Bryan. Mr. Wilson is the man who has dealt with things as they are; Mr. Bryan is the man who has tried to deal with things as he feels they ought to be. Both of these men are idealists, but I should say that Mr. Wilson's idealism is what mariners might call "corrected" idealism—corrected by application to the facts of the world as it is, whereas Mr. Bryan's idealism has received very little correction from the facts. And yet I am free to say that the very ineffectuality of the man makes him seem to me endearing.

I do not mean to say by all this that I do not think that Mr. Bryan is a politician. He is. And he has proved himself more than once a very adroit politician. He knows how to manipulate a convention. But when it comes to dealing with the practical principles of politics that lead to legislation and executive action, then he is the rather ineffectual idealist.

There seems to be no bitterness in the man ever. I remember how he talked about Champ Clark[36] in the same conversation which I had on the train going to Chicago back in the spring of 1913. He said: "Champ hates me terribly,[37] but I don't wonder at that; he has said much worse things about me than I have ever said about him, but the point is that he lost what he wanted at the convention, and I got what I wanted, and so it is very much easier for me to forgive him than it is for him to forgive me." I take it that was a typical Bryan attitude—broadminded and magnanimous.

23. Champ Clark, ca. 1912

In a speech which Mr. Wilson made to his fellow citizens of Princeton after his election to the presidency, he remarked that he had never been in the White House and he did not know how he was going to relish it.[38] His statement that he had never been in the White House caused curious laughs to ripple through the outdoor audience. He was speaking in front of the modest little cottage. Between that speech and the third of March, when he came to Washington, I heard more or less talk about arrangements for living in the White House. President Taft acted with his usual kindliness and consideration when he wrote a letter with his own hand,[39] not dictated, to Mrs. Wilson suggesting that she and Mr. Wilson pay him and Mrs. Taft a visit in the White House, as they would probably want to learn the details of the menage. This invitation, written in a beautiful and sincere spirit, was much appreciated by Mr. and Mrs. Wilson, but it did not seem possible to accept it. Then Mr. Taft wrote a second letter to Mrs. Wilson again in his own hand,[40] in which he described in considerable detail the arrangement of rooms in the White House. He told Mrs. Wilson that there was a congressional appropriation for fitting the upper story into rooms but that the actual work had not been done. I think I remember he stated that the White House did not have such a very great number of rooms and that the addition of the rooms in the top story would naturally add very much to their convenience.

All this is merely prefatory to saying that Mr. and Mrs. Wilson did not come to Washington until the third of March. I came with them. We were on a special train, which ran direct from Princeton to Washington. I remember it was said that it was not running on a schedule but would proceed as fast as was consistent with safety.

There were Mr. and Mrs. Wilson, the three girls, Miss Bones,[41] and myself in the immediate party which boarded the train at Princeton, but we were joined by Mrs. Howe and Mrs. Annie Cothran and her baby, and, I think, the two Howe boys—Wilson and George,[42] at West Philadelphia. The baby Josephine was the most conspicuous member of the company. She was a child in arms and seemed to think that the crowds at the railway station along the route were there for her special reception. The president was reading a good part of the journey, and as the train made no stops at the stations he made no special effort to acknowledge the crowds. But little Josephine, in her nurse's arms at the windows, was waving her salutes to them all. It was simply an ordinary railway journey. We arrived at the Union Sta-

24. President Taft greets Wilson at the White House, March 4, 1913

tion and proceeded to the president's room at the station, where there were greetings from officials, but who I do not remember, as I was in the background of the group. And then we proceeded to the Shoreham Hotel. The lobby was crowded. One of the first people that I met was Captain Bill McDonald from Texas, now United States marshal, who had taken on an extraordinary degree of flesh in the few months since he had been in Princeton, and who was the happiest man, I think, that I met in Washington during the two days.

That night Mr. John A. Wilson[43] gave a dinner to the Wilson clan but was good enough to include Mrs. Wilson's relatives among his invited guests, and so I was there. The president was rather quiet during the dinner and was obviously concerned with matters of state. He had a few interviews in the course of the evening, and then in the latter part of the evening he went to a Princeton reunion in some hall, but where I do not know.[44] I went myself but was driven there and don't know where the group was. I met there a great many friends, of course, and everybody seemed genuinely enthusiastic over the idea that a Princeton man was stepping into the presidency, though, of course, there must have been a great many of the alumni who had been among Mr. Wilson's enemies in the Princeton difficulties. His speech was brief but exceedingly genial, with no suggestion or reference to any of the questions that had divided the Princeton constituency. On the contrary, he told the assembled company that he would find many things strange in Washington, but with this group he felt no strangeness, but here he felt he was among old friends who understood him. He stressed that idea of "being understood" pretty hard in his speech, giving the impression that he felt that all the Princeton men who were with him or not at least knew him and would not have to be finding out what manner of man he was, as with the general public; and he seemed to take great satisfaction in the thought that there was this nucleus in Washington who would need little explanation of the character, personality, and motives of the new president.

Beyond that I remember nothing until the next day, except the good-night salutations in the hall at the Shoreham when we adjourned fairly early to our various bedrooms, nor do I remember anything about the next morning until we actually went to the Capitol. Mr. Wilson's first appearance was in the Senate chamber, where the oath of office was administered. Dr. Grayson, in the note which he has just dictated, spoke of the self-possession of the president as Dr. Grayson's own first impression of him when he met him the preceding afternoon in Washington. I who had known him all these years had that same paramount impression of his composure, as he and President Taft entered the Senate chamber that day. There was a naturalness and quiet confidence about him—an air as if all this was nothing at all unusual, as if he had been born to this very thing, and I could not help wondering at it, intimately though I knew him, that as he was stepping into this, the greatest office in the land and one of the greatest in the world, there was no expression of elation or embarrassment—he was just as natural as he would have been before a Princeton class. I viewed the scene from the gallery, where I was sitting with Mrs. House,[45] and I got my first sight of Speaker Champ Clark, and I was rather impressed with the dignity and also with the touch of sadness in the man. It was obvious that he was feeling the personal significance of the occasion on himself not being the center of the scene.

We then went to the east front of the Capitol and Mr. Wilson delivered his inaugural address, in which there occurred the famous phrase, since so frequently quoted, concerning "forward-looking men," whom he summoned to his side.[46] The presidential party were, of course, in the front seats among the audience, not on the rather high platform from which the president spoke. The result of this was that we got none too good a view of him. My own seat was on the end near to the Capitol building, so that I really could not see his full face as he spoke. I am speaking of these things now simply because of a characteristic but really unconscious performance of Mrs. Wilson's. Although she was naturally more advantageously seated than I was, still she could not hear everything he was saying or see his face clearly from her seat, and so, with absolute obliviousness to the fact that doubtless many of the people were watching the wife of the new president, she climbed up on a bench so that she could get her face nearly on a level with the platform, and from that vantage point both hear and see better than when she kept her seat. In other words, Mrs. Wilson as an auditor was as lacking in self-consciousness as the president himself had been in the Senate chamber.

After the inauguration exercises we made our way to the White House luncheon, which was a standup affair. I personally arrived a little late, and Mr. Taft was just leaving the dining room as I entered. Though he was taking his final departure from the White House, he wore his usual genial smile.

Speaking of Mr. Taft's departure reminds me of a ridiculous incident, which none of us knew about until a few days later. Mrs. Wilson's cousins, Miss Mary Hoyt and Miss Florence Hoyt,[47] are teachers in the Bryn Mawr School in Baltimore. Miss Florence Hoyt is a cripple, her leg having been amputated many years ago. This fact has to do with the story which I am about to relate. Several days after the inauguration, we were at the White House at a small family luncheon, Florence being among those present. Quite simply she asked the question: "Is there any marking on the White House automobiles by which the public knows that they are from the White House?" She was told, "Yes, it is the seal of the United States." She said: "That explains the deference shown to Mary and me when we rode to the station after the inauguration luncheon." And then she recited the following story, apparently not fully conscious herself of the absurd contrast each had presented. She and her sister had been at the Capitol at the inauguration exercises. By the custom of the nation, the entering president has no authority over any of the White House possessions or means of transportation until he has actually been inaugurated president; in other words, up to twelve o'clock that day all the automobiles belonging to the White House were under the authority of Mr. Taft; at twelve o'clock they passed from Mr. Taft's authority to Mr. Wilson's. Mr. Wilson had, therefore, no convenient means of providing vehicles and transportation for his relatives and friends. They who were invited to the White House had to get there the best way they could, and, though my memory is vague, I seem to recall that I rode down on a streetcar. Miss Florence Hoyt, being lame, and the crowd being great, her sister said that it would be necessary for them to find some other conveyance than the streetcar, for all automobiles and hacks were in requisition. So they found, drawn up by a curb near the Capitol, an excessively rickety old one-horse wagon, with an emaciated quadruped hitched to it, and an old Negro vendor of chestnuts in charge. The Hoyt ladies asked him if he could take them to the White House. He said he would be delighted to do so, so he took his stuff out of the wagon, spread some gunny sacks on the floor, and the two Misses Hoyt climbed into the wagon and rode into the White House. It was their intention to get out a block or two away and walk the rest of the distance, but their Negro driver had gotten so thoroughly interested in the situation that he insisted on taking them the whole way. Clearly there must have been less guarding of the gates at that time, because this vehicle was allowed to drive to the entrance to the White House. As they drove in, they met Mr. Taft driving out in one of the automobiles. This is the way they arrived. They departed in one of the automobiles, with policeman and lackeys waving the crowd away to make passage for them. This is one of the contrasts of life that the Misses Hoyt encountered at the inauguration.

It was after luncheon that we all adjourned to the reviewing stand in front of the White House and watched the inaugural parade. It is the only inaugural parade that I have ever seen, and so I do not know whether it was a fair sample, but certainly the one thing that stands out in memory, not only of myself but of many of my friends, was the amazing collection of passé horses that had been pressed into use. If the old fellow who drove the Hoyt girls up to the White House behind his starving beast had put his own horse into the military procession, it would have been in perfect keeping with most of the horse

25. Inaugural procession, March 4, 1913

flesh that we saw pass the reviewing stand that day. Some of the animals looked as if they would drop in their tracks. The one most striking contrast was that of Governor Mann[48] of Virginia, mounted on one of the most magnificent animals I ever saw. The most picturesque figure in the procession, not excepting Governor Mann, was Governor Sulzer.[49] I will never forget the jaunty figure and his elaborate pose as he went down the avenue. Of course, one saw many interesting sights, not the least being that of Murphy[50] and the Tammany crowd as they paraded in front of the stand. They, of course, are familiar with victory and defeat in politics, and they know how to play the game. It was very noticeable that neither Mr. Murphy nor his immediate lieutenants saw the grandstand as they passed. They were marching—and that was all!

That evening was to me personally a very thrilling evening, simply with the feeling that I was actually in the White House face to face with the actual possessions of many of the former presidents, and, southern though I am, nothing interested me quite so much as the reminiscences of Lincoln all through the house. Mr. Wilson and I spent perhaps half an hour examining the books in the study. It was a typical Wilson evening, which is to say a thoroughly domestic evening, with a few of the more intimate friends, and almost nothing of a political atmosphere about it. I remember particularly how Dr. Harry Garfield[51] and I sat on the rear veranda, or, what Vice President Thomas R. Marshall called the "back porch," when he said he was going out on the "back porch" and smoke his cigar. Dr. Garfield and I sat on this back porch for a couple of hours and he told me many interesting stories about his own recollections of it when it was his father's home. He gave me the only account given me, though I had been closely associated with him at Princeton, of the day his father was shot. He told me how he himself reached the station in time to take his father's head in his arms and hold it while they awaited the arrival of the doctors.

Mr. Wilson in August 1914
Sketches the League of Nations Idea.[52]

The President in August 1914 sketched not once but several times, and, of course, in different language, the situation and the program which has now been realized in the principles of the League of Nations.

As I reflect on these various conversations, I realize that there is only one of them which stands out with perfect clearness in my memory. And that is a conversation which he had in his study with me alone one morning early in August 1914, just after our entire party had returned from the funeral in Georgia.[53] Subsequent to this talk he sketched in fuller detail his ideas, once in a conversation with Dr. Grayson and myself, and again one evening in the study at the White House, when there were present, besides Dr. Grayson and myself, Colonel House, Colonel Ed Brown,[54] Miss Bones, and two of his daughters, Miss Wilson[55] and Mrs. McAdoo. But, as I have said, it is the first conversation which has made the most vivid impression on me, and which I shall undertake to give the substance of in these notes.

The scene comes rather vividly before my eyes. The president had been sitting at his desk—I was in a chair in another part of the room—when he arose from his desk, having completed whatever his task was, and began speaking rather abruptly. Of course, after the five years I shall not be able to reproduce his actual language, as I wish I might, but I think I can give the substance pretty clearly.

The first thing the president said was: "I am very much afraid that something will happen on the seas which will make it impossible to restrain our people." Beyond that I will not undertake to put the words in his mouth, but the idea was that the policy which Germany threatened to pursue with regard to shipping created a menace which might make it impossible for America to maintain that neutrality which the president was at that time urging on the country.

At this point it might not be amiss to add something which does not belong to the conversation which I am here rehearsing. It was in another talk with perhaps several of us that the president said that, though it was our duty to maintain our neutrality, we could not view with anything except apprehension the thought that, if Germany were victorious in the war, it would inevitably result in making America a military nation.

Returning to the conversation which I am trying to recall, the president said: "I have been thinking a great deal about a remark of Napoleon Bonaparte's that 'nothing was ever finally settled by force.'" And, again, in trying to report him, I must not give the impression that the language which I am now using represents him verbally. The thought was—whatever language he used to express the thought—that the great settlement of the world would not be by arms but by the negotiations which should follow the result of the battles in the field, in other words, the work of statesmen following the work of the soldiers.

Then it was that he said that four things are absolutely necessary for the ordering of the world of the future. And as he proceeded to talk, he developed the four points which I may here summarize as:

1. There must never again be a foot of ground acquired by conquest.
2. It must be recognized in fact that the small nations are on an equality of rights with the great nations.
3. Ammunition must be manufactured by governments and not by private individuals.
4. There must be some sort of an association of nations wherein all shall guarantee the territorial integrity of each.

What he said about the second point is least vivid in my memory, perhaps because to one born in America it more nearly resembled a truism than did the other two points. But I remember quite distinctly that the particular thought which he emphasized in this connection was that *small states should be put on an equality of rights with large states.* He developed at considerable length the idea that so much of the trouble in Europe in the past had grown out of the exploitation of small states by great powers. And the thought which I deduced from it all, though I do not remember that he stated it explicitly that morning, was that he was contending for an extension of the American democratic idea to nations at large. In America we had always contended for equal opportunity for all individuals. President Wilson was now contending for equal opportunity for all states; in short, for a world democracy.

The fourth point struck me then as the great new conception. Certainly, I myself at that time had never heard the phrase, League of Nations; and I am practically certain that I had never at that time heard of the League to Enforce Peace. Without using either of these terms, in fact without any technical phraseology at all, the president sketched the idea that it was absolutely essential that there should be a union of the governments of the world, all combined to protect the integrity of each, and that any country which should attempt violations on any other country would thereby automatically bring on war. He developed at some length the thought that modern conditions had brought the world into such a close neighborhood that never again would it be possible for the world at large to regard a quarrel between two nations as a particular and private quarrel, but that an attack in any quarter was an attack on the equilibrium of the world, and that the safety of the world demanded such a combination of the force of the nations as would maintain peace throughout all the world.

That is the substance of it. I am very sorry, indeed, that I cannot recall, after this lapse of time, the president's language, but this was the heart of what he said. And it struck me at that time, as, indeed, I have thought of it ever since, as one of the greatest utterances of one of the greatest conceptions that the world has ever known.

I remember distinctly, fully two years later, being at the White House (in the interim I had not been with the president very much, my work having kept me in other parts of the country), and saying to the president: "Do you remember a thought that you sketched for some of us back in August 1914, about a combination of world power for the preservation of world peace?" And when he answered that he did, I asked: "Do you still see the thing that way?" He replied, with that use of the vernacular that he sometimes indulges in: "You bet I do." And he added words to the effect that he was more emphatic in his belief than he had been at the outset of the war.

The *third* point he sketched more briefly, but I remember his peculiar appeal to me, because I found in this great man's thought a confirmation of a vague idea that I had had myself a great many years before; in fact, as far back as the Venezuelan imbroglio, when one of the firm of Cramps had issued a very bellicose statement in one of the Philadelphia newspapers.[56] I remember how I felt at the time that that was absolutely all wrong; that no one had a right to counsel war who was going to make profit out of the war; and so it was a great delight to me to hear the president say in his clean-cut way that in the future of the arrangement of the world it was essential that there should be no more manufacture of munitions of war by private enterprise, but that these things should be entirely the production of governments, of course, with the obvious implication that those who manufactured these things profited by them and naturally would aid and abet hostility in order that there might be a larger market for their wares. Again, I do not recall the language which he used at all.

When I come to dictate all this I find that the president's language is not in my memory at all, and I am sorry for it, but the thoughts are certainly there. These four things which he expressed in one of the very early days of August 1914 are perfectly clear to me; and from these things he has, of course, never swerved, though I believe in the councils in Paris he had to yield the matter of private manufacture of munitions because of the necessities of the small nations, which, if they were not allowed to purchase from commercial manufacturers, would be without munitions in time of war.

Notes on a Conversation One Sunday Night
in August 1919

There was a long conversation on the rear portico of the White House Sunday evening (no record of date) after dinner, there being present, besides the president, only Mrs. Wilson, Miss Wilson and myself, Dr. Grayson being still absent with his family in Connecticut. There was a good deal of talk about the third term, to which both Mr. and Mrs. Wilson are instinctively very much opposed, though Mr. Wilson's opposition to it does not rest on the two-term tradition. He said that if he were a younger man he would be inclined to break that tradition just for the sake of breaking it; that he thinks that the American people should always have the right to choose for president whomever they wished to choose. And he said that he finds that a good many of his close and sincere friends really hold an idea about the office of the presidency which he is sure is wrong, namely, that the office itself is so powerful that it would be dangerous to let any man occupy it for more than eight years. Said he: "I insist that the office in and of itself is not one of the most powerful of offices; it is nothing like so powerful as the premiership of England, for the simple reason that the prime minister of England can at any time dissolve Parliament and appeal directly back to the British people, and it is this knowledge on the part of Parliament that the prime minister can at any time make this appeal back to the people that undoubtedly whips Parliament into supporting the prime minister in many things in which they would not otherwise support him. And thus he has a hold on Parliament utterly unlike and superior to the hold which the president has on Congress." "Suppose," said he, "I could dissolve Congress now and appeal to the people to support the treaty, is there any question that the treaty would be immediately ratified? I would not have to dissolve Congress. The mere fact that I had the right to do it would bring Congress around at once." Surely this seems to be the soundest kind of analysis. Now, the president added to all this: "The presidency is what the incumbent makes of it. If he is a small and compliant man, it is a small office; if he is a real leader, it is an office of leadership. There is nothing dangerous about the office. The only danger is the man you put into office."

This conversation led to a consideration of presidential possibilities. The president asked me this question: "Suppose you yourself could name the next president of the United States (not considering his chances of being elected, not considering him as a candidate, but actually as president in the chair), whom would you name?" I replied: "You mean excluding yourself." He bowed assent. "Well," I said, "I know whom you would name, or I think I know that you would name one of two men, either Mr. Baker or Mr. Houston,[57] neither of whom could probably be elected president." Again the president nodded assent, it being his opinion that neither man has the qualities to make a winning candidate. I continued: "I do not know either of these gentlemen in the way in which you know them and, therefore, cannot have your conviction about the inherent qualities of each for the office, and I cannot help taking a very personal view of the matter and cannot rid myself of the thought and hope that if you are not available, Mac (meaning Mr. McAdoo) would be the nominee of the party for the next president." To this the president replied: "In anything that I have ever said about Baker or Houston I do not mean for a moment to rate them above Mac. I do not consider them abler men than Mac. But there is this one thought in my mind which troubles me: they are both *reflective* men, and I am not sure that Mac is a reflective man. There is no man who can devise plans with more inspiration, or put them into operation with more vigor, than can Mac, but I never caught Mac reflecting. Now, I may be wrong. It may be that when I have been with him, he has simply been so busy with the things in hand or immediately to come that I could not perceive the reflective elements in his nature. I am only saying, then, that dear Mac may not have the quality which I believe is going to be essential to a successful and wise administration in the near future. And I think Baker and Houston both have that quality— the quality, in short, of seeing the picture as a whole, the whole country in all its diverse elements, and understanding all these elements before they decide on any action at all. The action of the future may be very dangerous if it is precipitate and not based on long reflection on the condition of the country as a whole."

He then went on to make an analysis that was one of the most searching things I have ever heard even from him. He said: "The labor people are the only internationally minded people in our country. The rest of us (and he used the pronoun 'us') are provincials. The labor people see what the provincials do not see, that the fundamental questions of the future are questions which do not belong particularly to one country or another, but questions in which all countries are concerned. Now, this leads to a socialistic view, and I need hardly say that as between socialism and individualism, I favor individualism. But that does not mean that I do not see the inevitability of a part of the socialistic program in order to give just the opportunity to the individual that he ought to have. For instance, I am perfectly sure that the state has got to control everything that everybody needs and uses. This means that the state must control the means of distribution—the transportation facilities, the railroads; that the state must control the coal mines and the iron mines; that the state must control the water sources, the lighting facilities (he named several others, but I will not undertake to recall them)." Said he: "These things must be controlled by the state in order to secure equality of opportunity among individuals. For instance, the railroads under private management favor large shippers as against small shippers, give rebates, say that a man who takes a whole car should have more favorable rates than the man who sends only a single parcel. But on the principle of equality of privilege that is not true. The little man must have just the same rights as the big man, and state control provides for this." "Now," said he, "I go up to this point with the labor people, and, you may say, with the socialists, but there is a point beyond which I cannot go with the socialists, because in my opinion their further programs are not for the individual benefit of the individual. The man who is going to direct the future of America as an able president should always direct it, has got to be a man who reflects long and deeply on these complicated relationships of our time and the time immediately pending. He must not jump at conclusions; he must not be too speedy."

On Harding's Election

It seems to me that an even more remarkable example of Wilson's unwavering faith in the people was evident the day after Harding's election. Wilson had insisted up to the day of the election that Cox[58] would be elected. To me, it seemed not only pitiful but dangerous. I feared the consequences for his already shattered health when he should get the "returns" and see what most of us (including those of us who made no pretense of being politically wise) foresaw, that Harding would be not only elected, but overwhelmingly elected. I spoke with Grayson about the shock, then to Dr. Ruffin,[59] and suggested that, as his physicians, they prepare him for the shock. I "butted in" to do my own "preparing" of him. He would only smile on me, and say: "You pessimist! You don't know the American people. They always rise to a moral occasion. Harding will be deluged." Up to the last day I could make no impression on him. The day after the election I was so nervous about him that I called up the White House early and was told he was all right. As soon as I knew I could see him, I went over. He was as serene as in the moments of his own preceding victories (and the matter can't be stated stronger than that). His first words, after greetings, were (and I remember them verbatim): "I have not lost faith in the American people. They have merely been temporarily deceived. They will realize their error in a little while."

This was an *immediate* reaction. It seemed to me the test of the full measure of his faith in the people.

The Personality of Woodrow Wilson[1]

❧

THE ABYSMAL deeps of personality" is a phrase from Tennyson, who says that they "ever lie bare" before God. But these abysmal deeps are not equally clear to mortals, not even to the most sympathetic biographer. The conscientious portrait he draws may be unrecognizable by the man himself or the man's wife. Samuel Butler said that a portrait is usually a better picture of the painter than of his subject. Presumably he did not mean that the painter deliberately exploits his personality in the portrait, but that he necessarily gives his view of the man in his painting and thereby portrays something of his own habit of mind and observation, the sort of thing that interests him. Most portraits and biographies are interpretations, whether or not the painters and authors wish them to be so, and, insofar as they are interpretations, they are subject to the painter's and writer's limitations as interpreters.

Boswell had the right idea. He was the perfect biographer just because he was not metaphysical, because he was a good reporter. He entered daily in his diary the record of what Johnson had said and done that day, including whatever of foolishness or of wisdom the good doctor may have uttered. Johnson was sometimes morose, sometimes perverse, sometimes crabbed, sometimes bitter, sometimes narrow, sometimes unjust. Boswell set it all down, along with the record of Johnson's benevolence, generosity, kindliness, humility, and all his other robust virtues. Boswell achieved his masterly portrait—the most lifelike in literature—not by suppression of the faults and failings of his hero, but by telling everything he knew about him, apparently quite confident that the writer would be able to strike the balance for himself and see clearly how nobility preponderated in the doctor's complex personality.

But there was only one Boswell (the name has been loosely applied to many a subsequent biographer, but fittingly applied to none, for Boswell was in a class by himself), and certainly the writer of this book about Mr. Wilson has no expectations of challenging Boswell's fame. He has not the talent to rival him, and he has not the material out of which to imitate him, for, unfortunately, he did not keep a daily record of Mr. Wilson's utterances and activities throughout the long years of his association with him. Had he done so, he would have been able to give a more concrete picture of the man than is now possible. In the attempt of this chapter to explore the abysmal deeps of Mr. Wilson's personality, he is forced to strike the high spots, to analyze a bit here, to explain a bit there, and all the while offer an interpretation rather than a concrete record in the Boswellian fashion. Mr. Wilson's personality is more than ordinarily complex. It is the desire of the author to set it forth as much as possible in its own terms, with his expositions serving only as guide posts to the reader's understanding.

The personality of Woodrow Wilson has been much discussed, probably more than any other personality in the White House since Andrew Jackson, with the possible exception of Theodore Roosevelt. It is rather odd that this should have been the case, for Mr. Wilson himself shrank from exploiting his own personality. He disliked Colonel Roosevelt's frank methods of self-display. He shunned the cameramen, and he gave the newspaper boys comparatively little personal material, yet his personality was constantly discussed throughout the eight years of his administration—increasingly during the last two years of it. Much of the opposition to the League of Nations was based on dislike of Mr. Wilson's personality. His extreme enemies confidently summed up that personality in a few words of contumely, but those who have known him intimately know that it cannot be summarily accounted for in a few words either of dislike or admiration.

Mr. Wilson has been called a man of mystery, yet there was nothing Byronic about him, no dramatic assumption of mystery. He went about his daily task in the simplest and most unassuming fashion. As he did not care to exploit his personality, so he equally did not seek to veil that personality in romantic mystery. If he thought about the matter at all, it might seem that his attitude was: here I am, an American citizen living in the open, my personality accessible to any who may be interested in knowing it, but why should anyone be particularly concerned with my personality? I am charged with a great work to do. The work and not I is the important matter for consideration.

But the public would not have it so, neither his foes nor his friends. They wanted to know the man behind the work, and the more they sought to know him, the more they found themselves baffled and perplexed. There was something strange about him, people said; he was not like other men; he was hard to get at, so they called him austere.

Yet those who have known him intimately know that if by austerity is meant lack of natural affection, the word does not apply. In his younger days, he frequently signed his letters to men of his intimate acquaintance "affectionately yours," which is not the ordinary way in which men sign their letters, but it expressed the real impulse of a naturally warm heart. He was, particularly in those younger days, affectionate by nature.

One recalls a little incident of bygone days long ago, perhaps about 1888 or 1889, when Thomas Dixon,[2] subsequently famous as the author of *The Leopard's Spots* and *The Birth of a Nation*, was preaching in New York City and attracting huge congregations. Mr. Wilson and a friend went to hear him on Sunday night. The sermon was rather a sensational discourse, and the whole atmosphere was rather that of a public meeting than of a church; indeed, the service was not held in a church at all but in a large hall. When they left the building, the friend, knowing Mr. Wilson's strong Presbyterian predisposition towards "decorum" in religious worship, expected him to comment unfavorably on the sensationalism of the meeting, but instead Mr. Wilson simply said: "Tom Dixon is a lovely fellow. I see in him the same charm that endeared him to me at Johns Hopkins."

He loved and was devotedly loved by his classmates of the famous Princeton class of 1879. They called him "Tommy," and continued to call him "Tommy" after he was elected president of Princeton University. And though some of his classmates were weaned away by the Princeton controversy under Mr. Wilson's presidency, which rent the Princeton constituency in twain, others remained constant and continued to the end to think of him as "Tommy," whether they ventured to call him by that name or not to his face after he had become president of the United States.

He once said that he regarded it as a misfortune that his father had occupied several pastorates during his boyhood, for by moving from place to place he failed to take firm rootage in any one place and therefore failed to form the strongest boyhood ties of affection with other boys.[3] He would be just laying the foundations of life affections when he would have to pull up stakes, move to some other town, and form an entirely new circle of acquaintanceships. Without his knowing it, however, it is possible that there is right here the hint of a truth about Woodrow Wilson. Some boys take root quickly, and, after six months' residence in a small town, know every boy in the town, are passionately devoted to some and ardent enemies toward others, at any rate impersonal toward none. These are what is called in American parlance, "mixers." Mr. Wilson has never been exactly a mixer. He was too Scotch for that. This fact of Scotch blood must never be forgotten in assessing Mr. Wilson. He came of Covenanter stock. He referred to this eloquently on at least one occasion in defending the League of Nations before the American public. He said at Kansas City, Missouri, on September 6, 1919:

"My ancestors were troublesome Scotchmen, and among them were some of that famous group that were known as the Covenanters. Very well, then, here is the Covenant of the League of Nations. I am a Covenanter."

Notorious traits of the Scotch are caution and deliberation. Scotch emotion is deep rather than diffusive. The boy, Woodrow Wilson, descendant of that Woodrow who wrote *Sufferings of the Church of Scotland*,[4] was perhaps unconsciously influenced by the ancestors to move deliberately in forming his acquaintanceships with the little lads in the southern towns in which he lived, giving his friendship frankly but withholding his affections calmly.

In his younger days, at any rate, he was kind to all, genial with most, but demonstrative with few. In school and college he was popular with his associates, distinctly popular, regarded as a leader, elected to offices, called "Tommy," but with all that he did not acquire a vast number of lifelong friends of his bosom. Robert Bridges, Cyrus McCormick, Cleveland Dodge, Edward P. Davis, and a dozen others of the class of 1879 in Princeton, Moses Taylor Pyne, of the class of 1877, were intimate friends, valued friends, respected friends, and those who knew Mr. Wilson intimately knew what a wrench of the heart he suffered when the lifelong friendship with Mr. Pyne was broken in that fatal Princeton struggle.

If he moved somewhat slowly in forming affectionate friendships, it is equally true that the ending of those friendships cost him great pain. However, and this is one of the most painful aspects of Mr. Wilson's personality, when the friendship did end, it ended utterly. When he closed the door, it was closed for life. The action of his

mind—temperament, character, personality, whatever we call it—
was like the action of Fate, conclusive, irresistible. Maybe Scotchmen are like Indians in one respect—they do not forget easily. Those
who have loved Mr. Wilson without cessation have often wished, for
his own sake as well as for the sake of former friends, that he could
extend the olive branch or accept it when extended by others. They
have seen him torn, bleeding, and writhing under a severed friendship, and have wished, and sometimes even advised, that he go to
the estranged friend with open hands and say: never mind the past;
never mind how we have differed; let's forget all that; let's be friends
again and happy. But Woodrow Wilson would never do that. Perhaps
he could not. In time the pain would pass and it would be as if the
former friend were dead. He did not hate him; he simply ignored him
in his mind and consciousness. Occasionally he might refer to him,
seldom with bitterness, but with what was worse—that impersonal-
ity of fate, like the thunder cloud from which the bolt of lightning
has stricken a man dead and then passed on, with neither anger nor
remorse.

This is a part of the picture. This is true of the most devoted friendship he ever had with a man—one of his Princeton colleagues, John
Grier Hibben. It was Damon and Pythias; it was the complete refuta-
tion of the assumption that he was incapable of a devoted friendship
for a man. His intimates understood him, understood the intensity
of Mr. Wilson's nature, how he focused on a few—in that case on
one—how, relying so completely on the loyalty and sagacity of this
one man, he trusted him, he trusted him altogether, and seemingly
trusted him alone. He was letting his affection control his judgment.
The man was able, but there were other able men in the faculty; the
man was loyal, but there were other loyal men in the faculty; and
those who did not understand Mr. Wilson as his intimates understood him naturally became a little jealous, could not see why any
one man should be so obviously and emphatically preferred above
all others. But that was Mr. Wilson's nature. He had waited until he
was forty years of age to form a devoted all-involving, complete
friendship with a man, and to that friendship he in the unreleased
intensity of his nature gave all the ardor of affection which college
lads, but not he, are accustomed to give in younger days.

When the controversy arose over Mr. Wilson's proposal to reorganize the life of the college, the so-called quadrangle system, to
Mr. Wilson's amazement this gentleman espoused the cause of the

opposition. He was honest about it. He frankly and earnestly be-
sought Mr. Wilson not to take the step. He told Mr. Wilson, what
proved to be true, that he would rend the alumni community asun-
der, and that he could not engage the support of many prominent
alumni on whom Mr. Wilson supposed he could depend. It was an
honest difference of judgment. Mr. Wilson could not see his friend's
point of view, nor could his friend see his. Mr. Wilson thought that
his friend was timid, afraid to act boldly in an issue which so completely appealed to Mr. Wilson's reason that he was convinced that
boldness was the only possible course. What Mr. Wilson could not
understand was that the friend could ally himself with the opposition. There could be no doubt that the friend himself suffered much
in this crisis, and that he acted as he did because his judgment would
not let him act otherwise. But Mr. Wilson was almost stunned when
the friend arose in the faculty chamber and seconded the motion
which precipitated the great fight. Mr. Wilson's self-control was admirable. Though unable to credit his eyes and ears, he asked in a
steady voice: "Do I understand that Mr. Hibben seconds the motion
to, etc., (naming the motion)" and heard the response: "I do." Mr.
Wilson smiled pleasantly, but they who watched him intently saw
that he grew very pale. It was a dramatic moment, one of the most
dramatic in a career that was filled with dramatic incidents.

He received the shock from which in a deep sense he never recovered, because he never again gave that kind of friendship to any
other man. He said he could not. He said: "Hibben has shaken my
faith in friendship." He doubtless felt that in such an intimacy as had
existed between them for years it was impossible that his friend
should openly espouse the cause of the enemies who were trying to
crush him, if his friend had for him the sort of affection which he
himself had given and had thought he was receiving in return. He
doubtless felt that if the friend could not conscientiously support the
measure he was advocating, the friend should have signified his resignation from the faculty. Having given all to friendship, Mr. Wilson
could not understand how friendship could fail for any other consideration. It was the curious case of a man, who is called cold and austere, letting his affections, his emotions, control his reason. He said
on one occasion: "I suppose Hibben does not understand at all. I
suppose he thinks I am forward and stubborn, headstrong, and cannot understand how I am governed by a principle which I cannot
yield. But the agony of it is to find that such a friend could fail me in

a crisis." Mr. Wilson fell ill shortly after and his devoted wife, who had shared his affection for and confidence in this friend, exclaimed with the bitterness of a wife's devotion: "Mr. Hibben can thank himself for this illness of Woodrow's. Nothing else has caused it but the fact that his heart is broken."

There is no desire on the part of this biographer to reopen this old sore, or to parcel out blame between the two. The incident is referred to only because it illustrates certain qualities of a very complex man—the excess of affection of which he was capable, his sensitiveness to the wounds received from a friend, and his subsequent terrible unforgivingness. The friend made many overtures, sought in many ways to heal the breach, undoubtedly suffered grievously himself, showed himself magnanimous. But it was of no use. After the shock and the pain were ended, Mr. Wilson simply closed the door and never opened it.

One of the most painful of small episodes in Mr. Wilson's career was witnessed by the author of this book. He had gone with Mr. Wilson from Washington to Princeton when he, now president of the United States, had journeyed there to cast his vote in a national election.[5] Mr. Wilson, who had never lost his devotion to Princeton, was revisiting the old scenes, lingering with especial lovingness over the objects in old Nassau Hall, when he was told that a crowd had gathered in front of the hall to see him make his exit. With his characteristic instinct to avoid a spectacle, he asked one of his companions to see if a certain door at the rear was open so that he could slip out quietly and get to the train unobserved. Inquiry for this exit somehow caused a curious misinterpretation in the mind of an eager young alumnus who happened to be present and who in some mysterious way reasoned that Mr. Wilson's companion was looking for Mr. Hibben, Mr. Wilson's former friend. This young man hastened to Mr. Hibben's home, found him just starting for or returning from a horseback ride, and told him that the president of the United States was looking for him. As the president, his companions, and the secret service men were walking across the rear campus toward the train, they heard a clatter of horsehoofs and looking up were astonished to see Mr. Hibben galloping toward them at full speed. Mr. Hibben reined in his horse, swung himself out of his saddle, and said, his face flushed with excitement and probably with gratification: "I was told, Mr. President, that you were looking for me." The president, without extending his hand, with that cold, deadly smile, more dreadful than a frown, pursing his lips and arching his eye-brows, said slowly: "No, no, you are mistaken." And that was all. The little group stood a moment, all except the president, visibly embar-rassed. He, in a chilling voice, said: "Good afternoon, Sir," quietly turned and walked toward the train. Turning toward one of his com-panions who did not understand the incident, he said: "I must apol-ogize to you for my manner. The man who stopped and spoke to me was my friend. I did more to make him than I did for any other person in the world. I unbosomed my very soul to him. And in the crucial moment of my life, he turned against me. I can never for-give him."

It must be said that up to the present hour of this writing, the for-mer friend never fails to inquire solicitously about the president's health, and always in the tone of one who still loves him and would give much to be reconciled. But the past is dead—absolutely dead. That is Woodrow Wilson's way—it would be useless to comment on it—that is Woodrow Wilson's way.

A similar incident of a later time and a larger stage illustrates the same complexity of Mr. Wilson's mental and emotional constitution. This story involves a man, Colonel House, who played a conspicuous part in the Wilson administration. While Mr. Wilson never gave to this man or to any the same kind of romantic affection which he had given to his Princeton friend, he did give to him his confidence. He did prefer him above his other advisers, with somewhat the same result as in the Princeton case, of provoking hostility, suspicion, jeal-ousy among his constituted advisers. This gentleman, like the Princeton friend, undoubtedly in the beginning was devotedly at-tached to the president and desirous of promoting the president's policies and interests. Like the Princeton friend, he was sagacious, "steady," the reliable type that Mr. Wilson seemed to prefer for his closest advisers. The two worked in complete harmony for a long time, and, as this friend possessed engaging personal qualities, it is quite possible that the president might have given to him the depth of his affection had it not been for the former experience. He did give him friendship in abundance, and, in turn, he received a true friendship.

This gentleman was a constant visitor and always a welcome one in the White House. He was unobtrusive but always ready in counsel when called upon. As the national story unfolded, this gentleman be-came so marked a figure that the newspapermen naturally began to make "copy" out of him. After a while he, who had never sought the limelight, gave his consent to the publication of a book about himself and was privy to the writing of the book.[6] While the book was running in serial form in the newspapers, he was a guest at the White House. It was evident that he was in a low state of health. Never robust, he was obviously seriously ill. The president, always solicitous for the welfare of those around him, was earnestly concerned, and early one morning he talked with Admiral Grayson professionally about his friend. He said: "Have you ever seen a man so depressed in your life? I have never seen anything like it. Is there anything you can do for him?" Admiral Grayson said of course that he would see him at once and do what he could. The admiral was convinced from the guest's condition that something was weighing on his mind, and he knew that, if his offhand diagnosis was correct, he could be of little professional use to the guest unless the guest would unbosom himself. In other words, he must find the cause before he could treat the disease. Going to the guest's room, he by degrees drew from him a confession that he was greatly troubled in his thoughts and that the trouble concerned the book which was being serially published. Certain things in the book seemed to bear implications which he himself had not thought of in the process of writing, and he said: "I am sick over that book. I hope I shall never be connected with a book again as long as I live. I don't ever want to see my name in print again." The doctor found what he went to seek. He had made his diagnosis on the basis of the facts. He went directly to the president's library and said: "Mr. President, I found out what is the matter with Mr. House, and you are the only physician who can help him." The president said: "Why, what on earth do you mean?" And the doctor said: "It is that book which is bothering him, and, if it is possible, you should go and tell him not to worry about it." The president dropped his morning's work, laying his pen down, rose from his desk, and went straight to the guest's room, accompanied by the doctor. Seating himself at the guest's bed, taking the sick friend's hand in both of his and patting it gently, he said: "My dear fellow, if you are worrying about this book, forget it. I have never read the book and I don't intend to, and I beg that you will not have it on your mind at all. I believe in your friendship and your loyalty, and what I most want is for you to get well. Doctor Grayson has informed me that you need my treatment. I have given it to you. Forget it."

That night the guest was in his evening clothes at the dinner table, restored and happy.

This friendship seemed destined to continue so long as both men should live. The especial value of this gentleman to the president lay in the combined facts that he was a shrewd observer and assessor of men and motives, that he was sagacious in estimating affairs, and that above all he wanted nothing for himself personally. The president was accustomed to say that, as he mingled with men in public life, he found their views often distorted by their personal ambitions, but that here was a man without personal ambition, whose judgments were therefore clear and correct.

There can be no doubt that he played a large and valuable part in the earlier years of President Wilson's administration. There came a time, however, when very much, as in the Princeton case, his temperament and the president's led to diverse conclusions and modes of action. Those who have been most closely associated with the president, both in the educational and in the political world, have realized that the most difficult thing about him was his disinclination to compromise on what often to his advisers seemed to be details. As one of his old Princeton friends, one who remained loyal to him to the end, said: "He is the finest man in the world, but he does drive too hard." This was the general impression of the president's counselors.

The particular friend in question here was himself not aggressive. In a long experience of practical politics he had found that he got most by not demanding all. He had often compromised in what he considered unessentials. This is the key to that which is to follow.

The president was relying upon him, above all others, in the most important negotiations of his administration, at the Paris Peace Conference. In the absence of the president, this gentleman acquiesced in certain propositions of those with whom the president had been dealing.[7] Undoubtedly his motives were good. He thought that by yielding in what he considered minor details, he was oiling the track for the smoother running of the machine. But, on the president's return, he himself was shocked to find that what had been yielded for what his friend considered unessentials constituted to him the heart of the principle, and, added to that, was the fact that the distinguished people with whom the negotiations were being made had received the impression that the president had never intended to insist on his former demands. The friend's compromises had led them to the conclusion that the president formerly had been "bluffing"— demanding more than he really expected to receive. In short, the president found that the negotiations were in a bad tangle, and he foresaw failure unless action were taken speedily and emphatically. He asked one of his advisers to go to the gentlemen with whom the negotiations were being conducted and say to them that there was no bluff anywhere in his former proposal. Said he: "Tell them there is not a compromise corpuscle in my blood; that I meant exactly what I said—no more and no less—and that I will accept no less. What has been done by House must be undone immediately and finally."

An issue was thus created which never resulted in an open breach but did result in gradual estrangement. The friend was so convinced of the propriety and wisdom of his procedure that he ventured to say to the president on one occasion: "If you will go away and let me handle the situation, I think I can do it better than you." Unfortunately, this remark coincided with the tone of certain newspaper articles, which were saying that the president was only a politician and the friend was the real statesman; that if matters were left in his hands, they would be quickly adjusted, whereas the president himself was only confusing the picture. The deduction, justly or unjustly, seemed obvious that the friend himself had inspired these articles. And though there was no actual rift, as in the Princeton case, there was a slow drifting apart.

This story ends like the story of the Princeton friend. The political friend in this case was anxious for reconciliation or acknowledgment that there never had been a breach calling for reconciliation. He wrote to Washington suggesting that he call. The letter arrived after the president's grave illness had begun. The message was taken to him, but he said: "Don't let us discuss that any more. He is out of my life. The door is closed."

By the paradox of personality and life it was where his affections had been deeply engaged that he was most unforgiving. Browning says of Dante that he "loved well because he hated." When Woodrow Wilson's intense emotional nature was aroused, he was likely to love altogether or cease loving altogether. He was negative in nothing, positive in all things. But where his personal affections had not been markedly enlisted, he could be "a good sport." In the Princeton fight there was an opponent, Henry van Dyke, who was far more uncompromising in his opposition than the one-time friend referred to above. Van Dyke was an eminent member of the faculty with an extensive reputation. He was bitter in the speeches which he made against Mr. Wilson; the friend of the tragic experience recited above was never bitter. Indeed, it was this very gentleman who introduced in the faculty the motion, which Mr. Wilson's friend seconded, and whose second gave Mr. Wilson so much shock and pain. Yet Mr. Wilson cherished no animosity against the other gentleman, the introducer of the motion, and years afterward, when Mr. Wilson had become president of the United States, he appointed this gentleman minister to the Netherlands. This gentleman, a man of strong convictions, was in still later years an ardent and fearless champion of the League of Nations plan. His and Mr. Wilson's relations in Princeton had, up to the time of the controversy which split the college community, been pleasant, but not close. Opposition from him signified no rending of friendship. Hence Mr. Wilson could forget about that period of heated opposition when he was seeking a suitable man for a particular foreign post to which, as it happened, this gentleman was by ancestry and sentiment peculiarly fitted. But where his heart had been "garnered up," Mr. Wilson could not forget.

Once there was reported to him the mean and ungrateful criticism of him by a young man whom he had befriended in a marked manner, at the cost of considerable effort. When he heard the derogatory remarks of the young man, he merely laughed and commented: "It has been truly said that 'virtue is its own reward.' It hath no other." Mr. Tumulty has recorded how Mr. Wilson ignored the long, assiduous, and peculiarly venomous enmity of James M. Beck,[8] who began his assaults before Mr. Wilson entered political life, for reasons perhaps known to Mr. Beck, but never known to Mr. Wilson, or even inquired into by him, Mr. Beck and his opinions being of small concern to Mr. Wilson. Mr. Tumulty relates how a delegation, which included Mr. Beck, proposed to call on the president during the war, but how some of the delegates advised Mr. Tumulty that they feared Mr. Beck would be *persona non grata*, how Mr. Tumulty sent a note to the president to that effect, and how he received in reply a note telling them to bring Beck on, though his behavior had certainly earned for him little consideration, "but I ain't harborin' no ill will," said the president.[9]

Toward the various men, some young, some older, who had been affiliated with him and subsequently "flew the coop" with their sensibilities ruffled, Mr. Wilson cherished no anger, found excuses for some of them—considered, for instance, that Dudley Malone's mind had been poisoned by others, that W. F. McCombs was practically irresponsible—an invalid; of his former young friend and favorite, Henry Breckinridge, assistant secretary of war, he felt that Mr. Breckinridge had acted naturally in loyally espousing the cause of his immediate chief, Secretary Lindley M. Garrison.[10] Of Mr. Garrison himself, Mr. Wilson never spoke in bitterness, nor of Mr. Bryan. They had their opinions about public policies, he his. They had a right to theirs, he to his. There was nothing to get excited about. The case of Mr. Lansing was different; there he felt there had been duplicity, and that he would not forgive.

He was unfortunate in the selection of some of his advisers, so unfortunate that people said he was "a poor judge of men." He once commented on that himself, saying, "The Democratic party has been out of power for sixteen years, and therefore Democrats have not been trained to office like the Republicans. I have to take green men and try them out." But, with all that, resignations and removals were not more frequent under him than under other "strong" presidents.

Mr. Wilson has been equally blamed for "sticking by" appointees for whose removal public opinion clamored. When he had once given his confidence, he must have strong cause for withdrawing it. He retained some even after he had been disillusioned as to their personalities, if he felt they were "doing the job." He sometimes allowed his prejudices to lead him into personal coldness toward men whom he retained in office. Personally, he did not like them, and he allowed too much his dislikes as well as his likes to control his attitude, his personal demeanor, toward some men, but if the men were competent in office and loyal to the general plans of the administration, they could remain in office as long as they pleased.

There is a darker shading to the picture, however. There were some cases where he did not dislike the man, but where he did not like him as heartily as he should have done. Who can explain those "imperfect sympathies," of which Charles Lamb wrote, that slight maladjustment between personalities? Mr. Wilson's friends felt that of all the men in the cabinet, Mr. Franklin Lane was, by the literary cast of his mind, fitted to be one of the president's most cherished intimates. Yet for some mysterious reason they did not exactly "hit if off," and the fault, if fault there was, was Mr. Wilson's.[11] It is a pity that he did not give himself a chance to love Mr. Lane and be loved by him in turn. He was grieved when Mr. Lane died, but there had never been "the glad, confident" friendship between them which there should have been.

The author would not be faithful to his intention to write, in so far as his ability permits, the truth about his hero, in the confidence that he was so great and so good that the whole truth cannot hurt him, if he did not admit that Woodrow Wilson had strong prejudices, and, too often for so great a man, allowed a prejudice to control his personal attitude toward a man. Where a public policy was concerned, he acted with "even-handed justice," but he seemed to reason that his likes and dislikes were a part of his private possession and that he was no more bounden by duty than his old strong and opinionated father to pretend to like or try to like a man whom he did not like.

Dwell on Mr. Wilson's failings and you get the picture that some of his enemies, the more just of them, have drawn. (The unjust do not dwell on his real faults but invent faults in purest malice—Mr. Wilson has been the unconscious cause of more deliberate lying, on the part of his enemies, than any other American of his generation.) Dwell on his faults and the picture is distorted; deny the faults, and the picture is still distorted. Some able men are very vain, but their friends offset the vanity by calling attention to other and finer qualities of them. Some are unreliable, today favor one thing, tomorrow its opposite, but they have sturdier and handsomer qualities which help to make a better portrait. Some are insincere, say for political purposes what they do not mean, but in other ways they manifest something admirable, and so it goes. The only true portrait of Woodrow Wilson is a *balanced* portrait; he was sometimes prejudiced, sometimes caustic, sometimes impatient of what seemed to him stupidity; too often unforgiving; but, on the other hand, he was without petty vanity; staunch as the Rock of Gibraltar; utterly, even terribly sincere; relentless in pursuit of an object which he believed was for the welfare of the larger community; fearless; preferred devotion to the right, as he saw it, to transient popularity; unsparing of himself, his comfort, pleasures, and health in serving the public; devoted to the cause of democracy, the great inarticulate masses whose leader he conceived himself to be; and in his private relations, generous-handed, clean, affectionate, and considerate, even when the clouds of ill health and the exhaustion of his nervous energies tormented him, for those who knew him best learned to understand, in the latter years, that if he was exasperated by his condition to speak curtly one day, or be moodily silent, the next day or the next, he would be doubly tender.

Uncompromising, unforgiving, stubborn—yes, in drawing the true picture these things must be admitted. But after all, still drawing the true picture, one must bear in mind the strength and endurance of his great loves. To a few he gave all of his affection—to his father and his mother, to the first Mrs. Wilson and to the second, to the Princeton friends, and, of course, to his daughters. During his college days—the period in which young men are so likely to form affectionate and confidential relations with their fellow students—his real confidant was his father. Just after he had finished his university course he married and his wife became his actual confidante. It was possible that for one with so intense a nature as Mr. Wilson, he found one confidant at a time enough, and, therefore, did not form quite the kind of devoted and involving confidential relationship with young men of his own age that many other college students are so familiar with.

His love for his father has in the observation of all those who know him been one of his outstanding traits. His mental and temperamental resemblance to his father has grown stronger with his years. Those who knew Doctor Joseph Wilson have smiled secretly when President Wilson has said in his latter years: "I do not find any resemblance between my father and myself." The resemblance is so striking that it is funny. Doctor Joseph Wilson, whom people now alive knew only in his later middle life and in his old age, was, as is stated elsewhere in this book, a very great man, a fascinating conversationalist, a man very genial with a few, but withal a ruthless sort of man, and a man with a distinct streak of perversity in him. A cousin[12] who remembered him well, who loved him, and who loves the president even more devotedly, was commenting frankly on some of the more "difficult" aspects of President Wilson and said: "Of course, I know why it is. It is Uncle Joseph in him."

Doctor Wilson, like the president, was a man of strong convictions. Certain things he believed with all the intensity of his nature, and he justified his beliefs with all the power of a superior mind. Toward those who differed with him, he was sometimes ruthless. Like his son, he could not compromise with a principle. Also there was in him a certain savage humor which caused him to say sometimes cruel things even to those who loved him and whom he loved. Perhaps he did not know that he was being cruel, but it hurt.

Of all of Mr. Wilson's traits, the most painful to recall, and quite the most painful to record, has been a sporadic tendency to treat at times some of those near to him with that aloofness, which, without consciousness on his part, almost amounted to cruelty. This is not inconsistent with the fact that he was never harsh in his dealings with his family. He never was. But there is something that hurts more than harshness—apparent coldness toward the aspirations and thoughts of those who are dear to one. To account for this in Mr. Wilson is extremely difficult, and the writer of this book, who has for him a veneration mingled with the deepest love, would rather avoid this topic altogether but is induced to refer to it only because he feels that the portrait will be incomplete without it; and he has so much faith in the nobility and the splendor of him as a whole that he believes that the truest portrait he can draw will be a better tribute to his memory than any praise founded on fiction or suppression of the facts.

To get the perspective on this most painful matter, we shall have to go back to his young manhood, when nothing of the sort was visible in him—when, so far from being severe, he was almost deferential. It is perhaps difficult for those who have known him only in the days of his authority and crushing responsibilities and occasional severity to realize that as a young man, even after he was old enough to become a young married man, he was characterized by a considerateness for the feelings of others that was at times almost deferential. One can remember his constant habit of speech when propounding a proposition even to those who were his juniors, a habit of saying, "I think thus and so," and then, with almost an eager solicitude in his eyes and on his sensitive face, he would say, "Don't you think so?," as if he was anxious to avoid giving occasion for dispute or pain. His courtesy as a young man was very marked. It was courtesy to all without respect to age, position, or even sex, that is to say, he had that rare quality in America of being courteous to men as well as to women. It was no carpet-knight courtesy; it was no assumption of courtesy; it was no pose. It was the actual expression of a nature filled with loving kindness and sensitive consideration for the feelings of others. In one word, he was propitiatory. It marked him everywhere—in his home, in the classroom, in public conveyances, on the street. He was particularly gentle with the old. He was particularly deferential toward men sometimes not so very much older than himself but whose character and position he greatly respected. One recalls his attitude toward his wife's relatives, often a matter of jest among the newspaper paragraphers, but Mr. Wilson seemed to feel that as his wife's relatives they were deserving of all consideration and even affection. His wife's favorite uncle, Doctor Thomas Hoyt, quickly became a favorite of Mr. Wilson's. He called him "Uncle Tom," just as his wife did; loved him dearly. Mr. Wilson never saw much of another of his wife's much beloved uncle, Mr. Randolph Axson, but what he did see of him caused him to feel for Mr. Axson a great regard and affection. Mr. Axson paid only one visit to the Wilson household in Princeton, but he was a most welcome visitor, and, after he had gone, Mr. Wilson said to a friend: "I tried so hard to get him to call me Woodrow, because I so much wanted to call him Uncle Randolph, but he always insisted on calling me Mr. Wilson, and I did not feel I had the right therefore to call him Uncle Randolph."

His attitude toward all his relatives was not only considerate, but where need called was most substantially helpful. One could not name if he wished to all the relatives on his own side of the house who were his beneficiaries financially, when he himself was a very hard-working underpaid professor. He practically had to assume the sole support of several of them, and it was always given ungrudgingly. His house was the only home which his wife's younger brother and younger sister[13] had in their childhood, and it was periodically the home of the older brother, the author of this book. Indeed, one of Mr. Wilson's rebukes to this older brother was a sharp contention when this young man moved to Princeton as professor in the faculty and insisted on setting up his own bachelor quarters. Mr. Wilson said: "You ought not to do that; Ellen has her heart set on your living with us."

All these matters, and they could be multiplied by scores, indicate without comment the sweetness and beauty of Mr. Wilson's natural disposition. In outward generosity he never slackened. In that subtler thing of human sympathy, he perhaps stiffened as he grew older. Said his relative: "It is Uncle Joseph in him." Uncle Joseph grew stronger in him as his years increased, as the terrible responsibility of office pressed upon him, as he was in continual conflict, day after day, with individuals and groups of men, always battling. His first wife said, when he grew ill in the midst of the Princeton controversy: "He is too sensitive for all this battling; it will kill him." But it did not kill him. It made him sterner, more inflexible, less easy to express his sweetness of nature.

Now, mingled with all that, there is something very subtle, something we are fumbling after in trying to expound this man. There have been various types of men in the presidency of the United States. There has been the soldier in the presidential chair, and the rail splitter, and the frontiersman, and the tailor, and the professional politician. Just once thus far in our history has there been in the presidential chair the literary man, the artist, with all the artist's sensibilities, with all the artist's—what shall we say—nerves. Nobody who writes at all, with the artist's instinct to put the very best he has, even though that best be very little, into his writing, knows what a demand it makes on the vital forces, the terrible exhaustion of it, the agony of trying to make it come right when it won't come right, the artist's conscience, the artist's urge. All that was in Woodrow Wilson. In his younger days he toiled and travailed over his "style," his literary style. That does not need to be expounded: the people know what art means in literature, the striving to express himself in the best form possible, in the perfection of language, which his father had set before him as a standard. What has all this to do with what we are talking about? Possibly just this—that the irritability, the perversity, if we shall call it by so strong a term, sometimes observable in Mr. Wilson in his latter days is not only "Uncle Joseph" in him but is also the artist in him—the harassed nerves, the resentment at being torn away by an interruption from a line of intense, all-absorbing thought, being called on suddenly for a complete readjustment of his mind to some new set of topics. His is the creative mind, the mind clutched by an inspiration, the mind that follows the suggestion on to its finish. He never has been able to see things in parts—he has got to see it in the whole. That is one reason why his political associates have been unable to follow him. With them it is a little here and a little there. With him it is a whole plan—a pattern that must be worked out.

Now, approaching the matter a little more closely, suppose this creative, literary type of mind has been intensely absorbed all morning with a tremendous theme, an epic, to be written not in words, but in the deeds of a nation. Suppose after the morning's exhausting labors he goes to his lunch table and wants simply to relax, not have business follow him to the table; he wants to let his mind play, he wants to give it a thorough rest, he talks small talk with the members of his family, he recites limericks and makes puns and tells anecdotes; he does everything except be serious; the mind is crying for rest; his overwrought nerves cry for rest. Now, suppose a member of the family, a dear and valued relative, also full of his schemes, his plans, which he sees as the businessman, the man of affairs, the man of action—not the man of meditation, not the artist, not the literary man; suppose he insists on talking business—it is the president's business as much as his; it is the public's business; it is the business of the United States; why should it not be talked at the table? He never wearies of it. Here are two men, devoted servants of the public linked together by a common view of the necessities of the nation, linked together by ties of marriage, by admiration for each other, by affection. But how easy it is that the artist's mind and the business mind should come in clash. The business mind wants to keep on with business; the artist's mind wants renewal that comes from relaxation. The business mind belongs to the younger man. He, too, is intense, deeply in earnest. He wants to talk business, he insists on talking business. It rasps the older man, the literary man—why can't we drop business? At first he answers graciously by trying to avoid the topic. Then his tone takes a little edge on. Then he adopts that worst of all his defenses—silence. The silence of Woodrow Wilson is worse than the oaths of some men, more withering. The picture is not altogether fanciful.

The two men are Woodrow Wilson and William G. McAdoo. There have been ridiculous stories about the animosity between this father-in-law and son-in-law, grotesque newspaper canards, which friends have denied stridently. And yet it is curious how the newspapermen sometimes get a germ of the truth, though their conclusions may be so wide of the truth. There has never been the suggestion of a rift in the Wilson household, but that Mr. Wilson rather avoids serious discussion with Mr. McAdoo is true. How on earth did the newspapermen ever find that out? Nobody in the Wilson family talks of these things; nobody in the McAdoo family. Neither Mr. Wilson nor Mr. McAdoo would admit to themselves or to each other that there was any division, and yet—and this is coming back now to the point—Mr. Wilson has been perhaps without the slightest consciousness unkind to one of the most loyal men and to one of the most serviceable that has ever been engaged in service with him, and the devoted husband of an adoring wife, who is his loyal and devoted daughter. Here is a bit of a triangle. Without being conscious of it, Mr. Wilson has caused pain to one of his own blood whom he loves with a peculiar devotion. Nell, so she is known, has always been perhaps not his favorite daughter—he presumably would not admit that he had a favorite among the three—but his closest companion of the three, his chum, his little partner.[14] And yet he has hurt her—she is too loyal to admit it—but one does not have to be a clairvoyant to know it.

This is an example of what the author means by reference to the most painful aspect of Mr. Wilson's complex disposition. In his absorption in his great objects, in his nervous, literary constitution, in his increasing resemblance to "Uncle Joseph," he has in later years, and particularly after his great illness came upon him, been sometimes apparently oblivious of the fact that he was giving pain to others and to some of those dearest to him. Of course, the illness explains much. It is a well-recognized symptom of serious nervous disability that the patient frequently, as the phrase goes, "turns on" those he has loved most in health. There have been manifestations of this in Mr. Wilson's illness—never, for I am writing very frankly, toward his wife—for which his physician has thanked God repeatedly, for that too might have happened. It never has. There has never been a shadow of anything but docility under her management. He has obeyed her when he has rebelled against all others, but he has at times treated others with a lack of consideration which seems strange in one whose affections are naturally deep and tender. At the same time, he has continually shown in his illness flashes of all the old tenderness and consideration, perhaps the more tender after he has behaved with some asperity. He never apologizes for the asperity—that is not Woodrow Wilson's way. But it sometimes seems as if in his mind he determines to "make it up" by being particularly nice at the next meeting.

This perversity, if we call it so, has of course been accentuated by illness, but streaks of it were apparent some years before he became ill. It would show itself particularly with very important people—those who insisted and kept insisting that he do this or do that before the time had come when he was good and ready to do it. Left alone, he would probably do it in time, but abrupt insistence that he do it was the surest way of having him not do it. When he went to Paris, the French authorities insisted that it was his duty to go at once to

the devastated regions so that he could see "red" before the delibera-
tions of the peace conference commenced. The more they insisted,
the more he rebelled. Finally he said with firmness: "They cannot
make me go to the devastated region until I am ready." And he did
not go until just before departing for home.[15]

That perversity manifested itself occasionally from the time he became president of Princeton, and it practically never manifested itself before that, which may mean simply this, that up to the time he
became president of Princeton, he was the literary man doing his
literary work with the leisure that is necessary for the best consum-
mation of that work. When he entered administrative work, there
was superimposed upon him, as it were, a new nature, and out of the
superimposition there seems to have come a sort of irritability never
noticed in him in his earlier years.

Another famous Scotch son and his less famous father were
Thomas Carlyle and his father, James. The reverence of Thomas Carlyle for his father as indicated in that classic memorial which he
wrote of his own father after his death[16] is very like the reverence
which Woodrow Wilson always had for his own father, much more
distinguished than James Carlyle though much less distinguished
than the son, Woodrow Wilson. In that beautiful essay which
Thomas Carlyle wrote about his father, one notes with what relish
the son records examples of his own father's asperity, not in the least
apologizing for them, rather admiring them and commending them.
Why? Not merely because he was his father, but because Thomas
Carlyle had so much of the same asperity in himself, he was sympathetic with the traits of the father which he noted. It is a parallel to
Woodrow Wilson. He tells with greatest relish some of the caustic
retorts which his father was wont to make—it would never occur to
him to criticize his father for his biting habits of speech. He rather
admires him the more for this, exactly as in the case of the Carlyles.
This is due not only to the fact that he loves his father and his father's
memory, but that he also has in himself some of those same traits
which he admires in his father. None of this was in Woodrow
Wilson's own speech and conduct in his early years. There was no
resemblance to this side of his father in those days, when he used to
be so deferential even with people much younger than himself, but
the father has grown stronger in the son as the son has grown older.
It is "Uncle Joseph" in him.

The affectionate nature of Woodrow Wilson got its fullest expression in that relationship in which natural affection should have its

finest expression—in his marriage. When he fell in love, he fell in completely, head over heels. He was so impetuously in love that he wanted to get married at once, wanted to cut his education at Johns Hopkins short. Having fallen in love, he was convinced he had all the book learning that was necessary and was already ripe for teaching. He was eager for the plunge into his professional career, if only Ellen Axson would join him in the adventure. But she, with that wisdom which women seem to be able to combine with ardent loving, put a break on his impetuosity and told him that there was to be no marriage until he had completed the Hopkins course. The letter he wrote her in accepting the inevitable was a comedy. He was simply up against it and had to yield. So he got through at the Hopkins, and then he and she were married and went to Bryn Mawr where he began to teach. At Wesleyan he heard a lecture one evening by one of the friends whom he admired most, Professor Winchester—a great critic of literature and a great lecturer, but withal such a modest man that he was sometimes modest in the wrong place. Professor Winchester's subject was Robert Burns, and he was describing at one point the scene of one of Robert Burns' love poems with beautiful but controlled enthusiasm, and then, in his quiet, New England, and very modest way, he said: "Even one who was not a poet or a lover standing on this spot felt the inspiration of this scene." Mr. Wilson loved Mr. Winchester dearly, but for once he was provoked with him. As he walked home with his companion,[17] he said: "I think it was outrageous for Winchester to say that in his lecture. The idea! When he said he was neither a poet nor a *lover*, he as much as said he is no longer in love with Mrs. Winchester." His companion demurred saying: "Oh, I don't think you ought to take it that seriously; he didn't mean that." But the young husband flashed back: "But a husband should never forget that he is a lover, and if I had said that Ellen would have a right to think that I am no longer her lover." He was not only a lover throughout his married life, he was a romantic lover, with the tenderness, the considerateness, the memory for all anniversaries and special days and occasions of which husbands sometimes grow forgetful. But he never did.

Their first year of married life was spent in a boardinghouse at Bryn Mawr, but in the second year they set up housekeeping in a rented home with a family of five: themselves, their first baby, two of Mrs. Wilson's relatives—her cousin, Miss Mary Hoyt, and her little brother, Edward, both of whose parents were dead. Edward remained a member of the family until his graduation from Princeton eleven years later and was more like a son than a brother. Mrs. Wilson, one of the most unselfish of mortals, was continually planning for the welfare of others. She took Mary Hoyt to Bryn Mawr to get the college education for which Mary longed but had hitherto been unable to afford. It was probably at Mrs. Wilson's suggestion that George Howe, Mr. Wilson's nephew, became a member of the family when he was ready for boarding school at Lawrenceville and later for Princeton. He and Edward Axson were classmates. Later, after the death of Dr. Howe, his widow and her little daughter, Mr. Wilson's sister and niece, became members of the household for long periods. Dr. Joseph Wilson, the father, made his son's home his. Helen Bones, Mr. Wilson's cousin, was brought on from Chicago to attend Evelyn College in Princeton[18] and to make the Wilson home hers during all holidays and in as many weekends as school discipline allowed. At a later date one of Mr. Wilson's nephews, young Woodrow Kennedy,[19] was brought on from the West to live in the Wilson home and attend Princeton University. Mrs. Wilson's younger sister, Margaret Axson, who had been reared by an aunt in Georgia, became part of the Wilson household when she was in her early teens and remained in the home until her marriage.

For "society," in the smart sense of the word, the Wilsons cared little—who with minds to be fed can care much for it? But they *loved* people, Mrs. Wilson in particular, and her enjoyment of people stimulated in him a similar taste. During the twenty-nine years of their married life, they probably shared the majority of their meals at home with others. The guests were frequently house guests, many of them from the South, who in the old informal manner of southern hospitality arrived on invitations which set no limits to their stay. According to their inclinations and other engagements, they would linger several days or several weeks and sometimes several months. Occasionally there would be a "formal" dinner, formal only in the sense that evening clothes were worn, and the guests were numerous. Doctor Joseph Wilson would sometimes grumble at "so much company," but in his heart he enjoyed much of it—if he could hear what the guests said—not that he was deaf, he would insist, but that so few people took the pains to "ar-tic-u-late." The old doctor, himself a gifted conversationalist when he found a stimulating or receptive companion, enjoyed his own talk, but he enjoyed "Woodrow's" even more, and he had a pretty pride in his son as host when there was a large and interesting company at the table. "Did you see

26. Ellen Louise Axson Wilson at the White House, 1913

Woodrow at his own table when there were people there worth talking to, especially men?" he once asked a friend, and, without awaiting the answer, added: "He is *brilliant.*"

The love of Mr. and Mrs. Wilson for each other was complete but unselfish. It seemed to stimulate in them loving-kindness for others and to evoke loving-kindness from others. They were two strong personalities. Under Mrs. Wilson's gentleness, there was inflexible steel. With her principles there was no disputing, and she would yield her opinions only if, like the man from Missouri, she was "shown." She and he would discuss serious matters pertaining to his educational or political career very earnestly, and sometimes would differ widely, but there was never the edge of irritation in the tones in which they would express their differences of opinion. There was only mutual desire to get at the truth of the matter. The author of this book knew Mr. Wilson intimately in his family life, was at different periods and for many years practically a member of his household, met him three times a day at the family board, saw him in association with his wife and their daughters, and cannot recall ever having heard a harsh word from Mr. Wilson to any member of his family. These strong personalities never clashed. In quiet, even tones they would earnestly debate the matter under consideration, and he would sometimes say, with mingled affection and firmness: "You are wrong, my dear, you are wrong," and she in similar tone and spirit would reply: "Woodrow, I don't see how you can think that." But the adjustment was always arrived at without friction.

Doubtless all love involves sacrifice, and they made their daily concessions to each other, not as under the stern taskmaster, Duty, but in cheerful affection. Her supreme sacrifice, though she was probably never fully conscious of it, was to his public career. Undoubtedly, if she had wanted to choose the course of her own greatest happiness, she would have chosen that they should remain in the attractive house in Library Place, Princeton, which they built for themselves in 1896–1897. She was not given to morbid retrospection, but anyone who knew her well may be fairly confident in guessing that had she reviewed from the White House their married life, she would probably have said that they had never been so completely happy as when they were Professor and Mrs. Wilson of Library Place, living the quiet academic and domestic life with their three little girls, undisturbed by the tumults of the great world. In those days of his professorship he was seldom away from home except on brief lecture trips. In those simple days, they seldom left home for summer vacations. Their joys were quiet joys, reading aloud together in the winter before the pleasant open wood fire; in the summer, out on the lawn under the trees, usually with two or three friends to enjoy with them the things they read and discussed. The arrival of a new set of books was an event, or a newly acquired inexpensive but tasteful sketch or etching. One of the big little events of those days was a very small art loan exhibition set up for a brief while by Allan Mar-

27. The Wilsons at Prospect, the president's residence,
Princeton University, ca. 1910

quand in one of the university rooms. Among the pictures was a
Bouguereau Madonna, which Mrs. Wilson copied and which hangs
in Mr. Wilson's house today, along with a great number of landscape
paintings which she made in later years at Lyme, Connecticut. These
were the things that she loved more than the pomp and circumstances of official life. But Mr. Wilson's career was more important to
her than her personal gratifications, and so she threw herself with all
her enthusiasm and keen intelligence into the expanding career—as
president of Princeton University, as governor of New Jersey, as
president of the United States.

Indeed, she carried into the White House, as she had carried into
the presidential home, Prospect, in Princeton, the same human hospitality that she had practiced in the Library Place home, that is to
say, amid the distinguished guests, folk whom she must entertain,
there were constantly scattered many of the old friends whose only
claim to recognition was the human claim. She was the most loyal of
friends, as she was the most devoted of wives and mothers. He and
she conducted the social obligations of the White House with simple
dignity, recognizing what they owed the public, but resolutely de-
clining to make themselves a daily part of the White House exhibit.

28. Ellen Axson Wilson (*left*) and daughters Jessie, Margaret, and Eleanor
at the White House, 1913

There was sunshine in her disposition, and under that sunshine he
was constantly being melted to see people whom instinctively he did
not care to see. At her urgency he would sometimes reluctantly consent to have certain luncheon and dinner guests whom she proposed, but after having consented and met the guests, he would usually express himself as frankly pleased that she had insisted on his
doing the thing that he had done.

After her death, President Wilson said with much feeling to an intimate friend: "I don't know that I would be here in the White House
at all if it had not been for Ellen and the way that she has influenced
the growth of my career, and yet I sometimes regret that we ever
came here, for I almost fear the strain of it all has cost my darling's
life, and that if we had lived the old, quiet life she might be living still.
But now that she has gone, I feel that I ought for her sake to devote
myself more entirely to alleviating the suffering of the world."

It is significant that it was in the same month that he buried his
wife—that fatal month of August 1914—after the Great War had

begun, that in conversation with friends he laid down the basic conception, which was afterwards developed into the idea of the League of Nations. Possibly the president's thought was correct; possibly Mrs. Wilson would have lived longer if she had remained in the quiet home she loved so dearly in Library Place. Who knows? But one thing is certain: she would rather have died when and where she died than have lived at the cost of any diminution of the career in which her husband realized to the fullest his talents and his powers.

That summer of 1914 was a period of anguish for the president. The burdens of office were unusually heavy, because, added to pressure for patronage and the formation of national policies, he was harassed by the international situation. Mexico was aflame, and the war clouds of Europe were gathering. He was endeavoring in the face of persistent opposition to establish toward Mexico a new attitude in international relations based on fundamental justice and patience rather than on chauvinism. Nobody knew better than he how popular he could become by consenting to war with Mexico, but dearer to him than popularity or advancement was the fulfillment of what his conscience told him was right and just, and so he had to be calm while others were excited. From the first threats of war in Europe, he saw how precarious must be the position of the United States, and that if this country could be kept out of the conflict at all, it must be also by the exercise of great patience and wisdom. Added to these things, of which the country knew, there was that heartache of which the country knew little or nothing. Mrs. Wilson had been ill all through the winter and spring,[20] but early in the summer she had seemed to recuperate for a little while, and he had taken fresh hope. The improvement, however, was only temporary. Gradually he saw her failing and he began to fear the worst. He must not betray his personal sorrow in his public activities. In the White House office he would show a cheerful face to the importunate seekers for place, but when the morning's work was over he would hasten back to the White House and go directly to her room. Sometimes she was able to accompany him to lunch, sometimes not. Under the strain, he seemed to grow more patient, sweeter in all his contacts, though not less firm, where firmness was necessary. She in her own illness and suffering—and her physical suffering was very great—was constantly anxious about his health, and so she would insist that he should go to the theater, for she saw and said that he always came away from the theater rested. He would say to Admiral Grayson: "Will you go with me to the theater this evening? I don't want to go, but Ellen insists that I must." And, true to her prediction, he would seem to get a little benefit from the evening's relaxation. As the end drew on, he did as much of his writing as possible by her bedside. It was widely known throughout the country at the time that he was sitting at her side when he wrote the famous note in which he offered the services of the United States to the contending nations of Europe to adjust their difficulties and avoid the war.

His anxiety for her was intense, but he must not allow that to lessen his usefulness to the nation and the world. He was too courageous to want to be deceived about her condition, and he demanded that the doctor tell him daily the truth about it. Dr. Grayson long realized that the situation was very serious, and when he would go to the president's library each morning after his visit to Mrs. Wilson, he would say: "Mr. President, I am sorry, but I cannot make a very good report. She is not improving." The president would look up, listen intently, and then would heave a deep sigh and shake his head. Practically her last coherent talk was with Admiral Grayson. It was about three hours before her death. In a whisper she called him close to the bedside and bade him sit down. Feebly attempting to raise her head to look around the room and assure herself that there was no one else there, she said, placing her hands around his: "Doctor, I realize that I am going. You know him and he is devoted to you. Take good care of Woodrow." And as she said it she feebly patted his hand and smiled with that smile which all who remember her vividly recall. The doctor, controlling his emotion as best he could, presently summoned the family, for he knew as well as she that the end was not far off. The president sat beside the bed, softly patting her hands and calling her "dearie," as he had done day by day and many times a day throughout the prolonged illness. He and the girls controlled themselves until the end came quietly, peacefully. Then tenderly laying her hand across her breast, he walked to the window and for the first time broke down.

It was characteristic of his considerateness that he sent a telegram to Mrs. Wilson's only surviving brother, who was lecturing at the University of Oregon, carefully worded to prevent shock. The telegram was sent two days before Mrs. Wilson's death and simply said: "Ellen is not so well. If you can without inconvenience arrange to leave your work I should like to have you come to Washington." Even the summons to the absent daughters several days prior to this had been so thoughtfully worded as to give them no intimation that the anxiety was acute. Mrs. Sayre said afterwards that the message that came to her implied nothing more than that they would like to have her come on a little visit to Washington.

The beauty of the Wilson family life was due in large part to the fact that the discipline of the household was the discipline of love, not of law. The Wilson girls were docile, not because they lacked spirit, for they were high-spirited above the average, and not through fear of parental displeasure, for that was never displayed, but because they lived in an atmosphere of love, and because they were gently guided and never harshly driven. Mr. Wilson's attitude toward his daughters almost from their babyhood was that of a reasoning human being dealing with minds that ought to be reasonable. He did not issue commands; he merely talked with them naturally, letting them know his opinions as to how children ought to behave, and these opinions, so affectionately delivered, were translated into rules of conduct by the girls. Toward their father their attitude was complete devotion and respect mingled with affection. There was never placed upon them the severity of restraint, and yet there was always a sense of filial obedience in that household, the sweeter because cheerfully given. While their early instruction was left largely to their mother—afterwards, of course, to the governess and the teachers in their primary schools—he seemed desirous that an atmosphere of education and straight and high thinking should be thrown around them; in other words, in their presence he talked of the things of the mind, inducing them by easy degrees into a liking for intellectual matters, not talking down to them but talking with them with dignified simplicity. When they were still small children, but, as he believed, old enough to understand religious instruction, he instituted the good old Presbyterian fashion of family prayers in the home, saying that while hitherto he had not followed his father's custom of reading the daily chapter aloud from the Bible and offering extempore prayer for daily guidance, he felt that for the children's sake now this should be done, and for many years this custom was followed.

However, a picture only of pedantry and piety would be a misleading picture of the Wilson family household.[21] It was a home of laughter and sunshine, of continual joking, of limericks and puns, of nonsense and gaiety, interwoven with the serious things. A sense of humor characterized the whole family. Mrs. Wilson contended that she was very poor at making jokes herself or remembering other people's jokes, but she had an immense relish of the fund coined by others. If she truly did not remember jokes, that was perhaps fortunate, for, like many another dutiful wife, she had to laugh repeatedly at her husband's jokes reiterated to the different guests around the table. Sometimes the jokes were his own invention; sometimes they were anecdotes; sometimes they were family jokes of the sort familiar to all normal families. One of these that he long relished and often repeated was of the old servant at Bryn Mawr who was distinguishing between the older babies (Eleanor had not then yet been born), and who said: "Margaret is pretty like her papa, but Jessie is smart like her mama."

After some important history had been made the family would laugh at an amusing prognostication that Margaret had made when she was little more than a baby, many years before her father became president of the university. A little playmate, daughter of one of the professors, had one day pointed to Prospect, the president's house, and said: "We are going to live there some day, for my papa is going to be president of this college." And Margaret retorted: "That's nothing; my papa is going to be president of the United States," which would seem to go far toward qualifying Margaret as one of the "original Wilson men."

In the most important things, he allowed for his daughters' individual inclinations, as, for instance, in the matter of their education. Whether they should go to college or not was left altogether to their own choice and discretion, with the result that Jessie went through the four years of college life and graduated, Margaret took only two years in college, and Eleanor never went to college at all.[22] Margaret preferred to devote herself to music, Eleanor to painting, and, after graduation from college, Jessie to social work, and each was given full opportunity to develop her own tastes. After he had become president, one day, while on a long automobile ride, he told a friend that he naturally hoped his daughters would marry and yet he would be sorry when they did marry, but that he himself would never undertake to give them any advice in the matter; that he had talked with them often about different kinds of men, trying to insinuate into their minds sound notions as to the sort of men women should entrust their happiness to. But he said: "I am relying chiefly on the education they have had from their mother. If that does not lead them to a right choice, I do not see what can. They must make their own choice. Of course (and he smiled as he said it) no choice they make will satisfy me, but if they make a distinctly wrong choice, I shall never say anything about it. That is one time that I shall act a part of the liar to the end."

Though he has been constantly called the autocrat, he was certainly never autocratic in the management of his family, and, indeed, his supposedly autocratic behavior in public must be scrutinized to be understood. Back of that, as back of everything else in his personality, there is history and a rationale. The rationale is the rationale of leadership. His instinct for democracy involved the idea that, because a democracy is free, it is the more necessary that it be led. His faith in the people has never been a faith in the supreme wisdom of the people, but rather in the capacity of the people to be led right by those whom they elect and constitute their leaders. Violently opposed to the idea of a class whose privilege it is to rule, firmly believing as he himself has often said that a democracy is being continually enriched from its lower strata, that the leaders very often come from among the humble, yet leaders there must be. Neither timidity nor a fatuous faith in the infallibility of the people should obscure their obligation as leaders to precede the crowd, to blaze the way, to have the courage to propose new policies, and to fight doggedly for the things in which the leaders believe.

Mr. Wilson's whole campaign for the governorship of New Jersey was based on the proposition that he should lead and not follow, that he should be the prime mover in a program of legislation that would deliver the people and the state of New Jersey from domination by corporate interests. He called attention to the fact that the governor is the only state officer elected by all the people, that senators and members of the Assembly are elected by smaller groups in restricted geographical areas, but that all qualified voters vote for the governor, and that, therefore, the governor is in a peculiar sense the representative of the whole people, that in all his procedure he must insofar as possible think of the people as a whole and not of special groups among the people. The people as a whole should hold the governor to the strictest accountability. That was his philosophy of the office.

It was this conception doubtless that made him impatient of the individuals who undertook to press upon his attention their preferred claims for appointment to office or their special interest in a governmental policy. When he became president he gave scant consideration to those who were loudest in insisting on what they called a vigorous policy toward Mexico, for he realized that these were chiefly people who had land interests or mineral interests in Mexico, and he said with characteristic acidity: "I have continually to pause and remind myself that I am president of the United States and not of a special group of gentlemen who have financial interests in Mexico." A man who had special financial interests in Mexico on one occasion spoke heatedly to the president saying: "It is absolutely your duty to intervene in Mexico, to send soldiers there at once to protect American interests." The president, after listening with attention to the end of this gentleman's presentation of the case, said: "Very good, Mr. So-and-so, I will do that if you will consent to have your two boys put in the army and sent with the first contingent to Mexico." The man protested that this was not fair, that the president evaded the question, and the president replied: "No, somebody else's sons would have to spill their blood for your property. I presume that would be fair." Mr. Wilson had to be convinced that a given proposition was in the interest of the entire community before his imagination was inflamed or his interest engaged.

All this means that a good many men visited the White House offices considerably swollen with a sense of their importance and came away with the balloon badly punctured and proportionately irritated. People would sometimes say to him: "Why don't you flatter these people more than you do, even though you do not intend to do what they ask you to do? Why can't you bluff them a little and give them the impression that you were glad to hear what they had to say? Mr. McKinley used to do that, and he was a very popular man. Mr. McKinley would greet Tom, Dick, or Harry with the assurance that of all the men in the country he was just the man that Mr. McKinley was most anxious to see on that particular occasion. That sort of thing makes for popularity; that sort of thing makes the wheels go round smoothly." So they would say to him in effect, and he in effect would reply: "I cannot say what I do not mean; I cannot mean what I do not think; I cannot flatter; it seems to me unnecessary."

This leads to the second explanation, the historical. It was while engaged in the Princeton controversy that Mr. Wilson learned to despise flattery. During the prolonged struggle, he heard many speeches delivered across the banquet table to Princeton alumni and Princeton undergraduates, the burden of which was that Princeton men are the choicest men of all times and all climes, better fitted than any other men in the world to govern their own lives and direct their own destinies, and that any proposal to dictate to them their daily associates was an infringement of their popular rights as Princeton men. To his keen perception, all this was rank demagoguery—an attempt to defeat the policy which he had proposed in the interest of what he believed to be a better educational plan by an appeal to vanity, egotism, and passion. His sensitive mind, sensitive as it was strong, reacted once and for all against flattery. In his younger days he had been very gracious in his public speeches, which were marked by the courtesy and consideration which was natural to him, but, disgusted with the flattering tone of these Princeton speeches delivered for sinister purpose, he came to despise flattery in all forms, and in his intense nature he carried his reaction too far. He too frequently failed to say the pleasant thing when he could say it quite sincerely because of a sensitive, and, if one chooses to say so, an over self-conscious fear of imitating that form of speech which he had learned to loath.

It was in this same Princeton experience that the democratic tendencies of his nature were emphasized, when he found that it was vested interest and class pride that was resisting the reformation he was trying to enact in Princeton, that the club life represented the antithesis of the democratic spirit. It was in these circumstances that all the latent democracy in him flamed into activity. And, again, because his was an intense nature, he reacted too far. His sympathy for the humble people begot in him a corresponding dislike of the smart, wealthy upper crust. He could make exceptions in individual cases. He knew, for instance, that Cleve Dodge and Cyrus McCormick were very rich but quite unspoiled by wealth. But toward people of the same type with whom he had not the advantage of intimate and affectionate personal acquaintance, he was inclined to be suspicious. The man in big business he was likely to scrutinize very closely. He would give his confidence to an humble man more quickly than he would to a representative of the wealthy class of one of the great American cities. In short, he was sometimes prejudiced unjustly toward men whose fundamental sympathies were very like his own, but to whom he would not give an opportunity to show him their real natures.

Having reacted strongly against all forms of flattery, he too often neglected to say the kind word which the conduct of others had earned from him. This, combined with his habit of getting so absorbed in a plan as to forget personalities, led him on some occasions to give offense even to those who admired him and were fond of him. Brief words of commendation would have made him and his administration more popular. Unfortunately, he too often did not offer that word. A staunch friend in Chicago,[23] who has remained a friend through thick and thin but who is critical as well as friendly, relates how back in the Princeton days, he was summoned from Chicago to Princeton to confer with the president on a matter of Princeton policy. He found that other prominent Princetonians had been summoned from other cities—from New York, Philadelphia, Baltimore. They were joined by one of Mr. Wilson's staunchest supporters in the faculty, Dean Harry Fine. After they had assembled in the president's library he talked to them for two hours. He asked no questions, he gave no opportunity for interruption, but with his usual clarity and cogency of argument he presented to them the plan he had formed, and then he curtly bade them good morning, courteously but without expression of gratitude for the time and trouble they had taken to respond to his call. This Chicago gentleman said: "As we walked down the street, Harry Fine (whose loyalty to the president has never been exceeded by anybody's) was in a towering rage. He said: 'He might at least have thanked you fellows for the trouble you have taken.'" And said the gentleman from Chicago in telling the story: "Of course, he ought to have thanked us; that was the least he could have done; but, after all, how small it is to think about that. He was thinking of something big for Princeton; he knew our devotion to Princeton; he had been planning this thing through many hours of hard and wearisome thinking; through days and weeks he had not spared himself; he had not thanked himself; and it did not occur to him to thank us. He was thinking of Princeton as a whole; he was not thinking of the sensibilities of individuals."

On an occasion in Washington, a group of gentlemen from the "Hill" were summoned to the White House for a conference, among them Senator John Sharp Williams of Mississippi. They also sat in silence for an hour or so listening to the president expound a plan that he had in mind. They also were given no opportunity to question or suggest modifications, but when the president had finished what he had to say to them they were courteously bidden good-bye. As they left the White House, Senator Williams, most loyal of Wilson men, laughed and said: "And he calls that a conference." Doubtless Senator Williams would have made the same analysis that the Chicago friend did—that the man was too intent on a big policy to be thinking about the feelings of individuals.

This has characterized Mr. Wilson throughout his administrative career. He has given himself unsparingly to the work of his administration as president of Princeton University, as governor of New Jersey, and as president of the United States. He has thought closely, and he has generally thought far ahead of those who were associated with him. In his own heart he knew that what he was planning was not for self-advantage but for the common welfare, and he expected toward that common welfare the same devotion from others that he was so willing to give. But was there not a factor here to reckon with—that pervasive thing which we call human nature? Most honest men dislike to be flattered, but they like to be appreciated. If they have given themselves heartily to a piece of work, they like a word of commendation from the leader. It would have cost Mr. Wilson nothing to give that word, and in not giving it he often made the "going" for himself harder.

He was impatient of interference, but, on the other hand, he scrupulously refrained from interfering with others. When he had appointed a man to an important office, he expected that man to be as personally responsible for the right conduct of that office as he held himself responsible for the conduct of the larger office of the presidency. He refused consistently to deal with bureau heads direct, insisting that they must deal with the cabinet officer in general charge of the department, and that if there was anything to come beyond the cabinet officer up to him, it must be brought by the cabinet officer himself, not by one of his subordinates. The orderly mind of Mr. Wilson worked schematically: section officers were responsible to division officers, division officers were responsible to bureau chiefs, bureau chiefs were responsible to the secretary in charge of the department, the secretary was responsible to the president, and he (the president) was responsible to the American people.

He was impatient, doubtless too impatient, of small details. If the man whom he had appointed to an important office was continually bringing to him small perplexities, Mr. Wilson inevitably assumed that he had not selected the right man for that office, and, unfortunately, he often made it evident that he thought so, though it must be added that he was extremely slow to dismiss a man whom he had once appointed to office. Only in extreme cases did he ever take the initiative in preempting an office. There were many changes in the cabinet during his two administrations, but all these changes were by voluntary resignation, except in one case,[24] in which the president asked for the resignation.

With all the explanation that can be made, the fact remains that Mr. Wilson was often not politic where being politic would have been most helpful. That letter "s" makes a difference. Being politic is not necessarily playing politics. In his intensity of nature, in his engrossment in the great things he had in mind, in his fixity of purpose, in his determination to go to the objective, he did sometimes seem to go ruthlessly, to overlook the purely human qualities of human beings. It was not that he was averse to being gracious, it was rather that he was too busy, that he was himself so far above petty motives that he could not quite make allowance for the little genial weaknesses of human nature. A small incident will illustrate this.

One day a friend who had been dining at the White House on a Sunday suggested to the president that he call in for consultation the various heads of the various war activities and express to them his appreciation of what they were doing. This was in the midst of the war; in fact, it was in June 1918 when this friend presumed to offer a little advice. Said he: "May I suggest that you call these men together as a large family, address them as a family, tell them how much you appreciate what they have been doing, their loyalty to the country, their loyalty to the government without regard to party affiliation (for more of them are Republicans than Democrats), tell them that with all the splendid achievements of the army and the navy, the war could not have been prosecuted successfully thus far had they not performed their parts so well. I know some of these men personally. They are big men, tremendously able men, but they are very human. They like commendation. Some of them are not averse to a little flattery. They would be pleased with this personal contact. You could have them feeding out of your hands. Then, having told them how pleased you are with what they have done, go on and tell them that this is only the beginning, that this war has been prosecuted successfully thus far and will be prosecuted to a successful end, because men have forgotten their division—the party lines, the personal prejudices—and have united together in strong team play, but that when the war is over there will be a yet more important work to do, a work of rehabilitation, a work of international negotiation to prevent the recurrence of such a war in the future. For the war is only the first step; the greater and more important step is to follow. Tell them that

the later, greater work cannot be brought to a successful accomplishment without the same disinterested and unified effort as that which
has carried on the war; tell them that the country will need them,
that you will need them just as much after hostilities have ceased as
the country and you need them now. Inspire them with a vision, but
insist that the vision can be realized only by complete and harmoni-
ous cooperation of such leaders as they have shown themselves to
be. I repeat: address them as the family, and tell them you are relying
on the family."

The president was frankly interested. He said: "That's a good idea.
I don't think, though, how it can be carried out, for there are so
many of these men." Said the visitor, now thoroughly warmed to his
subject: "No matter how many there are, there are certainly not
too many to find standing room in the East Room. Crowd them in
there—the more the better. Let them feel that they are a part of
something tremendously big, even bigger than the war." "Yes," he
said, "I think that's worth thinking of."

It was obvious that the suggestion had made a real impression on
him, but he never carried it out. Why? Not because he was lacking in
appreciation of what these men had done, or lacking in the generous
instinct to let them have full share in great accomplishments, but
simply because he was too busy with what seemed to him larger and
more important matters than establishing the human touch between
himself and these leaders, and because he did not make full and due
allowance for that amiable human weakness which leads most men
to like to hear from their chief that they have done a good job. He
himself has not gone around seeking men's praise, though he himself experienced the sweetness of it when it came unsolicited; but he
never calculated on that for a motive for action, and, therefore, he
never made due allowance for it as a motive of action in other man.

Where Mr. Wilson failed, if he failed at all, was in just those points
where the most ordinary men succeed. The man in the street finds it
easy to clap the other fellow on the shoulder and tell him what a
good fellow he is. Mr. Wilson could never do that. Temperamentally,
he was not made that way. To say this is merely to say that Mr.
Wilson has not had all the qualities. He had the greatest, some of the
least he lacked, but if one man had in himself all the qualities, what
would there be on this earth for Almighty God to do!

To say that he could not counsel with other men his equals is simply to say what is not true. For seven months in Europe he was in

almost daily counsel with the actual governing heads of European countries. It was rough sledding at times. It called for all the conviction and the patience that he had in him: the conviction as to the main issue—the League of Nations—to prevent the recurrence of war, which had become the ruling passion of his spirit, and the patience to meet with and deal with objections, counterproposals, a hundred different devices to spoke the wheels.

One of the charges made against Mr. Wilson at home was that he proved to be compromising in Paris, he who had been so often denounced for his unwillingness to accommodate his views to the views of others. There was one big fundamental thing that he wanted to put over, there in Paris, compared with which most other things were of minor consideration, and so, holding firm to his principle, he yielded at many points for the sake of the end in view. His closest friends have felt that it was a pity that upon his return to America, he could not have continued to compromise. They felt that there was a time when, without relaxing anything essential in the Covenant of the League of Nations, he could have got a ratification from the Senate, for there can be little doubt that when he returned from Europe in July 1919, the sentiment of the country at large was overwhelmingly in favor of the League of Nations. And yet later, after a campaign of adroit and infamous misrepresentation, there was a different story to tell. The people's minds had been poisoned, but the very unyieldingness of Mr. Wilson in the earlier stages of the controversy had unhappily played into the hands of his enemies. It must be remembered, however, that Mr. Wilson was ill, that the strain of Paris had sapped him, that he came home without the elasticity which had been so marked in Paris; he was a worn-out man, and before long there was to be a great collapse. When the debate in the Senate reached its crisis, he was flat on his back. A sick man is seldom sweetly reasonable. A sick man with the will of Woodrow Wilson is most unlikely to be extremely accommodating. He was prostrated, but his will was regnant, and from his sick bed he issued manifestos which were like a rallying battle cry. But by that time he was leading a forlorn hope. His strategy was bad, his purpose was splendid. It might be said of him as is said of another: "It is splendid, but it is not war." He could die in the ditch, but he could not in the circumstances lead his forces to a victory. Yet who shall say in the long run that he was wrong and his more politic friends right?

Time has passed now, and we find the Republicans, the opposition, engaged in fresh international negotiations,[25] and every success that they make is an approach to the thing that Mr. Wilson proposed and they rejected, and every day the sentiment for Mr. Wilson grows stronger, the admiration of him greater. And part of that admiration is based on the idea in the picture of a soldier who fell at the front fighting for his cause, of one who would not compromise, of one who had a purpose so great that he could yield nothing of it, of one who believed that he had found the thing that would save the world, and that this, and nothing else, should be accepted by his own nation. It is the picture of that battle-scarred warrior who fought all but to the death, literal death, physical death, for a cause that has stirred the hearts and minds of the American nation. These things must be calculated in the long view, not in the short view. It is possible that Woodrow Wilson, failing magnificently, has done more for the cause of the world's salvation than a triumphant Woodrow Wilson would have accomplished, for men now regard him as they regard the great champions in the history of the world's struggle for betterment, and nearly every one of those champions has been a martyr. It is the meritorious crown, not the victor's, which sits upon the brow of the world's supreme servitors. A hundred years from now, when the world is really at peace, and armies and navies have been scrapped, and the nations are united in a resolute purpose to preserve the order of the world, men will point back to that figure which they called tragic in 1920—the broken figure of Woodrow Wilson—as the man who gave the impulse to this whole thing, and loved it so greatly and fought for it so stubbornly that he broke, but the cause went on.

It is impossible in any chapter, even a very long chapter, to make the portrait of Woodrow Wilson's personality complete. The attempt has been made in this chapter not to defend him and not to praise him, but to point out insofar as the writer could what he essentially was. He was a man with a mission; he was a man, who, like all of the greatest reformers, has been obsessed with the idea that the world must be changed, that in stagnation is ruin, that things left to themselves tend to grow continually worse, and that only by great effort and devotion and courage and battling can things be made better.

As one looks back on the Woodrow Wilson of, let us say, 1890, the gentle, considerate, kindly, humorous, affectionate young man, and then views the Wilson of 1921, grim and isolated and sometimes sardonic, he realizes that Mr. Wilson has come a long course, that in some ways he has changed. He is not so amiable now, not so gracious now, not so propitiary now as he was thirty years ago. What is this change but the price, the terrible price, that he has had to pay for a great accomplishment? He, like the first Mrs. Wilson, would probably be personally happier now if he had never moved out of Library Place in Princeton. His disposition would be sweeter probably, but he could not stay there. There were voices calling him. He heard the voices, and he followed them. He was led over rough roads and through terrific struggles, and he has been wounded, wounded in the spirit of him as well as in the flesh, and yet, though he has grown somewhat as his Scotch ancestors called "dour," though the "Uncle Joseph" has grown stronger in him, to the cost of some of that boyish sweetness that characterized him in 1890, he has done things for the world without which the situation of the world would be ghastly.

Bad as has been the world situation following the armistice, how infinitely worse it would have been if there had not been some one to point the way of hope. And it was Woodrow Wilson, and practically Woodrow Wilson alone, who pointed that way. The very reproach led against him in Europe was that he was insisting on his own idea—the League of Nations—rather than giving full attention to those very "practical" interests for immediate rehabilitation; in other words, to set the nations as quickly as possible on their feet so that they could proceed as quickly as possible to sow the seeds of new wars and fight them yet to more ghastly finish. This one man insisted, amid all the confused voices, on one thing which alone could prevent the repetition of the disaster. He had to fight his way to that, and in the long fight he has suffered grievously. Everything has to be paid for with a price, and the greater the thing the higher the price. Woodrow Wilson has paid everything for the one purpose which he had in mind.

Biography should not be written as if it were psychology, especially if the biographers are not psychologists, but in attempting to explore "the abysmal deeps of personality" in Woodrow Wilson, one must lay stress on his unusual power of concentration. It was part of his philosophy of leadership that the leader must be capable, not only of firm decisions and swift acts when the occasion calls, but also of long periods of concentrated meditation. His companions knew that his prolonged unbroken silences betokened travail of thought, and they scrupulously respected his silent mental laborings. Frequently on long automobile rides he would lapse into silence, which he himself might break at intervals with a brief remark, like a diver coming up to breathe before replunging into silence and the deep. What he said might furnish a hint as to what road his mind was traveling—a word about the necessity of such and such a public policy, or about the character and mental traits of someone with whom he must wrestle in pending legislation. At other times his remarks would be trivial and irrelevant, a brief comment on a face or inanimate object by the roadside, or a whimsical joke, perhaps a breathless reading of the full name on the Von Steuben statue as the automobile swept round the corner of Lafayette Square: "Frederick William Augustus Henry Ferdinand Von Steuben." Mr. Tumulty, Mr. Ray Stannard Baker, Mr. Thomas Lamont,[26] and many others have disposed of the foolish legend that Mr. Wilson "would not take counsel," have shown that he sought and welcomed advice. But the final decision must be his, and therefore he must think hard as well as listen.

He never said a truer thing of himself than that he had "a one track mind." Silly distortions of this metaphor have been made by some who could not and others who would not understand his real meaning. He meant that when his tenacious mind grappled with a difficult idea, it was temporarily immune to other ideas. He was like a man climbing a difficult cliff who sweeps aside detritus to get a firmer footing for the next step. His mind is not on the detritus except as interference with the one thing on which his mind is fixed—getting to the top. The Princeton clubs were not the primary object of his concern; his quarrel with them was secondary to something which he considered bigger and more important; they were merely interferences with a plan for a reorganization of college life which he was convinced would be for the good of Princeton and American education in general. In Paris, everything else was incidental to the objective, a league of nations, which he believed with all his soul would bring to the world justice and order; temporary and partial adjustments were less important than a final adjustment of the whole world.

In his concentration on the iniquity of war and the necessity of measures to prevent its wholesale repetition, he did not have to visit battlefields and work himself into a frenzy over stories of German atrocity, in the manner of "four-minute speakers" selling Liberty Bonds and Red Cross subscriptions. He knew well enough what Germany was doing, what *war* was doing. It was not his business to churn himself into frantic excitement over individual incidents. He must keep cool in order to think straight. His mind must dwell less on the horror of the disease than on the remedy, like a surgeon who must remain calm when the patient is screaming with agony, for the surgeon needs all his wits about him to operate for the patient's cure.

Superficial critics said that because Mr. Wilson had no son to send to war he did not fully appreciate the anguish of war, was calmer than others because he felt less than others. They did not realize, did not try to realize how much more abhorrent to him than to the average man is war and the suffering it entails. He had a deep and painful sense of his personal responsibility for the death or hurts of every fallen American soldier. "I sent those boys over there," he would say repeatedly in the grave tones of one suffering deeply under an unavoidable necessity. His tender sympathies and keen sense of responsibility were deeply stirred when got the news in 1914 that some marines had been killed at Veracruz:[27] "I sent them there," he said solemnly, and repeated the remark when he attended their funeral in New York—against the advice of the secret service officers who had reason to suspect a plot against his life on that occasion. "I sent them to their deaths; of course I will attend their funeral, no matter what happens."[28] In the Great War, he avoided as much as possible the details of suffering and death in the American army, for he knew he would be unnerved if he allowed his active imagination to dwell on details. They had been sent where duty called them; he was heart and soul behind every intelligent, concerted plan to alleviate their sufferings in field and hospital; he lent an attentive ear to every individual complaint when he believed that anything could be done in justice to diminish the anxiety and suffering of parents or young wives; but he must not go over and over and over accounts of the suffering in detail. That would unfit him for the plan and action he had in mind to prevent recurrence of the tragedy. His abhorrence of war was so great that he was resolved that, God helping, the boys of the next generation should not be called to arms. On his western tour in behalf of the League of Nations, he was always deeply moved by the crowds of schoolchildren who greeted him in the streets. "I am the attorney of these children," he said repeatedly, "I am the trustee of their future. I must guarantee that they shall not be summoned to do and suffer what their parents and elder brothers have suffered!"

His love of the American soldier was deep and his admiration for him was boundless. When he got the news of Château-Thierry, his eyes flashed and his face flushed with pride. After the later developments, he often said in private, "Our boys turned the war!" He was too just to say, even in private, that they had *won* the war, but he gloried in the thought that it was they who gave the *turn* from defeat to victory. There is robust partisanship in Woodrow Wilson. When he was the sedate president of Princeton University, he rejoiced in a Princeton football victory or was dejected by a Princeton defeat as much as any undergraduate. He *felt*—it was too irrational to be called *belief*—that Princeton men were a little bit superior to anybody else as athletes. So toward the American soldier boys, he felt in his heart, though he was too diplomatic to hint it aloud, that they were unquestionably the best soldiers in Europe. In France he took pride in the "set-up" of the American soldier in contrast with the soldiers of the other countries.

After the termination of his presidency, much of his voluminous correspondence was with the former service men, particularly the invalided. Between him and them there was a mutual recognition of comradeship—they had been broken in the same cause. Some of them wrote him charmingly naive letters, badly spelled, atrociously "slangy." Sometimes there was doggerel verse in the letters, ranging in theme from "Old Glory" to "cooties." One of the latter inspirations described the cootie in terms of affection, as "one that sticketh closer than a brother." One of the war stories that Mr. Wilson loved was about a doughboy who stooped down in the trench to remove a biting "cootie" from his leg; at that instant a "whiz-bang" passed over his head and exploded. Stooping had saved his life; the "cootie" had caused him to stoop; so he took the "cootie" from the ground and put it back on his leg—the insect had earned the right to continue its meal! That story was calculated to appeal to Mr. Wilson, because, in addition to its grotesque humor, it carried the idea of *justice—even* to a "cootie."

Every letter, even every newspaper that arrived for him by post at 2340 S Street[29] received some kind of acknowledgment—usually dictated to his secretary and brother-in-law, Mr. Randolph Bolling, to be signed by him, for Mr. Wilson "saved his hand" as much as possible in his illness, but the thoughts and the salient words of each letter were his, scrupulously preserved by Mr. Bolling. None of the letters was more welcome or more cordially responded to than those from the former service men. He frequently addressed them as his "comrades," he *always* thought of them as comrades. In his automobile rides around Washington, he would sometimes, if absorbed in conversation or meditation, fail to see people who bowed to him, though he was always anxious to acknowledge every salutation, but he seemed to have a clairvoyant intuition for the presence of the uniform of a soldier, sailor, or marine, and would salute every service or ex-service man he passed, often when he was not seen or recognized by the young men themselves.[30]

A wounded soldier on the roadside was always a signal for the chauffeur to stop the car. There was many a chat between Mr. Wilson and the men. Some of the encounters were pathetic, some humorous. He had a meeting over in Virginia with Angus MacGregor about which he would tell with gusto, for Angus was an upstanding fellow, even though he couldn't stand at all, but had to swing himself along on his crutches, his shattered feet merely brushing the ground. Angus had been an aviator and was brought down over the lines by a German plane: "He got me, but I got him, too," said Angus, "and by dropping him and his plane, I saved the lives of a lot of our fellows, for he was out to bomb our trenches." Of course, Mr. Wilson liked that, liked also the indomitable optimism of Angus. It was on a Sunday afternoon, December 1921, that they met. Mr. Wilson's classmate, Cleveland Dodge, was spending the day with him—a happy day for Mr. Wilson, who fairly bubbled with laughter and anecdote in the warming presence of this beloved friend. After lunch Mr. and Mrs. Wilson and Mr. and Mrs. Dodge went for a ride in Virginia. At the rickety old bridge which crosses Hunting Creek, they got their first sight of Angus MacGregor, swinging himself by his shoulders and his crutches along the bridge. Of course the car stopped, and Angus was bidden to get in, which he did with the assistance of Mr. Dodge. Angus talked freely. He was on his way back home to Suffolk, Virginia, a hundred or two miles away. "Surely not afoot!" Mr. Wilson exclaimed—if Angus' mode of locomotion could be called "afoot." Well, Angus "expected" people would give him lifts along the way, people were "mighty good about that." He had spent all his money getting to Washington to see his sister, but he had arrived only to find that she had closed up the house and gone to Suffolk. So he had turned around and was on his way back. Mr. Dodge, who had joined in the conversation, ranging wide over Angus' war and hospital experience, told Angus that he wanted to pay his railway fare back to Suffolk. Angus said he couldn't take the money unless Mr. Dodge would give him his address so he could return it. "Oh," said Mr. Dodge, "never mind the address; I am just an old gray Santa Claus; if you must regard the money as a loan, pass it on to some other soldier in need of a lift." Before Angus left them to take the train, Mr. Wilson requested that he write to him and tell him how he fared on the journey. In due time the letter arrived.[31] It was from the Jefferson Hotel in Richmond. That was probably like Angus, the blessed optimist. Penniless on the roadside one day, the next day a guest at the Jefferson. Angus will always encounter Santa Claus somewhere. He deserves to. And he will be Santa Claus to the other fellow if he has any money, as Angus would probably say, "in his jeans." Mr. Wilson loved Angus and remembered him. I wonder if he chanced to recall the meeting his poet Wordsworth had with the leach gatherers. The leach gatherer was old, Angus young, but in some respects they were alike, both had been "done in," one by war, one by age, and both were irrepressible optimists, both unconsciously taught the lesson of "Resolution and Independence," as Wordsworth worded it in the title to his poem.

When Mrs. Wilson told the story of Angus to Mr. and Mrs. Charles Dana Gibson, Mrs. Gibson exclaimed: "Fancy being picked up on the road by Woodrow Wilson and Cleveland Dodge! It was worth being smashed up for." But Angus was only one of a multitude of soldier friends that Mr. Wilson acquired in his days of relaxation after leaving the White House.

If in some ways he grew more severe as he grew older, in other ways he grew more tender. He had more "moods," or at least indulged them more, after his illness began. High strung and intense of nature, ill, broken in nerves, it would have been strange if he had not sometimes been caustic and impatient and severe. But at other times, and quite as frequently, he would be tender as a child, sympathetic as a woman, and sometimes with a kindness that radiated to all around him.

To see him in one of those moods of sunshine was to see a lovely and memorable spectacle. Seated in the library in S Street, always in the same chair, in exactly the same nook by the fireplace, an armchair, varnished oak frame, upholstered in brown leather, well worn, he would turn on everybody in the room in rotation, a face that shone with loving-kindness, a face that seemed more placid after the expressions of pain and severe thought had passed from it. There was much of the old-time consideration in the tone and manner with which he would talk to his visitors or to members of the family, a touch now and again of the old propitiatory tone, genial warmth, and the old captivating smile. In these latter days he was less calcula-

29. Edith Bolling, engagement photograph, 1915

ble than in the early days, when he was always lovely, but his moods of loveliness in the latter days were not less winning than of old, only different. His long, hard battles for the things in which he believed changed him in some ways on the surface, but in the depths of him there was something unchanged. The sunshine was still there, though at times it might be temporarily concealed by clouds of sorrow, pain, and grim purpose.

Good fortune and misfortune have mingled in Mr. Wilson's career, but he would say doubtless that good fortune has predominated, and he would count it among the greatest evidences of his good fortune that he met and loved and won the love of her who is now Mrs. Woodrow Wilson. Without love Woodrow Wilson simply could not live. He who seems so stern is to an extraordinary degree beyond

30. Wilson and his fiancée Edith Bolling at a baseball game, 1915

that of most men dependent upon love, close personal love, daily love. Mrs. Ellen Wilson knew that and gave the supreme testimony to her own self-effacing love for him when she expressed to him the hope that when she was gone he would marry again. He said to an intimate friend in anticipation of his second marriage: "Doubtless the country will be shocked at my marriage, but I know that if Ellen's spirit perceives, she would have it so."

What he would have done without Mrs. Edith Wilson in the terrible years when America was engaged in the war, and yet more terrible years personally when his health broke, must make any friend shudder merely to contemplate. Of course, the fact is that he could not have gone on without her. Her strength of character, her strength of mind, and, added to all else, the strength of her physical constitution, has brought her through, and brought her smilingly through, a terrific experience, which to her has doubtless not seemed terrific because sweetened and sanctified by perfect mutual love. Few women are made by nature to *look* so completely the part of a great man's wife as she. There is something royal in her bearing and royal radiance in the smile that she turned upon the crowds in the capitals of Europe and at home. She fascinated the people of France just by the dignity of her bearing, the beauty of her smile, and perhaps one might add without seeming to descend to levity, the perfection of her clothes. She was made to adorn a great place, and yet great place is quite unimportant to her, quite negligible among the things she really values. What she cares most for is home and her husband and her kin. She once remarked that she would have only one regret when they left the White House, and that was "moving out of this very comfortable house," as she said.

She does not feel that regret now, for the modest home in S Street is a source of unfailing joy to her. She continually congratulates herself and him on their good luck in stumbling quite accidentally on this place when they were looking for another. His dependence on her is complete, and she has made herself practically his prisoner, which is to say, love's prisoner. Her whole day is measured and ordered according to his needs. She makes appointments to see visitors only at such times as he will not be in need of her. That is a very small portion of each day; all the rest of the day belongs completely to him.

Notes

∾

Chapter One
Woodrow Wilson and His Father

1. Woodrow Wilson's father was Joseph Ruggles Wilson, who was born at Steubenville, Ohio, on February 28, 1822, the son of James Wilson and Anne Adams Wilson, both of whom were immigrants from Ulster. Joseph Ruggles Wilson attended the local academy in Steubenville and was graduated from Jefferson (now Washington and Jefferson) College as valedictorian of his class in 1844. A candidate for the Presbyterian ministry, he attended Western Theological Seminary and Princeton Theological Seminary from 1845 to 1847. After teaching in Steubenville, he was ordained in 1849 and began his ministry in a small church in Pennsylvania. From 1851 to 1855, he was professor of chemistry and natural science at Hampden-Sydney College in Virginia and pastor of a nearby country church. He had meanwhile married Janet, or Jessie, Woodrow on June 7, 1849.

Wilson's real ministerial career began in 1855, when he was called to the pastorate of the First Presbyterian Church of Staunton, Virginia. Mainly through the efforts of his brother-in-law, James Woodrow, he was called to the large and prestigious First Presbyterian Church of Augusta, Georgia, and was pastor there from 1858 to 1870. He was professor of pastoral and evangelistic theology at the Columbia Theological Seminary, 1870–1874; pastor of the First Presbyterian Church of Wilmington, North Carolina, 1874–1885; and professor of didactic, polemic, and historical theology at the Southwestern Presbyterian University, 1885–1893. After his retirement from this latter position, he lived in New York, Columbia, South Carolina, Richmond, Wilmington, North Carolina, and Princeton. He died in Woodrow Wilson's home in Princeton on January 21, 1903. He received the degree of Doctor of Divinity from Oglethorpe University in 1857 and was thereafter always known as Dr. Wilson.

Dr. Wilson was one of the founders of the southern Presbyterian Church; in fact, that denomination was organized in his church in Augusta in 1861. Dr. Wilson was permanent clerk of the General Assembly of that denomination from 1861 to 1865; stated clerk, 1865–1898; and moderator of its General

Assembly in 1879. For an excellent discussion of Dr. Wilson's career, see John M. Mulder, *Woodrow Wilson: Years of Preparation* (Princeton, N. J.: Princeton University Press, 1978), pp. 3–28.

2. He probably referred to Dr. Grayson.

3. Axson here refers to Wilson's maternal grandfather, the Reverend Thomas Woodrow, who was born in Paisley, Scotland, in 1793, was pastor of the Annetwell Street Congregational Church of Carlisle, England, 1820–1835, and moved with his family to New York and Canada and thence to Chillicothe, Ohio, in 1835–1837.

4. Janet (always called Jessie) E. Woodrow Wilson, born in Carlisle on December 20, 1830. What Axson says about her in the following paragraphs was undoubtedly true; however, Axson's description is somewhat idealized. She was shy, sensitive to alleged slights, given to periods of depression, and seems to have been utterly without a sense of humor. Her relationship to her son Woodrow was that of an overprotective mother who managed in many subtle ways to keep her son emotionally attached to her until his marriage to Ellen Axson. Jessie Wilson died from an unknown disease on April 15, 1888.

5. Joseph Ruggles Wilson and Jessie Wilson had four children. The oldest was Marion Williamson Wilson, born at Chartier's Manse, Pennsylvania, on October 20, 1851. She married the Reverend Anderson Ross Kennedy in 1872 and moved with him to the southwestern frontier in Arkansas. She and her husband died in 1890, leaving three children to be cared for by Kennedy relatives. The second Wilson child was Annie Josephine, born at Hampden-Sydney College on September 8, 1853. She married George Howe, M.D., of Columbia, South Carolina, in 1876. Widowed in 1895, she and her family afterward lived largely upon the largesse of her brother Woodrow. She died on September 16, 1916. Thomas Woodrow Wilson, the third child, was born in Staunton, Virginia, soon after midnight on December 29, 1856. The fourth child was Joseph R. Wilson, Jr. (he always signed himself with a middle initial), who was born in Augusta on July 20, 1867. After an undistinguished preparatory schooling, he attended Southwestern Presbyterian University and was graduated from that institution in 1888. "Josie" or "Dode," as he was diminutively called, did not have the intellectual qualities of his father and brother. Even so, he had a fairly successful career in journalism in Clarksville, Tennessee, and Nashville. He married Kate Wilson in 1892 and was in business in Baltimore from 1913 until his death on February 26, 1927.

6. Wilson did not learn his letters until he was nine and did not learn to read until he was twelve. Edwin A. Weinstein, in *Woodrow Wilson: A Medical and Psychological Biography* (Princeton, N. J.: Princeton University Press, 1981), pp. 14–19, has concluded that Wilson most probably suffered from developmental dyslexia, and this conclusion is strongly supported by another eminent neurologist, the late Dr. Norman Geschwind of the Harvard Medical School. N. Geschwind to A. S. Link, August 13, 1982 (letter in Link's pos-

session), and N. Geschwind to August Heckscher, May 12, 1983 (letter in Heckscher's possession).

Wilson attended Joseph T. Derry's "select classical school" in Augusta from 1865 to 1870 and Charles H. Barnwell's school in Columbia from 1870 to 1873. Thus he had had only eight years of formal schooling when he entered Davidson College in 1873, at which time he must have met that institution's entrance requirements in Latin, Greek, and other subjects. He did well at Davidson in all subjects except mathematics (during the first term of his freshman year). Alexander L. George and Juliette L. George, in *Woodrow Wilson and Colonel House: A Personality Study* (New York: The John Day Co., 1956), pp. 6–7, suggest that Wilson's lateness in learning to read was an unconscious form of rebellion against an overbearing father who put tremendous emphasis upon learning in general and on the correct use of the English language in particular.

7. He referred (Baker interviews, February 8, 10, and 11, 1925) to Richard Theodore Ely, about whom see chapter 3, note 16.

8. Woodrow Wilson's uncle, James Woodrow, was a man of many parts. Born in Carlisle, England, May 30, 1828, he graduated from Jefferson College in 1849, studied under Louis Agassiz at Harvard in 1853, and went on to receive the Ph.D. degree in science from Heidelberg University in 1856. He taught at Oglethorpe University, then in Alabama, from 1853 to 1861 and was ordained to the Presbyterian ministry in 1859. He served as Perkins Professor of Natural Science in Connection with Revelation at the Columbia Theological Seminary from 1861 until he was driven from his chair in 1886 because he was a leading proponent in the United States of theistic evolution. Among his many other activities, he was editor and publisher of *The Southern Presbyterian*, professor at and president of South Carolina College (now the University of South Carolina), and president of a bank in Columbia, South Carolina. He received many honorary degrees and was elected moderator of the Synod of South Carolina in 1901 in spite of his allegedly heretical views. He died in 1907.

Dr. Woodrow took a special interest in his nephew, Woodrow Wilson, and Woodrow respected, even revered, his uncle until the latter's death. Like his father, Woodrow Wilson strongly supported his uncle in his long-drawn-out controversy with church authorities over his views on evolution.

9. He could have been the Reverend Dr. Francis McFarland, moderator of the General Assembly of the Presbyterian Church in 1856, who was pastor of Bethel Church in Virginia from 1823 to 1835 and 1841 to 1871.

10. That is, Stockton Axson.

11. "Old Dr. Wilson was not a fundamentalist in religion. He had areas of questioning that he never brought into the light. He undoubtedly grew more liberal as he grew older, disliking the extreme theological type. Religion became more and more simple with less ado about forms and ceremonies. At

his best he was a powerful preacher and a strong personality. He was a much wider reader than his son chiefly in theology and history." Baker Interviews, February 8, 10, and 11, 1925.

12. James Henley Thornwell, D.D. (1812–1862), like Dr. Wilson, was one of the founders and luminaries of the southern Presbyterian Church. He was, among other things, professor of theology at the Columbia Theological Seminary from 1855 until his death in 1862.

13. Benjamin Morgan Palmer, D.D. (1818–1902), pastor of the First Presbyterian Church of Columbia, South Carolina, and professor at the Columbia Theological Seminary, then pastor of the First Presbyterian Church of New Orleans from 1856 to 1902. He was the biographer of Dr. Thornwell and the author of numerous devotional works. He died after being struck by a streetcar.

14. He was Ellen Axson Wilson's uncle, the Reverend Thomas Alexander Hoyt, who had grown up in South Carolina, been a pastor in Louisville and Nashville, and who was pastor of the Chambers Presbyterian Church in Philadelphia from 1884 to 1902. He was moderator of the General Assembly of the southern Presbyterian Church in 1880. One of Woodrow Wilson's favorite stories concerned a visit of Hoyt and his wife to the Wilsons in Middletown, Connecticut. Hoyt, thinking that the Wilsons had a manservant, left his boots outside his bedroom, whereupon Wilson, not wishing to embarrass him, blackened the boots himself.

15. That is, Axson.

16. This was a story about a mule which, becoming tired of pulling the streetcar, climbed up on the driver's platform for a rest. In Dr. Wilson's expanded version, the mule took over the driver's control and steered the streetcar himself.

17. Joseph Patrick Tumulty, about whom see chapter 7, note 9.

18. About which see chapter 5, note 21, and chapter 7, note 2.

19. He greatly scandalized the family by moving in with Mrs. Elizabeth Bartlett Grannis of 33 East 22nd Street, New York, during summers and vacation times from 1889 to 1893, and then on a regular basis after his retirement from 1893 to 1894. Mrs. Grannis, widow of Colonel Fred W. Grannis, was editor of the New York *Church Union* and of the *Children's Friend and Kindergarten Magazine*, founder and president of the National Christian League for the Preservation of Purity, and active in the movement for the sterilization of habitual criminals and mental defectives. There is reason to suspect that the relationship between Dr. Wilson and Mrs. Grannis was something more than platonic. Joseph R. Wilson, Jr., insisted that Woodrow Wilson persuade his father to remove himself from Mrs. Grannis' home, but Woodrow Wilson refused to interfere. However, when Dr. Wilson severed his relationship with Mrs. Grannis, Woodrow Wilson wrote to his wife: "The breach with 'that household' is something to be profoundly grateful for: I rejoice over it

from the bottom of my heart. It was nothing less than a tragedy to see so fine a mind, and so elevated, under such influences, under the spell of all the namby-pamby thought of the day." On another occasion, Wilson wrote to his wife: "Take it all in all, I think Mrs. Grannis is about as undesirable a companion as one could find in the ranks of chaste women,—as demoralizing as anyone could well be to one's manliness and self-respect."

20. A cathartic.

21. He was undoubtedly the Reverend Henry Clay Cameron, professor of Greek language and literature when Woodrow Wilson was an undergraduate at Princeton. In a diary entry for September 11, 1876, Wilson tells about a terrible argument between his father and Cameron on the "southern question" and refers to Cameron as a "*jackass.*"

Chapter Two
Health and Recreations

1. The Squeers of Dickens' *Nicholas Nickleby.*

2. A tincture used as a counter irritant.

3. W. B. Hale, *Woodrow Wilson: The Story of His Life* (Garden City, N. Y.: Doubleday, Page & Co., 1912).

4. Jessie Woodrow Bones, Wilson's first cousin, was the daughter of James W. Bones and Marion Woodrow Bones. Bones was a commission merchant in Augusta at this time and later moved to Rome, Georgia.

5. This address to the Atlantic Fleet, delivered on August 11, 1917, is printed in Arthur S. Link et al., eds., *The Papers of Woodrow Wilson*, 69 vols. (Princeton, N. J.: Princeton University Press, 1966–1993), vol. 43, pp. 427–31.

6. Axson here refers to Wilson's idea of preventing the exit of submarines from the North Sea by laying a barrage of nets and mines from Scotland to Norway, and to the support that Wilson gave to Assistant Secretary of the Navy Franklin D. Roosevelt in carrying out this plan, over the initial opposition of the American naval commander in the European theater, Admiral William S. Sims, and British naval authorities.

7. Robert Brodnax Glenn, governor of North Carolina, 1904–1909.

8. As the reader will see, Axson was never sure about the disease that is supposed to have caused Wilson to withdraw from Davidson College at the end of his freshman year in 1874. As a matter of fact, Wilson had a good year at Davidson and certainly was not subject to any serious illness. If he had a serious disease, it occurred during the summer following his departure from Davidson. But there is no evidence to support such a supposition. Dr. Weinstein (in *Woodrow Wilson*, p. 23) concludes that Wilson withdrew from Davidson on account of homesickness and emotional immaturity.

9. Wilson did suffer from a nervous stomach toward the end of the first term of his second year at the University of Virginia, but, as Weinstein (ibid.,

pp. 52–53) points out, he withdrew from the university, not on account of illness, but because he was bored with the study of law, at odds with his professors, and lovesick.

10. He was Abraham Thew H. Brower, who is a somewhat shadowy figure and seems to have been in some kind of business (Axson later calls him a banker). He and Jessie Bones were married about December 1881. The Browers later moved to Chicago, and their marriage ended in divorce.

11. Margaret Wilson, born April 16, 1886.

12. This brings up the matter of Wilson's health problems, about which we will have a good deal to say from time to time. Let it suffice to say here that Wilson complained increasingly of severe headaches while he was a student at the Johns Hopkins, and these headaches were accelerating at this very time. We can only speculate about the reasons for this affliction. One possible reason was that Wilson had been doing extensive reading in preparation for his final Ph.D. examination at the Hopkins in 1886. Although he wore glasses for reading at this time, his light might have been poor, and the strain of so much reading might have produced the headaches. This supposition does not seem to hold water, because the headaches persisted for years afterwards.

It has now been well established that Wilson suffered from severe hypertension, most likely since his young manhood. As we will see, he also suffered from severe stomach disorders from the 1880s until many years later. Dr. Grayson later told Ray Stannard Baker that one of the first things he did when Wilson came under his care in 1913 was to stop his use of "coal-tar medicines," that is, aspirin and other analgesic derivatives from coal tar, for headaches. It seems to us very likely that Wilson was overdosing on analgesics and continued to do so, much to the discomfort of his stomach. Much more will be said about his stomach problems later on.

13. Caleb Thomas Winchester (1847–1920), professor of English literature at Wesleyan. He remained a close friend of Wilson until Winchester's death in 1920.

14. Alois P. Swoboda, of Chicago, was probably the leading medical quack of his day. He combined a course of exercises with the prescription of drinking four pints of water a day to cure almost any illness. Swoboda claimed that drinking water freely after food was well digested would add to the quantity of one's blood supply. Wilson was under Swoboda's care, so to speak, from 1901 to 1902.

15. Edwin Curtis Osborn.

16. Peter Alfred V. van Doren, who was counsel to the borough of Princeton.

17. Wilson had a nervous tic under his right eye which, actually, was caused by pressure on a nerve and did not signify any neurologic problems.

18. Axson here refers to an illness that Wilson suffered in 1896. On about May 27, 1896, he suffered the loss of the use of his right hand and perhaps the

use of his right arm, and the disability in his right hand continued for about eight months. There has been some controversy about the etiology of this attack, which Bert E. Park, M.D., *The Impact of Illness on World Leaders* (Philadelphia: University of Pennsylvania Press, 1986), pp. 331–32, reviews. All neurologists who have studied Wilson's health history agree that he suffered from hypertension and that it was the basic cause of his neurologic illnesses. Weinstein (*Woodrow Wilson*, pp. 141–46) says that the incident of 1896 was probably a small stroke occasioned by the breaking off of an embolism in Wilson's left carotid artery, which found its way to his brain. Park (*The Impact*, pp. 332–33) says that it is more likely that Wilson had suffered a small stroke due to a small-vessel lacunar infarction, which in other language means that one of the small vessels in the brain on the left side had occluded or ruptured. From later excellent medical evidence, we know that Wilson was afflicted with hypertension, carotid artery disease, and atherosclerosis (a disease of the inner layer of the arteries) for a long period, and that he had a number of small strokes on account of either or all these conditions. Thus it is impossible to know precisely what caused the attack in 1896, but it was probably the first such incident, although Weinstein says that he may have suffered one in 1891.

19. Francis Delafield, M.D. (1841–1915), whom Wilson had first consulted in the autumn of 1895. Dr. Delafield told Wilson that he should wash out his stomach every morning with a siphon.

20. S.S. *Ethiopia.*

21. Regarding this change in Wilson's personality, Axson added the following (Baker interviews, February 8, 10, and 11, 1925):

Dr. Axson commented upon a subtle change which came over Mr. Wilson after the return from the trip to Europe in 1896. He cannot altogether explain it but says that it was notable. Before that time Mr. Wilson loved to "loaf and invite his soul." He said that he and old Dr. Wilson and Mr. Wilson often sat in Mr. Wilson's study and talked for hours. Both Dr. Wilson and Dr. Axson smoked, although Mr. Wilson did not. These were triangular talks up to 1896 and ranged over every possible subject. During these years also—from 1890 to 1896—he and Mr. Wilson would go for long bicycle rides and sit down by the roadside and talk. He remembers on one of these occasions of Mr. Wilson's having outlined the essay which he afterwards called "Mere Literature." Old Dr. Wilson was a fine talker, somewhat like Dr. Samuel Johnson, with a dash of Dean Swift, and his son always held him in the profoundest regard.

But after Mr. Wilson got back from his vacation in 1896 it was Dr. Wilson and Axson who would sit and talk after meals. Mr. Wilson was up and away on some of his many enterprises. Old Dr. Wilson often complained that Woodrow was getting away from his old interests. It was from 1896 until 1902 that his fame outside of Princeton began to grow.

22. William Ward Van Valzah, M.D., who had earlier treated Ellen Axson Wilson for various ailments. Weinstein (*Woodrow Wilson* p. 149) says that Dr. Van Valzah took Wilson off the stomach siphon.

23. James Holmes Wikoff, M.D., whom Wilson often referred to as "Herr Doktor" Wikoff.

24. This, Wilson's most serious illness before 1919, has been the subject of some controversy as to its etiology. Every medical specialist who has studied this incident agrees that Wilson suffered a retinal hemorrhage during the night of May 27–28, 1906. All of them agree that the hemorrhage was caused by an occlusion of the central retinal vein in the left eye. The retina of that eye was so scarred that Wilson thereafter had only peripheral vision in it. Weinstein (ibid., pp. 165–67) attributes the attack to blockage of the left ophthalmic artery by platelets breaking off from the right carotid artery. So also do Kenneth R. Crispell and Carol F. Gomez, *Hidden Illness in the White House* (Durham, N. C.: Duke University Press, 1988), pp. 36–39. Dr. James F. Toole, head of the Stroke Center at Bowman Gray Medical School, strongly supports this diagnosis in several unpublished papers. Park (*The Impact*, p. 333) says that hypertension was probably the cause of the retinal hemorrhage and was definitely a manifestation of a broader cerebrovascular disease. It might be added that there is a good deal of contemporary evidence to support the latter hypothesis. Certainly Wilson suffered a serious vascular accident in 1906.

There is also a great deal of evidence that the incident and its sequelae had a profound effect upon Wilson's behavior during the controversies at Princeton over the so-called quadrangle plan and the graduate college and school. August Heckscher, *Woodrow Wilson: A Biography* (New York, etc.: Charles Scribner's Sons, 1991), pp. 143–47 passim, deals with this matter very well.

25. John Grier Hibben, class of 1882 at Princeton. After a brief career as a Presbyterian minister, he received the Ph.D. in philosophy at Princeton and was at this time Stuart professor of logic. Axson will have a great deal to say about the friendship between Wilson and Hibben and its tragic breakup, and it will suffice to say here that, before 1907, Hibben was Wilson's dearest friend on the Princeton faculty.

26. A man of great wealth, accumulated originally by his maternal grandfather, Pyne was a member of the class of 1877 and was elected to the Princeton board of trustees in 1884. His estate in Princeton, Drumthwacket, was one of the showplaces of the town. He gave large sums of money to the university and was generally known as the leading trustee and alumnus. He was originally a strong supporter of Wilson as president of the university, but broke with him over the quadrangle plan, and, during the fight over the graduate college, was the person who organized and led the group supporting Dean Andrew Fleming West, about whom much more will be said later.

27. That is, Madge Axson.

Chapter Three
Woodrow Wilson's Educational Career

1. Axson was in error here. Wilson was managing editor in 1878–1879 of *The Princetonian,* the weekly college newspaper, founded in 1876.

2. The Rev. Dr. James McCosh (1811–1894), president of the College of New Jersey, 1868–1888. He was born in Ayrshire, Scotland, became a minister of the Church of Scotland, and was one of the founders of the Free Church of Scotland in 1843. He was professor of logic and metaphysics at Queen's College, Belfast, 1852–1868. He wrote numerous books on Christianity, philosophy, and psychology and was perhaps the most influential advocate of theistic evolution in the Anglo-American world in the nineteenth century. McCosh was chiefly responsible for the revival of the College of New Jersey after the Civil War and for laying the foundations of its later eminence as an educational institution. He was also a great teacher and a striking, if somewhat austere, personality who made a lasting impression on the faculty and students alike. Axson told Baker that Wilson said that McCosh was "a dominating, self-determining and uncompromising old Scotchman, full of humor without having any humor." Baker interviews, February 8, 10, and 11, 1925.

3. Wilson performed well in his Princeton courses in history, philosophy, and classical languages. He did poorly in science courses. His grade average at graduation was 90.3, and he was ranked thirty-eighth in a class of about 167 men.

4. Axson was also in error here. The debater's medal, which was indeed the "chief distinction of this sort" at the University of Virginia, was awarded to William Cabell Bruce in the spring of 1880. Wilson won the orator's medal, which was generally regarded as a second prize for the annual debate.

5. Wilson testified briefly before the Tariff Commission in Atlanta on September 23, 1882. He confined himself to very general arguments against protective tariffs and for free trade. He advocated the repeal of protective tariff laws and the establishment of a tariff for revenue only. His testimony is printed in *The Papers of Woodrow Wilson,* vol. 2, pp. 140–43.

6. John William Henderson Underwood.

7. This and the following ten paragraphs are from a chapter entitled "Reaction and Progress" of Axson's biography of Wilson, a manuscript in the Stockton Axson Papers in the Fondren Library of Rice University.

8. Edith Gittings (Mrs. Harry Fielding) Reid, the wife of a longtime professor of geology and geography at The Johns Hopkins University. She and Wilson first met in 1894, and they became frequent correspondents for the rest of his life. She recorded their friendship and her estimate of Wilson in *Woodrow Wilson: The Caricature, the Myth and the Man* (New York: Oxford University Press, 1934). Axson's quotations from Mrs. Reid in this and the following paragraphs are from her book.

9. Arthur Brooks. He was actually a colonel in the Colored National Guard of the District of Columbia.

10. Actually, Wilson heard this limerick at the wedding of Madge Axson and Edward Graham Elliott at Old Lyme, Connecticut, on September 8, 1910. The limerick runs as follows:

> For beauty I am not a star.
> There are others more handsome by far.
> But my face, I don't mind it,
> For I am behind it,
> It's the folks out in front that I jar.

11. Daniel Coit Gilman (1831–1908), president of the Johns Hopkins from its inception in 1875 until 1902. He developed the plan of the institution as the first American university devoted primarily to graduate study and research and selected its initial faculty. He was also the driving force in the founding of The Johns Hopkins Medical School, which opened in 1893.

12. John William Davis, United States ambassador to Great Britain, 1918–1921, and Hugh Campbell Wallace, United States ambassador to France, 1919–1921.

13. Georg Jellinek (1851–1911), for many years a professor of constitutional law, international law, and politics at the University of Heidelberg, author of many important works on constitutional and international law. Wilson frequently cited and quoted from Jellinek's books in his own scholarly writing and teaching.

14. Henry Augustus Rowland, professor of physics, 1876–1901, a leader in the study of electricity and magnetism, spectrum analysis, and physical measurements.

15. Henry Newell Martin, professor of biology, 1876–1893, a pioneer in the teaching and study of physiology in the United States.

16. Herbert Baxter Adams (1850–1901). Following graduate study at the Universities of Berlin and Heidelberg, Adams became a fellow at The Johns Hopkins University in 1876 and advanced through the ranks to that of professor of history, which rank he held from 1892 to 1900. He was a founder of and secretary of the American Historical Association, 1884–1900.

Adams was the first great organizer and promoter of historical study in the United States. His reputation as the most influential graduate teacher of American history derived from his emphasis upon original work in the sources and the study of history as a science, as well as from the work of his students who, as the first generation of professional historians, laid the foundations of scientific historical work in the United States.

17. Richard Theodore Ely (1854–1943). A.B., Columbia University, 1876; Ph.D., University of Heidelberg, 1879. Head of the department of political economy at The Johns Hopkins University, 1881–1892; professor of political

economy, University of Wisconsin, 1892–1925; professor of economics, Northwestern University, 1925–1933. A founder of the American Economic Association, which he served as secretary, 1885–1892, and president, 1899–1901. Distinguished author in many fields of economics.

Wilson characterized Ely in 1883 as "a hard, conscientious worker." However, he also described him as "a man stuffed full of information, but apparently much too full to have any movement which is not an impulse from somebody else." On another occasion, Wilson noted that Ely's style was "not forceful." "He," Wilson wrote, "has too unerring a scent for the weaker forms and combinations of our tongue ever to achieve any reputation for brilliancy of treatment. But he writes smoothly, clearly, and grammatically and is quite full of encyclopaedic matter and Germanic Doctrine."

18. James E. Rhoads, M.D. (1828–1895). He gave up medical practice in 1862 after suffering a stroke and thereafter devoted himself to philanthropic and educational work. He became the first president of Bryn Mawr College in 1883 and served until 1894.

19. Martha Carey Thomas (1857–1935). A.B., Cornell University, 1877; graduate study at The Johns Hopkins University and the University of Leipzig; Ph.D. with highest honors, University of Zurich, 1882. Appointed dean and professor of English literature at Bryn Mawr College in 1883, she did much of the work of selecting a faculty before the opening of the college in 1885. She was president of Bryn Mawr, 1894–1922.

20. Actually, he was appointed as associate in history. He was promoted to associate professor of history and political science in 1887.

21. Mary Eloise Wilkins Hoyt, daughter of William Dearing Hoyt, M.D., of Rome, Georgia.

22. Edward William Axson, then age eleven, also came to live with the Wilsons in Bryn Mawr in the autumn of 1887. He continued to reside with them in Middletown, Connecticut, and later in Princeton until his graduation from Princeton University in 1897. After graduate work there and at the Massachusetts Institute of Technology, he went to work for a mining company in Tennessee in 1899. He was married on April 9, 1901, to Florence Choate Leach, a violin teacher of Boston. Their only child, Edward Stockton Axson, was born on June 2, 1903. Later that summer they moved to Creighton, Georgia, where he became superintendent of the Franklin Gold Mining Co. Edward, his wife, and their son were drowned in a freak accident involving a horse-drawn carriage and a ferry on the Etowah River near Creighton on April 26, 1905. Edward made a valiant effort to save his family by swimming with them to shore, but his strength gave out before help could arrive.

23. Francis Amasa Walker, *Political Economy*, 3d ed., rev. and enlarged (New York: Henry Holt, 1888).

24. Ellen Wilson had spilled boiling lard on her foot on or about Decem-

ber 31, 1889. The severe burns healed very slowly and it was only on May 2, 1890, that Wilson could report in a letter to a friend that her foot was "almost entirely well at last."

25. The Conversational Club, organized in 1862, a group of Wesleyan University faculty and townspeople who met informally in members' homes. Wilson was elected a member on December 31, 1888, and was president, 1889–1890.

26. James Cooke Van Benschoten, who was actually professor of Greek language and literature at Wesleyan from 1863 to 1902.

27. Alexander Johnston, professor of jurisprudence and political economy at Princeton University, 1884–1889. Actually, he died on July 20, 1889. Negotiations between Wilson and Francis Landey Patton, the president of Princeton, looking toward Wilson's selection to replace Johnston, began immediately. However, the Princeton board of trustees did not elect Wilson to the position until February 13, 1890.

28. There were six Poe brothers who played football at Princeton between 1882 and 1901, all sons of John Prentiss Poe of the Princeton class of 1854, attorney general of Maryland and a cousin of the writer Edgar Allan Poe. The best known of the six was Edgar Allan Poe, class of 1891, later also attorney general of Maryland.

29. James Maclin Brodnax, A.B., Princeton, 1894, who was actually from Mason, Tennessee. He went on to study at Princeton Theological Seminary from 1894 to 1898, was secretary of the Y.M.C.A. at the University of Virginia from 1898 to 1900, and served briefly as pastor of the Presbyterian Church in Richmond, Kentucky, before his untimely death in 1904.

30. On April 26, 1892, Wilson had been startled by two members of the board of trustees of the University of Illinois who accosted him at his Princeton classroom door to interview him for the "regency" (presidency) of their institution. Four days later, one of them wrote him from New York and offered him the position at an annual salary of $6,000, twice what he was then being paid at Princeton.

The University if Illinois at that time was a small institution of about twenty-two faculty members, approximately five hundred students, and five buildings in the small town of Urbana, Illinois. The trustees had explained to Wilson that, while the school had hitherto been primarily a technical and agricultural college, they now hoped to develop it into a major institution with a strong emphasis on the liberal arts.

Woodrow and Ellen Wilson considered and debated the proposition during the first two weeks in May, but Wilson rejected the offer on May 12 on the ground that the presidency would too seriously interfere with his plans for scholarly research and writing.

31. Wilson first consulted with representatives of the University of Vir-

ginia about the "presidency" of that institution in August 1897. He then advised against the creation of the office as then proposed. When Wilson actually received an offer on March 21, 1898, it consisted of a professorship in the university's law department and the chairmanship of the university faculty. However, the committee making the offer had been authorized to "define more clearly" the duties of the chairman, and Wilson was assured that he, as chairman, would "largely assist" the committee in this process. He was also promised carte blanche to teach whatever subjects he wished. Both the committee and personal friends of Wilson at Virginia assured him that he was the unanimous choice to lead the institution into a new era.

Wilson considered the offer very seriously, partly because of his loyalty to and esteem for the venerable Virginia institution, partly because of dissatisfaction with recent actions and inactions of the administration and trustees at Princeton University. However, he also had a strong bond of loyalty to Princeton. Moreover, a new factor entered the situation when several wealthy Princeton alumni proposed to raise a fund to supplement Wilson's salary at Princeton. As it turned out, the fund was raised and Wilson, on April 22, 1898, informed the Virginia authorities that, after much soul searching, he had decided to remain at Princeton.

32. Winthrop More Daniels, A.B., Princeton 1888; A.M., 1890; instructor in economics and social science, Wesleyan University, 1891–1892; assistant professor of political economy to professor at Princeton, 1892–1911; member, Board of Public Utility Commissioners, New Jersey, 1911–1914; member, Interstate Commerce Commission, 1914–1923; professor of transportation, Yale University, 1923–1936.

33. Actually, it was the family of Cyrus Hall McCormick, Jr., Wilson's classmate of 1879, which in 1896 endowed the McCormick professorship of jurisprudence as part of the sesquicentennial celebration of the founding of Princeton University. A year later, at Wilson's request, the words "and politics" were added to the title of the professorship.

34. Andrew Fleming West (1853–1943). Actually, although the establishment of a graduate school had been under discussion since 1896, the board of trustees did not formally establish the school until December 13, 1900, at which time West was chosen as its first dean. However, very little was accomplished toward making the institution a reality between 1900 and 1905.

West received his A.B. degree from Princeton in 1874 and the Ph.D. from Princeton and was appointed professor of Latin in 1883. He remained at Princeton as professor of Latin and dean of the graduate school until his retirement in 1928.

35. Francis Landey Patton (1843–1932). Born in Warwick, Bermuda. After holding pastorates in New York, Nyack, Brooklyn, and Chicago, he began his academic career in 1872 as professor of didactic and polemical theology at

the Presbyterian Theological Seminary of the Northwest (later McCormick Seminary) in Chicago. He soon became well known as a defender of Presbyterian orthodoxy against the liberal thought that was then influencing the church. Princeton Theological Seminary called him in 1881 to fill a new professorship of the relation of philosophy and science to the Christian religion. A year later he began teaching a course on ethics and the philosophy of religion at Princeton University.

Patton was a brilliant and often witty speaker, but he was also somewhat notorious as a heretic hunter. It was the conservative-fundamentalist faction on the Princeton board of trustees who pushed through his election as president in 1888. He was the latest in an unbroken line of ministers to head the college.

Wilson and Patton usually managed to avoid any confrontation over religion at Princeton. Upon Wilson's election as a professor in 1890, Patton wrote to Wilson that there had been some criticism of him because of his alleged belief in naturalistic evolution and his failure to give sufficient attention to Christianity as a reforming force in history. Patton went on to warn Wilson that the trustees were determined to maintain Princeton as a Christian college and expected him to highlight theistic and Christian suppositions in his teaching, and that academic freedom would not protect Wilson if he did not heed this warning. F. L. Patton to Woodrow Wilson, February 18, 1890, *The Papers of Woodrow Wilson*, vol. 6, pp. 526–27.

One incident nearly led to a break between Wilson and Patton. Wilson was eager to attract Frederick Jackson Turner, the distinguished historian, then at the University of Wisconsin, to Princeton. Patton fell in with the plan in 1896, and Turner agreed to come. Then it became known that Turner was a Unitarian, whereupon Patton canceled the offer. Wilson was so outraged that he nearly resigned. Axson, commenting on the manuscript of Baker's second volume, had the following to say about this incident: "With regard to the theological conservatism of Princeton, Wilson was impatient when his recommendation of Professor Frederick Turner for a new chair in history was rejected on the ground that Turner was a Unitarian. He exclaimed, 'They would accept an agnostic, but not a Unitarian. Unitarianism is their *bête-noire*.'"

It might be added that Wilson was a person of very broad and tolerant sympathies and attitudes toward persons outside the mainstream of Protestantism—Jews, Catholics, and nonbelievers. He appointed the first Catholics and the first Jew to the Princeton faculty. Moreover, when Andrew Carnegie established the Carnegie Foundation for the Advancement of Teaching to provide pensions for retired professors in 1905, Wilson, in 1906, in order to qualify Princeton as a participant in the Carnegie plan, had the trustees adopt a resolution declaring that Princeton University was a nonsectarian institution, and that no denominational test would be imposed in the choice of trustees or teachers, or in the admission of students, and that no distinctively denominational tenets or doctrines would be taught to students.

However, Wilson had no intention of shedding Princeton's religious, particularly Presbyterian, heritage and traditions. About this and the Carnegie matter, Axson made the following comment on the manuscript of Baker's second volume:

> When I learned that Princeton was to be put on the Carnegie foundation I expressed my surprise to Wilson, but I knew the original nonsectarian provisos in the foundation. "Have you ever read the Princeton charter?" he asked me. I admitted that I had not. "It is one of the most liberal documents in our colonial history," he said proudly, "absolutely nonsectarian; its only limitation is that a certain proportion of the trustees shall be from New Jersey."
>
> When the great expansion began in the early years of Wilson's presidency of the university, "Momo" Pyne and some others of the "Episcopal persuasion" started a movement to buy the First Presbyterian Church (which you remember is surrounded by the college campus) with the idea of having a new church erected at a distance from the campus, avowedly to relieve the college of its Presbyterian associations. Mr. Wilson said to me, "I shall never consent" (this was before the first breach in the college community), and added, "Princeton is not a Presbyterian college, but I am not going to permit a break with its old tradition of Presbyterian *affiliation*. It is not a question of denominationalism, but of keeping faith with the past. Presbyterians made the college though they were broad-minded enough *not* to make it a *Presbyterian* college."

36. This and the following eight paragraphs are from "Reaction and Progress," a chapter in Axson's manuscript biography.

37. Frederick Scott Oliver, *Alexander Hamilton: An Essay on American Union* (New York: Putnam, 1906).

38. Published in Wilson's *Mere Literature and Other Essays* (Boston: Houghton Mifflin and Co., 1896), pp. 104–60.

39. Jerry Simpson, Populist politician of Kansas, who served in the United States House of Representatives, 1891–1895 and 1897–1899. He was usually known as "Sockless Jerry" because of a newspaper reporter's misinterpretation of a remark of Simpson's to mean that he owned no socks.

40. About Wilson's earlier approval of Cleveland, Axson wrote in a commentary on Baker's first volume:

> Almost with a pang I recall Woodrow Wilson's *first* letter to me. It was just after the 1884 election and he was all elation over a *Democratic* victory. Doubtless because I was only a freshman in college, he did not

betray his deeper yearnings for a *new* party, or more far-reaching governmental policies than were in sight. It was a *gleeful* letter about party victory and Grover Cleveland.

In the summer and early autumn of 1888 I was with him constantly in Bryn Mawr and Middletown. He looked forward with confidence to Cleveland's reelection. By that time, you will remember, the tariff issue had been clarified, was clean-cut. It overtopped the old civil service reform issue. But both, mingled with the idea that machine politics, spoils politics, domination of government by special interests, would be checked if not overthrown by "four more years of Cleveland," and Wilson felt, I am sure, that Cleveland's reelection in 1892 meant something genuine. He was immensely interested—and confident. I remember him saying one day, "*The Evening Post, Harper's Weekly,* and *Puck* are all for Cleveland. That's a combination hard to beat!" *Puck* was something of a power in those days. Its "infant industries" cartoons were effective. Wilson cut a picture from *Puck,* and pinned it on the wall—colors harsh, but drawing attractive—Cleveland, with "fair round belly," but not gross, smiling happily, stepping forward, silk hat in hand to salute the electorate.

41. Wilson did indeed vote in 1896 for John McAuley Palmer and Simon Bolivar Buckner, the presidential and vice presidential candidates of the National Democratic party, the so-called "gold Democrats."

42. John Huston Finley (1863–1940). President of Knox College, 1892–1899; editor of *Harper's Weekly* and *McClure's Magazine,* 1899–1900; professor of politics, Princeton University, 1900–1903; president of the College of the City of New York, 1903–1913; commissioner of education, New York State, 1913–1921; associate editor, *The New York Times,* 1921–1937; editor in chief, 1937–1938.

43. In the first days of June 1915, then Secretary of State Bryan found himself in disagreement with Wilson over the text of the second note to Germany on the subject of the sinking of the British ocean liner, *Lusitania.* Bryan feared that the note, as drafted by Wilson, would lead to the breaking of diplomatic relations between the United States and Germany and hence to war between the two nations. When Wilson refused to modify the note to meet Bryan's objections, Bryan decided on June 5 that he must resign as secretary of state. Bryan formally submitted his resignation on June 9, 1915, and Wilson accepted it on the same day.

44. William Gibbs McAdoo (1863–1941) married Eleanor Randolph Wilson at the White House on May 7, 1914. The groom, a widower, was then fifty years of age; the bride was twenty-four.

McAdoo, born near Marietta, Georgia, practiced law in Chattanooga and moved to New York in 1892, where he established a successful law practice.

Between 1901 and 1905 he organized and became president of several com-
panies which built and operated four rapid transit tunnels under the
Hudson River between New York and Hoboken and Jersey City, thus com-
pleting a project at which others had attempted and failed.

McAdoo had long taken an interest in Democratic party politics, and in
1911–1912 he played a key role in the nomination and election of Wilson to the
presidency. Wilson then selected him as secretary of the treasury, and he
served in that post from 1913 to 1919. The scope of his activities greatly increased after the entrance of the United States into the war in 1917. In addition to his duties at the Treasury, he was chairman of the Federal Reserve
Board, the Federal Farm Loan Board, and the War Finance Corporation. He
was also the director general of the nation's railroads after their takeover by
the federal government in 1917. He left government service in January 1919 in
order to recoup his personal finances. He moved to Los Angeles in 1922 to
practice law and continue his pursuit of the presidency. He and Eleanor
Wilson McAdoo were divorced in 1934.

45. This and the following paragraph are extracted from "Reaction and
Progress."

46. In a commentary on volume 4 of the manuscript of Baker's biography,
Axson embellished this paragraph as follows:

> During and immediately after the war, Wilson was belligerent—re-
> gretted he was not free to enlist in the armed forces and fight—read
> each day's news with the eagerness of a boy. He was a hero-worshipper
> of [George] Dewey especially—at later date was very friendly toward
> Roosevelt. "He will make a good president," he remarked after the Buf-
> falo tragedy. He was sympathetic with McKinley during negotiations,
> though recognizing McKinley's limitations—said, humorously, "How
> can a *good* Methodist and the Spanish diplomats understand each
> other?" (with humorous emphasis on "good"). Had he voted for McKin-
> ley in 1896? I don't know—very possibly he had. Of course he deprecated
> Mark Hanna's influence. He was much impressed by prowar speeches
> of Senator [John Tyler] Morgan of Alabama—their unimpassioned pres-
> entation of the situation in Cuba. I rather think he was a champion of
> Schley in the Sampson-Schley controversy, enthusiastic about Hobson
> (who, by the way, in 1911 was a visitor more than once to Sea Girt, and for
> a time a Wilson-for-president enthusiast). He did not seem to be agi-
> tated by expansionist policy. Wainwright was one of his war heroes—he
> was immensely interested in the actual sight of Wainwright's small ship
> *Gloucester*, which he saw in Gloucester Harbor: when someone re-
> marked that it seemed too small for effective fighting he answered, "Not
> when Wainwright is in command." I fancy never again or before was he
> so nearly a "Jingo." He was cordial, gratified about England's attitude—

said when Boer war broke out that it would be shameful if our country should be anti-British in this conflict, after England's attitude toward us in the Spanish-American war.

Schley was Commodore Winfield Scott Schley, commander of the Flying Squadron in 1898. Sampson was Commodore William Thomas Sampson, commander of the Atlantic Squadron. The controversy was over which man was responsible for the destruction of a Spanish fleet off Santiago, Cuba, on July 3, 1898. Hobson was Richmond Pearson Hobson, a young naval officer who, during the War with Spain, became a national hero by sinking a collier, U.S.S. *Merrimac*, in Santiago Bay. He served in the United States House of Representatives from 1907 to 1915. Wainwright was Commander Richard Wainwright, who took part in the destruction of the Spanish fleet as commander of U.S.S. *Gloucester* and was advanced ten numbers in rank "for eminent and conspicuous conduct in this battle" and was presented with numerous tributes on his return home.

47. Wilson certainly was not an imperialist in the common meaning of that word. He had grave doubts about the wisdom of acquiring a colonial empire but concluded that the United States had no alternative. For a good discussion of this subject, see Heckscher, *Woodrow Wilson*, p. 129. Perhaps it is not inappropriate to add that, as president of the United States, Wilson was the first effective anti-imperialist statesman in modern history.

Chapter Four
Social Disposition and Habits

1. Albert Lefevre, assistant professor of philosophy, Cornell University, 1902–1903; professor of philosophy, University of Virginia, 1905 until his retirement. On this trip, in 1899, he was on his way to study at the University of Berlin.

2. Axson underwent an operation for appendicitis, just before peritonitis set in, on a table in the Wilsons' house on February 8, 1900. Princeton had no hospital at this time, and Dr. Robert Fulton Weir, professor of surgery at the College of Physicians and Surgeons of Columbia University, was called down to Princeton to perform the surgery.

3. *A Farewell.*

4. Sir William Grantham, judge of the high court of justice, queen's bench division.

5. Albert Venn Dicey, Vinerian professor of English law at Oxford.

6. He was probably Francis Albert Christie, professor of church history at Meadville Theological Seminary.

7. The Rev. Dr. Charles Cuthbert Hall, president of Union Theological Seminary in New York.

Chapter Five
Ellen Axson Wilson and Woodrow Wilson

1. The Wilsons had three daughters: Margaret Woodrow Wilson, born in Gainesville, Georgia, April 16, 1886; Jessie Woodrow Wilson, born in Gainesville, Georgia, August 28, 1887; and Eleanor Randolph Wilson, born in Middletown, Connecticut, October 16, 1889.

2. Randolph Axson.

3. We do not know when this exhibition was held at the University Art Museum. Frances Wright Saunders, *First Lady Between Two Worlds: Ellen Axson Wilson* (Chapel Hill, N. C., and London: University of North Carolina Press, 1985), p. 113, says that the following incident occurred about 1896. Bouguereau was Guillaume-Adolphe Bouguereau (1825–1905).

4. About this accident, see chapter 3, note 22.

5. Actually, Mrs. Wilson went up with her daughters and Madge Axson to Old Lyme, Connecticut, in the summer of 1908, while Woodrow Wilson was in Great Britain. Miss Florence Griswold housed a large colony of artists there during the summers in a kind of summer art institute. Ellen Wilson's special teacher was Frank DuMond, but there were a number of other painters there, all of them of the American impressionist school. The Wilsons went back to Old Lyme in 1909 and 1910. Some of Ellen Wilson's paintings done at Old Lyme are reproduced in vol. 30 of *The Papers of Woodrow Wilson*.

6. "I know that you are interested in the Berry Schools and that you know that Mrs. Ellen Ax[s]on Wilson sold her pictures and endowed a day here, $1250., in memory of her brother. The amounts that have come to me in this way has [sic] built up our endowment, and the interest on such amounts is used to help pay the expenses of boys and girls who are not able to pay." Martha McChesney Berry to Woodrow Wilson, November 14, 1921, *The Papers of Woodrow Wilson*, vol. 67, pp. 456–57.

7. Probably Dr. Thomas A. Hoyt.

8. The address, "Should an Antecedent Liberal Education Be Required of Students in Law, Medicine, and Theology?" is printed in *The Papers of Woodrow Wilson*, vol. 8, pp. 285–92; the cartoon is reproduced in ibid., p. 286.

9. It is printed in ibid., vol. 10, pp. 11–31.

10. This passage reads as follows:

I have had sight of the perfect place of learning in my thought: a free place, and a various, where no man could be and not know with how great a destiny knowledge had come into the world:—itself a little world; but not perplexed, living with a singleness of aim not known without: the home of sagacious men, hard-headed and with a will to know, debaters of the world's questions every day and used to the rough ways of democracy; and yet a place removed—calm Science seated there, recluse, ascetic, like a nun, not knowing that the world passes, not caring, if the truth but come in answer to her prayer; and Literature, walking within her open doors in quiet chambers with men of olden time, storied walls about her, and calm voices infinitely sweet; here "magic casements, opening on the foam of perilous seas, in fairy lands forlorn," to which you may withdraw and use your youth for pleasure; there windows open straight upon the street, where many stand and talk intent upon the world of men and business. A place where ideals are kept in heart in an air they can breathe; but no fool's paradise. A place where to hear the truth about the past and hold debate about the affairs of the present, with knowledge and without passion; like the world in having all men's life at heart, a place for men and all that concerns them; but unlike the world in its self-possession, its thorough way of talk, its care to know more than the moment brings to light; slow to take excitement, its air pure and wholesome with a breath of faith: every eye within it bright in the clear day and quick to look toward heaven for the confirmation of its hope. Who shall show us the way to this place?

11. *A Farewell.*

12. Emile Legouis, professor of English language and literature at the Sorbonne, 1904–1932.

13. *La Jeunesse de William Wordsworth* (Paris: G. Masson, 1896).

14. Roosevelt was shot in the chest by a fanatic as he left his hotel in Milwaukee on the evening of October 14, 1912, on his way to a speaking engagement. He was not seriously wounded and made his final campaign speech in Madison Square Garden on October 30.

15. About whom see chapter 7, note 16.

16. The following section constitutes the main part of a letter that Axson wrote to Ray Stannard Baker on September 6, 1931. It is a handwritten letter included in the Axson commentaries in the Baker Papers in the Library of Congress. Axson wrote it after reading the manuscript of vol. 4 of Baker's *Life and Letters* and was prompted to do so particularly after reading the sections of that volume on life in the White House and on Mrs. Wilson's death in 1914. In the foreword to the main part of the letter, Axson said that he felt that Mrs. Wilson did not quite come alive in the Baker biography; hence he wrote the essay which follows.

17. Mary Allen, who married Thomas Harbach Hulbert in 1883, who died in 1889. Left with an infant son, she married Thomas Dowse Peck, a wealthy textile manufacturer of Pittsfield, Massachusetts, in 1890. Wilson met Mrs. Peck in Bermuda in 1907 and was smitten by her. The friendship between the two became serious in the early months of 1908, and there is reason to be-

lieve it caused a crisis in the relationship between Woodrow Wilson and Ellen Wilson. It is not known how far that relationship went, but Wilson saw Mrs. Peck frequently and wrote her numerous letters which were, as he once said, "more warm than discreet." The Wilsons visited Mrs. Peck in Pittsfield in October 1909. Mrs. Peck may have visited the Wilsons at Prospect, but Axson's statement to this effect is not supported by evidence. However, she did visit the Wilsons at Sea Girt in the late summer of 1911, and Ellen Wilson invited her to the White House for a visit in May 1913.

For a fine article on Wilson and Mrs. Peck, see Frances W. Saunders, "Love and Guilt: Woodrow Wilson and Mary Hulbert," *American Heritage* 30 (April/May 1979): 68–77. Heckscher, *Woodrow Wilson*, passim, also has a fine discussion of this matter.

18. William Cooper Procter, a member of the Princeton class of 1883, one of the principals of the graduate college controversy of Princeton, about whom much will be said later. Procter had been an executive of the Procter & Gamble Company since his graduation.

19. Mrs. Wilson had William Jennings Bryan to dinner to meet her husband for the first time at the Princeton Inn on March 12, 1911.

20. George Brinton McClellan Harvey, editor of *Harper's Weekly* and an early supporter of Wilson for the presidency of the United States (more will be said about him later), spoke on March 17, 1910, at the Present Day Club at Princeton, a women's club which Mrs. Wilson had helped to found in 1898. Harvey spent that evening as a guest of the Wilsons at Prospect.

21. Wilson's objections to Tumulty on social grounds were certainly not very strong. He later conceded to Edith Bolling Wilson, his second wife, that Tumulty was "common," as she had said, but he then went on in this exchange to explain Tumulty's extraordinary usefulness to him and the Democratic party. There were occasional criticisms of Tumulty because he was a Roman Catholic and charges that he would therefore leak all state secrets to the Pope. Wilson realized that this was a political problem, but he was as ecumenical and sympathetic toward other religious groups, including Jews, as any leader of his generation. For a brief biography of Tumulty, see chapter 7, note 9.

22. The Baltimore convention was the Democratic national convention of 1912, at which Wilson was nominated for the presidency. The story that Axson tells below relates to the crisis period of that convention. It came on the tenth ballot, when Champ Clark of Missouri, speaker of the House of Representatives, won a majority, but not the then necessary two-thirds majority, for nomination. It is true that Wilson drafted a message of withdrawal, and that his chief campaign manager, William Frank McCombs, had given up the fight. Wilson did not send the message, and Axson's statement that it was Mrs. Wilson who persuaded him not to send it may well be true.

23. Allan Bartholomew Walsh.

24. Ruth Cleveland, daughter of Grover Cleveland and Frances Folsom Cleveland, who died of diphtheria on January 7, 1904, at the age of twelve.

25. The following miniessays were written as commentaries after reading the manuscripts of Baker's first, third, and fourth volumes. They are the longest pieces that Axson ever wrote on Wilson's general reading; they are too long for footnotes; and, since Axson has a good deal to say about Ellen Wilson's influence on Wilson's reading, we print them here as addenda to this chapter.

26. Miss Murfree's pen name.

27. Again, *A Farewell.*

Chapter Six
President of Princeton University

1. Nathaniel Burt, "The Princeton Grandees," *Princeton History* (1982), pp. 1–27, has written about them and their great estates: the Moses Taylor Pynes of Drumthwacket; the Allan Marquands of Guernsey Hall; the George Allison Armours of Allison House (now called Lowrie House); the Junius Spencer Morgans of Constitution Hill; and the Archibald Douglas Russells of Edgerstoune. Constance Greiff has an article on these five houses in the issue of *Princeton History* cited above.

2. William Francis Magie, professor of physics.

3. A crisis in Patton's presidency had been developing at least since 1896, on account of Patton's failure to provide leadership, his resistance to meaningful efforts to improve the curriculum, and a general decline in scholarly standards among the students. Although he was usually dilatory in all matters, he was an exceedingly clever politician and usually managed to head off or defeat efforts at reform. He did appoint a faculty committee of the affairs of the university in 1897, but always managed to diffuse its criticisms. The "committee on inquiry," which Axson refers to, grew out of a special committee of the academic faculty and one of the science faculty, which combined in 1901 to form the university committee on scholarship, with Magie as chairman.

4. Alexander Thomas Ormond, McCosh professor of philosophy.

5. Henry Burchard Fine, at this time Dod professor of mathematics. Wilson appointed him dean of the faculty in 1903, and the two men collaborated in building up what were among the great mathematics and physics departments in the world. Fine, a man of absolute integrity and courage, was a strong but not uncritical supporter of Wilson during later controversies at the university. In 1913 Wilson tried hard but unsuccessfully to persuade Fine to accept the ambassadorship to Germany.

6. So serious had the crisis in presidential leadership become by 1902, that a group of trustees, led by Cyrus Hall McCormick, Jr., of Chicago, in effect bought out Patton's contract in order to persuade Patton to resign. They agreed to give him a sum in cash which would equal his salary as president of the university for six years (Patton, who became president in 1888, had said that he had planned to be head of Princeton for twenty years). Patton was elected to the new office of president of the Princeton Theological Seminary in the fall of 1902 and continued in that position until 1913. Another concession that the Princeton trustees made to Patton was to agree to promote his son, George Stevenson Patton, from assistant professor to professor of Bible. Axson's statement in the following sentence that Patton was asked to resign was incorrect. He was simply bought off, much to his benefit and undoubtedly to his peace of mind.

7. Wilson presented the committee's report to the university faculty on April 16, 1904; it was adopted with minor amendments on April 25, 1904.

8. Henry Bedinger Cornwall, professor of analytical chemistry and mineralogy, who had joined the Princeton faculty in 1873.

9. This cartoon is reproduced in *The Papers of Woodrow Wilson*, vol. 14, p. 384.

10. Wilson had this fence constructed around Prospect in the summer of 1904.

11. Students dug out a portion of the fence in the autumn, and several days later unknown persons vandalized 1879 Hall. The fence was restored, and repairs were made to 1879 Hall soon afterward.

12. He was Arnold Guyot Cameron, professor of French literature, and son of Henry Clay Cameron, Wilson's old professor of Greek. Wilson regarded the younger Cameron as a "mountebank." When Wilson assumed the presidency of Princeton, the trustees authorized him to remove any professor at his pleasure. He informed Cameron of his dismissal in the spring of 1904 and, as Axson says below, offered him a year's leave of absence with pay. Cameron's dismissal was greatly resented by members of his class of 1886. Cameron continued to live in Princeton but, until the end of his life, never set foot on the Princeton campus again. Although he and his family had fallen on very hard times, he, like the Reverend Josiah Crawley, M.A., perpetual curate of Hogglestock, of Trollope's Barsetshire novels, would destroy baskets of food left on his back porch by kind neighbors rather than accept charity. He sent his several sons to Yale, it might be presumed, on scholarships. When the editor of this volume knew him, he wore a French-like flowing cape, beret, and mustache and was known for his flamboyance and exaggerated manners.

13. Axson wrote the following commentary on the Cameron affair after reading the manuscript of Baker's second volume:

I have often puzzled over these things, for on the surface everything seemed so smooth and amicable. I was first apprised of a change of attitude toward him in the *student* body when an undergraduate newspaper correspondent came to my room one night and told me that there was ready for the wire a red-hot sensational article based on President Wilson's request for Guyot Cameron's resignation. I was shocked and showed my agitation. The student said "You don't realize how unpopular he (Wilson) is with the students." Fortunately I was able to put the Cameron matter before him in a way that caused him to suppress the article.

Of course you know how brave and honorable President Wilson was in the Cameron matter. He had nothing against Professor Cameron except that he did not believe his somewhat sensational classroom lectures were a healthy scholastic influence—that while Professor Cameron's character was above reproach, he was so eccentric that he should not be retained in Princeton. It was all rather intangible, and nobody with less powerful convictions than President Wilson would have done anything. Certainly few college presidents would have acted with such honorable courage. Professor Cameron, suspecting nothing, applied for leave of absence. President Wilson told him that he could have the leave, but that a year after his return (I *think* that was the time set) he (President Wilson) would ask him to resign, and he thought it only fair to advise him in advance so that he could be looking for another position. Professor Cameron became furious—was extremely popular among the students. A big sensation—lots of trouble.

It all illustrated President Wilson's courage, conviction, and fairness. It would have been so much easier to allow matters to "rock along," and certainly so much easier to let Professor Cameron go away and then *write* to him. But that wasn't President Wilson's manner. He took the bull by the horns. He knew Cameron's popularity, but was convinced of his "general disqualifications," and he wasn't afraid of results.

14. Wilson presented his report on the social coordination of the university to the trustees on June 10, 1907. The minutes of the board of trustees say simply that the report was "adopted." As Axson notes below, only Joseph Bernard Shea voted against the motion of approval.

15. Archibald Douglas Russell and Albertina Hine Russell were, as we have said, among the grandees of Princeton. Mrs. Russell was a sister of Moses Taylor Pyne.

16. George Lansing Raymond, who gave up his professorship of aesthetics in 1905 to reside in Washington and teach at the George Washington University.

17. Josephine Ward Thomson (Mrs. Thomas) Swann, a wealthy widow

who died on March 2, 1906. Her will provided that Princeton University should be the residuary legatee of her estate and that the proceeds be used to construct "upon the grounds of the said University" a residence for graduate students to be named the John R. Thomson Graduate College of Princeton University in memory of her first husband.

18. George McLean Harper, who had begun his teaching career at Princeton in 1889 and was at this time professor of English literature. He was a noted Wordsworth specialist and author of the famous *William Wordsworth, His Life, Works and Influence* (New York: Charles Scribner's Sons, 1916). The Harper and Wilson families were intimate, and the Harpers visited the Wilsons in the White House.

19. Aside from Wilson, he was probably the best known man on the Princeton campus at this time on account of his leadership roles in the Presbyterian Church, U.S.A., and his writings. A graduate of Princeton in 1873, he was ordained to the Presbyterian ministry in 1879 and held several important pastorates before becoming professor of English literature at Princeton in 1900. He was minister to The Netherlands and Luxembourg, 1913–1917, by Wilson's appointment. Probably the best known of his numerous books is *The Other Wise Man* (1896).

20. Walter Augustus Wyckoff, who was appointed assistant professor of political economy in 1898 and was the first and for a long time the only sociologist on the Princeton faculty. He died of heart disease in 1908.

21. Leah Lucile Ehrich Wyckoff.

22. Cyrus McCormick has already been identified. Cleveland Hoadley Dodge, Princeton 1879, was one of Wilson's closest friends. Edward Wright Sheldon, also of the class of 1879, was another close friend of Wilson's.

23. Axson probably refers to Varnum Lansing Collins, although we have never heard him referred to as "Wilkie." He was at this time preceptor of modern languages.

24. Actually, Procter withdrew his offer on February 6, 1910.

25. Axson does not follow exact chronology in the following account. There was a special meeting of the faculty on the quad plan on September 26, 1907. Winthrop More Daniels introduced a resolution approving the quad plan and calling for the appointment of a special faculty committee to cooperate with the university authorities to carry it out. Theodore ("Granny") Whitefield Hunt, professor of English, seconded the motion. Then, Henry van Dyke introduced a motion asking the board of trustees to appoint a joint trustee-faculty committee which, together with the president of the university, should investigate "the present social conditions of the University in conjunction with representatives of the Alumni and students and consider the best method of curing the evils which exist and of maintaining and promoting the unity, democracy, and scholarly life of the undergraduate body." Hibben seconded the motion, as did Howard McClenahan, professor of

physics, although Wilson reminded him that the motion did not require another second. The great debate over the motion took place four days later, on September 30. Wilson spoke at length. We do not have a transcript of his speech, but one of the faculty members present wrote in his diary that it was "one of the most wonderful speeches" he had ever heard. The vote was on the Van Dyke resolution, which lost by a vote of twenty-three to eighty.

26. Edward Graham Elliott, of the Princeton class of 1897, had received the Ph.D. in political science at Heidelberg in 1902 and was at this time preceptor in history, economics, and politics. Wilson appointed him first dean of the college in 1909. He married Madge Axson in 1910 and went on to become a professor at the University of California and a prominent banker in the San Francisco area.

27. Edward Capps was a distinguished professor of Greek language and literature at the University of Chicago, whom Wilson persuaded to come to Princeton in 1907. He led the team that excavated the Agora in Athens. Wilson appointed him minister to Greece in 1920. Edwin Grant Conklin, who was probably the most outstanding biologist of his time, came to Princeton from the University of Pennsylvania as professor of biology in 1908, mainly on account of his admiration of Wilson.

28. The *Princetonian*, now a daily newspaper, held an annual spring dinner of its editors and board. Axson below relates events of the tenth annual banquet of the *Daily Princetonian* held at the Princeton Inn on April 10, 1908. There is a brief account of this affair in *The Papers of Woodrow Wilson*, vol. 18, p. 260, but Axson's account is much more complete.

29. Isaac Chauncey Wyman, class of 1848.

30. Axson is essentially right in this statement. There were all sorts of rumors in the press that the Wyman estate would be worth eight to ten million dollars. West, upon conveying the news of the bequest to his ally, Pyne, said that its value would run between two and three million dollars; he expected that the total would be three million dollars, "with chances of going up." It actually amounted to about $800,000.

31. A member of the class of 1919, he was afterward a lawyer and businessman of Baltimore.

32. Axson, curiously, says very little more about Woodrow Wilson's religious faith and convictions in this memoir. However, in response to questions from Baker, or when prompted to do so by reading Baker's manuscripts, Axson did comment on what all Wilsonian biographers agree was the supreme intellectual and ideological force in Wilson's life, namely, his Christian faith and his unshakable belief in God's providence and loving control over the destiny of people and nations.

We have culled the following from the Baker interviews and from Axson's various commentaries:

In one of his commentaries, Axson remarked on Wilson's devotional life, saying that, on the trip to Scotland and England he and Wilson took together in 1899, Wilson read a chapter of the Bible every day and prayed on his knees before going to bed. Elsewhere, he remarked: "Mr. Wilson read a chapter of the Bible every day and was given to regular prayers." Baker interviews, February 8, 10, and 11, 1925. In another commentary, he wrote: "To the end, it seemed to me, that Wilson's critical mind was never so uncritical as when he attended a church where the preacher spoke simply and expounded the Presbyterian doctrines. Wilson sat like a docile child. And after the service he almost invariably spoke in admiration of the sermon. There was one powerful Presbyterian preacher, Dr. Maltbie Babcock, in Baltimore in the early nineties (later pastor of the Brick Church in New York) whom Wilson (Mrs. Wilson also) admired intensely as a preacher and cherished as a friend."

Axson's most often quoted remarks were made to Baker in an interview on February 24, 1925, as follows: "Dr. Axson was interesting in his comments upon Mr. Wilson's religious beliefs. He thought them not only strong but formal and stern. The idea of an all merciful God was, I believe, to him a piece of soft sentimentality. I have always thought that he not only believed in a future life but in a Hell. Margaret [Wilson] thinks not; that in his later years he softened; that Hell became to him a mere state of mind. I remember distinctly his comment on Bob Ingersoll's death. Some newspaper had commented that he, Ingersoll, "was quite unafraid to go." Mr. Wilson commented on this: "By now he probably knows the difference between a Christian and an agnostic. He is where he will learn it." Robert Green Ingersoll, the great agnostic lecturer and writer, died on July 21, 1899.

It is needless to say that the above comments fail to do justice to the complexity and depth of Wilson's religious beliefs. Dr. Mulder's book, mentioned earlier, is very strong on the subject, and the reader will find convenient brief accounts in Arthur S. Link, "Woodrow Wilson: Christian in Government," in George L. Hunt, ed., *Calvinism and the Political Order* (Philadelphia: Westminster Press, 1965), pp. 157–74, and "Woodrow Wilson and the Reformed Tradition," manuscript in Link's possession.

Chapter Seven
Politics, 1910–1913

1. George Brinton McClellan Harvey was, in 1906, owner and editor of the *North American Review*; president of Harper and Brothers, publishers; and editor of *Harper's Weekly*. He had played a significant role in the nomination and election of Grover Cleveland to the presidency in 1892 and would do the same for Warren G. Harding in 1920.

Harvey's "personal and informal nomination" of Wilson for the presidency took place on February 3, 1906, at a dinner in Wilson's honor given by the Lotos Club, a social organization of artistic and literary men of New York. Harvey, who had recently become interested in Wilson and his career, hailed him as a man "by instinct a statesman." "As one of a considerable number of

Democrats," Harvey said, "who have become tired of voting Republican tickets, it is with a sense almost of rapture that I contemplate even the remotest possibility of casting a ballot for the president of Princeton University to become President of the United States." Harvey's speech was widely quoted and discussed in the American press, and the favorable response encouraged him to undertake a publicity campaign looking toward a Wilson presidential candidacy. His complete remarks are printed in *The Papers of Woodrow Wilson*, vol. 16, pp. 299–301. For the background and impact of the speech, see Arthur S. Link, *Wilson: The Road to the White House* (Princeton, N. J.: Princeton University Press, 1947), pp. 97–100.

2. Perhaps this comment was also inspired by the Lotos Club speech. However, it could have referred to an earlier mention of Wilson for the presidency by an anonymous "Old Fashioned Democrat" in a letter to the editor of the *Indianapolis News*, dated May 1, 1902, and published in that newspaper on May 5 of that year. This writer suggested that the Democratic party should break away from its old leaders and nominate someone "wholly unidentified with past quarrels." The new man should be a person of ability and character and one steeped in "Democratic principles." Woodrow Wilson, he said, was such a man. The letter was quite remarkable, in view of the fact that Wilson had at that time not yet been chosen president of Princeton University. It is printed in *The Papers of Woodrow Wilson*, vol. 12, pp. 356–58.

A portion of the "Old Fashioned Democrat" letter was reprinted in the *Princeton Alumni Weekly*, May 31, 1902, p. 580. The cover of that issue, listing the contents, included the phrase "Woodrow Wilson '79 for President."

3. On or about December 26, 1906.

4. James Smith, Jr., a wealthy businessman of Newark, was for many years the Democratic boss of that city and of Essex County, New Jersey. He had been a United States senator from New Jersey from 1893 to 1899. His support was crucial to Wilson's nomination as the Democratic candidate for governor in 1910. He broke with Wilson soon after the gubernatorial election when the governor-elect opposed his ambition to return to the United States Senate. About Smith and his relations with Wilson, see the index references under his name in Link, *Wilson: The Road to the White House.*

5. Lawrence Crane Woods or his brother, Edward Augustus Woods. They were insurance brokers.

6. Wilson's acceptance speech, delivered at the convention on September 15, 1910, is printed in *The Papers of Woodrow Wilson*, vol. 21, pp. 91–94.

7. On September 28, 1910. This speech is printed in ibid., pp. 181–91.

8. About these speeches, actually two in number, see ibid., p. 191, n. 1.

9. Joseph Patrick Tumulty (1879–1954) was a lawyer of Jersey City who served as a Democratic member of the New Jersey Assembly from 1907 to 1910. Though initially opposed to Wilson's gubernatorial candidacy because of his sponsorship by political bosses such as James Smith, Jr., Tumulty was

soon won over and became both politically and personally devoted to Wilson. He served as Wilson's personal secretary during his governorship and as secretary (chief of staff) to the president from 1913 to 1921. Tumulty was one of Wilson's principal advisers on political matters during all these years.

10. This speech of October 3, 1910, is printed in *The Papers of Woodrow Wilson*, vol. 21, pp. 229–38.

11. Malone, city attorney of New York in 1910, was active in Wilson's gubernatorial and presidential campaigns.

12. 25 Cleveland Lane.

13. Parker Mann, an artist who specialized in landscapes. Wilson characterized his paintings as "quite indifferent affairs." *The Papers of Woodrow Wilson*, vol. 23, pp. 424–25.

14. Lucy Marshall Smith and Mary Randolph Smith were daughters of the Rev. Dr. Henry Martyn Smith, pastor of the Third Presbyterian Church of New Orleans, 1857–1888. Following the deaths of their parents in 1894, they continued to live together in New Orleans. Neither ever married. The Wilsons had met them in the summer of 1897 when all were vacationing at "Mountain View," a guest house located at Markham, near Front Royal, Virginia.

15. Jessie Woodrow Wilson and Francis Bowes Sayre first met in the spring of 1912 and became engaged on October 29 of that year. They were married in the White House on November 25, 1913.

16. Edward Mandell House (1858–1938). Born in Houston, Texas, he attended Cornell University for two years. A man of inherited wealth, House maintained residences in Austin, Texas, and New York and devoted much of his life to the study of political, social, and economic questions and to advising candidates and elected officials. Between 1892 and 1902 he served as campaign manager for and adviser to four Texas governors. He became interested in Wilson as a presidential candidate in 1911. His contribution to Wilson's campaign for the Democratic nomination consisted of a small financial donation and occasional political advice. It was only following Wilson's nomination on July 2, 1912, that the two men began to develop the close personal relationship that was to make House a principal adviser of Wilson until 1919.

House and Wilson first exchanged letters in mid-October 1911. They met face to face for the first time at House's apartment in New York on November 24, 1911.

17. McAdoo's courtship of Eleanor Wilson began some time in 1913. As has been noted, they were married in the White House on May 7, 1914.

18. The Wilsons believed that he was Nicholas Murray Butler, president of Columbia University.

19. Actually, as has been noted, Wilson and Bryan had met at Princeton on March 12, 1911.

20. Wilson's speech at the Jackson Day dinner is printed in *The Papers of Woodrow Wilson*, vol. 24, pp. 9–16.

21. Wilson spoke to a Sunday School rally of approximately six thousand persons at the Second Regiment Armory in Trenton on October 1, 1911. His address is printed in ibid., vol. 23, pp. 372–80.

22. Longtime newspaper editor, who became professor of politics at Princeton University in 1908. Wilson appointed him New Jersey commissioner of banking and insurance in 1912.

23. "Beautiful Isle of Somewhere."

24. The words of the hymn were by Jessie Brown Pounds; the music was by John Sylvester Fearis.

25. Wilson, Harvey, and Watterson met at the latter's apartment in the Manhattan Club in New York on December 7, 1911, to discuss practical details, including finances, of Wilson's presidential nomination campaign. Watterson was the long-time editor of the Louisville *Courier-Journal.*

26. Watterson was indeed "a dupe in the master hands of Harvey" in this affair. Harvey made repeated efforts to get Watterson to make a public statement on the Manhattan Club conference which would indict Wilson for his alleged ingratitude to Harvey. However, when Watterson finally did give out his version of the conference on January 17, 1912, it proved to be sufficiently truthful that it served chiefly to exonerate Wilson of the charge of ingratitude. For a detailed account of the Wilson-Harvey-Watterson affair, see Link, *Wilson: The Road to the White House*, pp. 359–78.

27. Printed in *The Papers of Woodrow Wilson*, vol. 25, pp. 512–13.

28. November 5, 1912.

29. Lyman Abbott, the editor of *The Outlook*; William Peterfield Trent, a professor of English literature at Columbia University; and Wilson met with Roosevelt at his home in Oyster Bay, New York, on July 26–27 to discuss ways and means of involving college men in reform politics in both major parties.

30. Dodge wrote as follows: "Theodore told us how much he admired you, your writings, your ability, &c. '*But* I cannot say that I like his political utterances.'" C. H. Dodge to Woodrow Wilson, December 13, 1908, *The Papers of Woodrow Wilson*, vol. 18, p. 546.

31. Taft's speech at Winona, Minnesota, on September 17, 1909, was a lengthy defense of the recently enacted Payne-Aldrich tariff act. While he did not deny that the measure had its defects, he insisted that it represented, taken altogether, a downward revision of the tariff rates. One sentence in the speech, reproduced or paraphrased in endless newspaper headlines, was to haunt Taft through the remainder of his administration: "On the whole, however, I am bound to say that I think the Payne bill is the best bill that the Republican party ever passed."

32. Undoubtedly William Edward Dodd, professor of American history at the University of Chicago, who published *Woodrow Wilson and His Work* (Garden City, N. Y.: Doubleday, Page & Co., 1920).

33. Bryan arrived in Sacramento, California, on April 28, 1913. Wilson had sent him to attempt to persuade the California legislature and Governor Hiram Warren Johnson either to delay passage of a bill excluding foreigners not eligible to citizenship from owning land in California or to reword the legislation in such a way as not to offend the Japanese government and people. Bryan appeared twice before executive sessions of the legislature and also conferred with Johnson, but he was unable to prevent the passage of a bill which did contain language offensive to the Japanese. On the California land legislation and the diplomatic crisis which it created between the United States and Japan, see Arthur S. Link, *Wilson: The New Freedom* (Princeton, N. J.: Princeton University Press, 1956), pp. 289–304.

34. Franklin Knight Lane, Secretary of the Interior, 1913–1920.

35. The New York *World*, in a front-page editorial entitled "The World to Mr. Bryan," published September 17, 1913, offered Bryan $8,000 a year during his incumbency at the State Department if he would devote his full time to the duties of his office and refrain from delivering lectures and other addresses for which admission fees were charged. There is no evidence beyond Axson's statement below to indicate that the *World* sent an emissary to Bryan.

36. James Beauchamp Clark, always known as Champ Clark, Democratic congressman from Missouri, 1893–1895, 1897–1921; speaker of the House of Representatives, 1911–1919. Clark was a leading contender for the Democratic party presidential nomination in 1912 and led in the early ballots at the party's national convention in Baltimore.

37. Bryan, at a critical point in the balloting for the presidential nomination at Baltimore on June 29, 1912, announced that he was switching his vote from Clark to Wilson because the New York delegation had swung its votes to Clark. The clear implication of his words was that Clark was now under obligation to Tammany Hall and Wall Street. See Link, *Wilson: The Road to the White House*, pp. 452–55.

38. Wilson said this in farewell remarks to his neighbors in Princeton on March 1, 1913. See *The Papers of Woodrow Wilson*, vol. 27, pp. 142–44.

39. Taft's letter is missing, but see Wilson's reply of December 2, 1912, printed in ibid., vol. 25, p. 574.

40. Actually, W. H. Taft to Woodrow Wilson, January 6, 1913, printed in ibid., vol. 27, pp. 16–18.

41. That is, Helen Woodrow Bones.

42. Wilson's sister, Annie Josephine Wilson (Mrs. George) Howe; her daughter, Annie Wilson Howe (Mrs. Perrin Chiles) Cothran; her granddaughter, Josephine Cothran; and her sons, James Wilson Howe and George Howe III.

43. John Adams Wilson, a first cousin of Woodrow Wilson, oil broker of Franklin, Pennsylvania.

44. A reception and smoker in Wilson's honor, held at the New Willard

Hotel under the auspices of the Princeton Alumni Association of the District of Columbia. Some eight hundred alumni from all parts of the United States attended, and Wilson is reported to have shaken hands with all of them. For Wilson's remarks on the occasion, see *The Papers of Woodrow Wilson*, vol. 27, pp. 147–48.

45. Loulie Hunter (Mrs. Edward Mandell) House.

46. "I summon all honest men, all patriotic, all forward-looking men, to my side. God helping me, I will not fail them, if they will but counsel and sustain me!" *The Papers of Woodrow Wilson*, vol. 27, p. 152.

47. Florence Stevens Hoyt, first cousin of Ellen Axson Wilson, younger sister of Mary Hoyt. She graduated from Bryn Mawr College in 1898. Her leg was amputated above the knee in 1901 as a result of tuberculosis of the bone.

48. William Hodges Mann, governor of Virginia, 1910–1914.

49. William Sulzer, governor of New York from January 1, 1913, until October 17 of that year, when he was removed from office as the result of an impeachment proceeding. Sulzer had a tall, ungainly figure and facial features which some persons found reminiscent of Henry Clay. He deliberately imitated the Kentucky statesman's dress and unruly shock of hair.

50. Charles Francis Murphy, New York political boss, leader of Tammany Hall from 1902 until his death in 1924.

51. Harry Augustus Garfield, former professor of politics at Princeton, at this time president of Williams College. He was the son of President James Abram Garfield.

52. This and the following essays are discrete memoranda and are manuscripts in the Wilson Collection in the Seeley G. Mudd Library, Princeton University; the last item is a commentary on the manuscript of Baker's fourth volume.

53. That is, the burial of Ellen Axson Wilson in Rome, Georgia, on August 11, 1914.

54. Edward Thomas Brown, a first cousin of Ellen Wilson, at that time a lawyer of Atlanta.

55. That is, Margaret.

56. Axson refers, of course, to the diplomatic dispute between the United States and Great Britain in 1895 over the boundary line between British Guiana and Venezuela. The "bellicose statement" was undoubtedly made by a member of the firm of William Cramp & Sons' Ship and Engine Building Company, of Philadelphia, at the time one of the nation's largest builders of naval vessels.

57. Newton Diehl Baker and David Franklin Houston, at this time secretary of war and secretary of agriculture, respectively.

58. James M. Cox, the Democratic presidential nominee in 1920.

59. Sterling Ruffin, M.D., of Washington, Mrs. Wilson's personal physician and one of Dr. Grayson's consultants during Wilson's illness following his large stroke on October 2, 1919.

Chapter Eight
The Personality of Woodrow Wilson

1. Axson wrote this chapter, or essay, in December 1921, and it is probably fair to say that he was influenced by his frequent association with Wilson during the period following Wilson's vascular illness during the summer of 1919 and his large stroke of October 2, 1919. That stroke not only had devastating effects on Wilson physically, but also left him severely crippled psychologically. As is common with victims of massive stroke, Wilson could often be petulant and extremely difficult to get on with. Axson was in the White House a good deal during 1920 and 1921, and one wonders whether he really understood what had happened to Wilson physically and psychologically. However that might have been, the relative six-year hiatus (1913–1919) in their relationship allowed Axson an opportunity to identify Wilson's premorbid personality as different from his personality as affected by cerebrovascular disease from the summer of 1919 until the end of 1921.

2. Thomas Dixon was a North Carolinian who had practiced law, studied for a year at the Johns Hopkins with Wilson in 1883–1884, served in the North Carolina legislature, and entered the Baptist ministry in 1886. After serving churches in Raleigh, Boston, and New York, he turned to lecturing and the writing of novels, two of which, *The Leopard's Spots* (1902) and *The Clansman* (1905), were extremely anti-Negro and glorified the Ku Klux Klan as the savior of the white civilization of the South. It was through Dixon's influence that Wilson received his first honorary degree of LL.D. from Wake Forest College in 1887.

3. If Wilson said this, he was referring to his adolescence, not his boyhood. As has been said, the Wilsons lived in Augusta from 1858 to 1870 and moved to Columbia when Woodrow Wilson was thirteen. He lived in Columbia four years, 1870–1874, and in Wilmington, North Carolina, about two and a half years between 1874 and 1885.

4. Robert Wodrow, *The History of the Sufferings of the Church of Scotland, from the Restauration to the Revolution: Collected from the Publick Records, Original Papers, and Manuscripts of That Time, and Other Well Attested Narratives*, 2 vols. (Edinburgh, 1721–1722).

5. The following incident occurred on September 23, 1913, when Wilson went to Princeton to vote in a Democratic primary election. Wilson, writing to his wife on September 28, 1913, wrote about his visit to Princeton and said: "Unfortunately I ran across Hibben just before leaving. Stock. says that I behaved pretty well, and did not freeze him as I did Richardson who seemed, in his infinite stupidity, quite taken aback by my manner towards him." Richardson was Ernest Cushing Richardson, librarian of Princeton University. One can only say that there was considerable difference between Wilson and Axson in their perceptions of what occurred.

Margaret Axson Elliott, *My Aunt Louisa and Woodrow Wilson* (Chapel Hill,

N. C.: University of North Carolina Press, 1944), pp. 267–68, tells the story of a second meeting of Wilson and Hibben. She says that she and her husband met Wilson in Princeton, where he had gone to vote on November 3, 1914, and that they rode down to Washington with him in his private car. She writes that as they were all standing about the car before it left the university station, Hibben came rushing up and told Wilson that a student had said that he was asking for him. Wilson, in a courteous manner, but unbelievably remote, looked at Hibben and said just one word—"No."

It does indeed seem that there were Wilson-Hibben encounters both in 1913 and 1914. Wilson was certainly in Princeton on September 23, 1913. Although the *Princeton Press*, the village weekly, does not record the fact, Wilson also came to Princeton to vote on November 3, 1914. The White House Diary records that the Elliotts joined him there, rode back with him in the special car, and were guests at the White House through November 4.

6. Arthur Douglas Howden Smith, *The Real Colonel House* (New York: George H. Doran Co., 1918). There is contemporary evidence that House was considerably embarrassed by the newspaper notices of this book. The incident that Axson relates here occurred on April 7, 1918.

7. Wilson left Paris on February 14, 1919, to return to the United States for the end of the session of Congress and returned to Paris on March 14, 1919. During his absence, he had designated House as his principal spokesman and had been in frequent telegraphic communication with him. Contrary to Wilson's explicit instructions, House had given the impression that Wilson would consent to certain French demands and to the separation of the Covenant of the League of Nations from the peace treaty with Germany. Axson is correct in saying below that this did not result in any open break between the two men, but it did mark the beginning of Wilson's loss of confidence in his hitherto trusted adviser.

8. James Montgomery Beck, lawyer and Republican politician of Philadelphia, later solicitor general of the United States and member of the United States House of Representatives.

9. Wilson to Tumulty, c. January 15, 1918, *The Papers of Woodrow Wilson*, vol. 63, p. 625.

10. Henry Skillman Breckinridge, who resigned on February 10, 1916, on the same day that Secretary of War Lindley Miller Garrison resigned in protest against Wilson's acceptance of a compromise army reorganization bill.

11. The chief problem in their relationship was the fact that Lane had no sense of confidentiality and was the source of leaks to newspapermen and friends.

12. Helen Woodrow Bones.

13. That is, Edward William Axson and Margaret Axson.

14. Writing soon after Eleanor's marriage to McAdoo in 1914, Wilson said, "She was simply part of me, the only delightful part." Axson, in a comment

on the manuscript of Baker's fourth volume, was frankly puzzled by this comment and tried to explain it as follows:

> Was the master of words using an inaccurate word, "delightful"? Did he perhaps mean "frolicsome"? For at least twenty years, and I think longer, Mrs. Ellen Wilson was his delight. He rejoiced in Margaret's eager, impulsive conversations, in Jessie's serious discussions. Mrs. Wilson felt that Jessie's mind was more like his than that of any of the other girls', and occasionally expressed regret that he had not more time to fit his mind to hers (Jessie's) in long conversations.
>
> Possibly Jessie was a little too much bent on "discussions" when he wanted to relax. I could see that McAdoo, so full of projects, sometimes irritated him *at meals* by persistently talking of affairs of state when Mr. Wilson wanted small talk and relaxation.
>
> It was obvious that he loved to frolic with Eleanor ("Nell," we all called her). A typical remembered picture is of him and Nell trotting down the long second story White House hall, "chicken-fighting," as we used to call it in the South, their arms folded, bunting and bumping each other from side to side. I remember smiling and thinking to myself, "What would the great American public think if they could see their 'austere' president now?"

15. Axson is here thinking of Wilson's trip to Belgium, June 18–19, 1919. He had actually visited some of the battlefields of France on March 23, 1919.

16. "James Carlyle, of Ecclefechan," in James Anthony Froude, ed., *Reminiscences by Thomas Carlyle* (New York: Charles Scribner's Sons, 1881).

17. That is, Axson.

18. Evelyn College was founded in 1887 by the Rev. Joshua Hall McIlvaine as a school for girls, with the hope that it would become affiliated with the College of New Jersey. It closed its doors in 1897 after McIlvaine's death that same year.

19. Wilson Woodrow Kennedy, who entered Princeton in 1899 as a sophomore and was forced to withdraw in 1900 on account of ill health. He died on November 8, 1900.

20. She suffered from chronic nephritis and died, probably of Bright's disease, on August 6, 1914.

21. George Howe III described the Wilson household in an interview with Baker on February 24, 1925, as follows:

> George Howe gives a most amiable picture of the easy joy and friendliness of the Wilson household at Princeton. He lived in the home during much of his college course. He said that Mr. Wilson had a playful nature, playful both of mind and body. He loved to tease the young people who were about him, but unlike his father, the teasing was never pain-

ful. It was a household which radiated the easy hospitality of the South. People were always running in and out or stopping informally to meals. The conversation at table was amusing and delightful. Mr. Howe said that Mr. Wilson was always sending some one of the girls or the boys for a book, often a dictionary, to prove his case, or to furnish a bit of information. He said that Mr. Wilson teased him out of the "mammy" dialect which he brought up with him from the South. He did it by mimicking him from time to time. He would often after dinner insist upon dancing about the room with the children, a sport in which "Aunt Ellie," as Mrs. Wilson was called, never joined. She often stood by smiling and sometimes, when the fun grew too furious, she would cry out: "Woodrow, what is the matter with you?"

22. Jessie graduated Phi Beta Kappa from the Woman's College of Baltimore (now Goucher College) in 1908; Margaret attended the Woman's College of Baltimore from 1903 to 1905, after which she began professional musical study at the Peabody Conservatory of Music in Baltimore; Eleanor attended St. Mary's School, an Episcopal boarding school and junior college for girls in Raleigh, North Carolina, from 1906 to 1908.

23. He probably referred to Cyrus H. McCormick, Jr. We can find no evidence to support the following account of a special meeting of prominent Princetonians or others called by Wilson to consider "a matter of Princeton policy." In fact, we can find nothing that even remotely resembles such a meeting. It is possible that Axson was confabulating and had transformed a meeting of Wilson and his friends following a meeting of the board of trustees. Nor do we know anything about the alleged White House conference, mentioned below, at which John Sharp Williams was present.

24. He referred of course to Wilson's request on February 13, 1920, for the resignation of the secretary of state, Robert Lansing.

25. Axson was writing during the middle of the Washington conference on the reduction of naval armament and the settlement of outstanding far eastern questions that had arisen among the United States, Great Britain, Japan, and China. President Harding had called this conference with the enthusiastic support of Republicans in Congress and throughout the country.

26. Axson referred to Joseph P. Tumulty, *Woodrow Wilson As I Know Him* (Garden City, N. Y.: Doubleday Page & Co., 1921); Baker's *Woodrow Wilson and World Settlement*, 3 vols. (Garden City, N. Y.: Doubleday Page & Co., 1922–1923), which was at this very time being serialized in newspapers; and Thomas W. Lamont, "Reparations," in Edward M. House and Charles Seymour, eds., *What Really Happened at Paris: The Story of the Peace Conference, 1918–1919 by American Delegates* (New York: Charles Scribner's Sons, 1921), pp. 259–90.

27. At the climax of his campaign to oust the Mexican military usurper, General Victoriano Huerta, from power, Wilson, on April 21, 1914, had or-

dered marines and naval forces to occupy the Mexican port of Veracruz. American casualties were nineteen dead and seventy-one wounded.

"I was present (who else if any, I do not recall) when the president said, in effect: 'I cannot shake off the thought of those boys killed in Mexico. It was right to send them there, but that does not mitigate the sorrow for their deaths, and *I* am responsible for their being there.'" Axson's commentary on the manuscript of Baker's fourth volume.

28. Axson, commenting on the manuscript of Baker's fourth volume, wrote the following:

> About his going to New York to take part in the parade: I was at the White House (had gone up to the McAdoo wedding, and lingered a few days). He summoned me to his "study" (private office in the main building). His face was serious. When he said what he said, I interpreted it as an injunction on me to assume my responsibility to the family in case the worst should befall. Closing the door, he said: "The secret service men have discovered something and are trying to persuade me not to ride in the procession, but to review it from a stand where they can better protect me."
>
> I asked him if he should not heed their advice, adding "the country cannot afford to lose its president."
>
> His rejoinder was, "The country cannot afford to have a coward for president."
>
> He rode.

29. The home in Washington which Wilson bought with the help of friends in 1921.

30. According to Axson's commentary on the manuscript of Baker's fourth volume:

> After he recuperated sufficiently from his last (mortal) illness to ride out, I was frequently in the car with him and Mrs. Edith Wilson. He usually sat slumped in lethargy, unheedful of citizens who would salute him from the sidewalk. Frequently Mrs. Wilson, alert, would nudge him to a response. His response would be a weary gesture, usually too late for the pedestrians to see it. *But* he would see for himself a lad in service uniform many yards ahead, would straighten in his seat, and give a full salute. I recall one occasion when a number of young soldiers were lounging in a group. The president saluted them almost vigorously. They did not return the salute. Looking back, I could see them staring stupidly at the car. It was obvious that they had no idea who the broken old man was who had been so attentive to them.
>
> For young soldiers of other nations he had a similar regard. Away back in 1899, when attending church in Edinburgh, he was deeply interested in a detachment from the Gordon Highlanders or Black Watch (I

don't remember which). During the Boer War, an illustrated London paper carried a picture of young men from this unit who had been killed, and Mr. Wilson used to study that picture, declaring that he could recognize some of the faces he had seen in the Edinburgh church.

This pity, *personal* grief, for young blood shed for a cause not of the young man's making was one strong mark of the deep sympathetic humanity in Woodrow Wilson's stern nature.

31. Angus C. MacGregor to Woodrow Wilson, December 11, 1921, the Papers of Woodrow Wilson, Library of Congress.

Index

❧

Note: Notes are indexed. Page references to notes which place a comma between the page number and "n" cite both text and note, thus: "418,n1." On the other hand, absence of the comma indicates reference to the note only, thus: "59n1"—the page number denoting where the note number appears.